TESTING THE SPIRITS

Elizabeth L. Hillstrom

INTERVARSITY PRESS
DOWNERS GROVE, ILLINOIS 60515

InterVarsity Press® is the book-publishing division of InterVarsity Christian Fellowship®, a student movement active on campus at hundreds of universities, colleges and schools of nursing in the United States of America, and a member movement of the International Fellowship of Evangelical Students. For information about local and regional activities, write Public Relations Dept., InterVarsity Christian Fellowship, 6400 Schroeder Rd., P.O. Box 7895, Madison, WI 53707-7895.

All Scripture quotations, unless otherwise indicated, are taken from the HOLY BIBLE, NEW INTERNATIONAL VERSION®. NIV®. Copyright © 1973, 1978, 1984 by International Bible Society. Used by permission of Zondervan Publishing House. All rights reserved.

Cover illustration: Roberta Polfus
ISBN 0-8308-1604-6

Printed in the United States of America ∞

Library of Congress Cataloging-in-Publication Data

Hillstrom, Elizabeth L., 1941-
 Testing the spirits/Elizabeth L. Hillstrom.
  p. cm.
 Includes bibliographical references.
 ISBN 0-8308-1604-6
 1. Parapsychology—Religious aspects—Christianity. 2. Occultism—
Religious aspects—Christianity. 3. New Age movement—
Controversial literature. 4. Experience (Religion)—Controversial
literature. 5. Unidentified flying objects—Religious aspects—
Christianity. 6. Apologetics. I. Title.
BR115.P85H55 1994
261.5'1—dc20   94-41678
           CIP

17	16	15	14	13	12	11	10	9	8	7	6	5	4	3	2	1
09	08	07	06	05	04	03	02	01	00	99	98	97	96	95		

To Ken, Diane, Gary, Brian,
Amy, Niel, Lisa and all our grandchildren
with gratitude for your patience, prayers,
love and encouragement

1 The Current Shift Toward Mysticism _____ 9

2 New Age Thought & Its
Contributions to the New Mysticism _____ 23

3 The "Higher Self" & Subconscious Processes _____ 37

4 Altered States & Extraordinary Experiences _____ 58

5 Near-Death & Out-of-Body Experiences _____ 80

6 Eastern Meditation & Mystical Experiences _____ 107

7 Are Human Beings Developing
New Powers of Mind? _____ 133

8 Healings _____ 155

9 Communication with Spirits _____ 176

10 UFO Experiences _____ 195

11 The Larger Picture _____ 210

Notes _____ 225

1

The Current Shift Toward Mysticism

The Chinese used to curse their enemies with the words "May you live in interesting times," by which they meant times of deep uncertainty and disturbing changes. By this measure our times are exceedingly "interesting." Not only are we confronted with overwhelming social, economic, health and environmental challenges, but in Western nations there are indications that some of our fundamental beliefs may be changing in significant ways as well. In many quarters there has been a discernible shift away from traditional Western systems of thought—including Christianity, Judaism and secular materialism—and toward a worldview that is nonlogical, subjective, experience-oriented and mystical. This newer perspective bears some resemblance to New Age thought but is less extreme, less obviously tied to Eastern religious dogma, more eclectic and much more compatible with important Western beliefs. Thus it appeals to a much broader range of Westerners.

This new mystical outlook, which I shall call "New Mysticism," has definitely borrowed some of its content from New Age thought, but it is too broadly based and too eclectic to be considered just the newest permutation of the New Age movement. In part, it probably represents an adaptation of certain concepts that were popularized by New Agers, a "mainstreaming" of New Age notions into a form that appeals to a much broader segment of Western populations.

This developing perspective has several distinctive themes. It assumes that the spirit realm is real, including both the spiritual aspects of human nature and the existence of other spiritual beings. It exalts human nature, emphasizing human worth and potential and affirming our power to control our own destiny. It anticipates hidden powers in the human psyche, like clairvoyance, mental telepathy and the ability to heal and to contact the realm of spirits. Its notion of life after death is linked with universalism (the belief that everyone goes to heaven regardless of their beliefs) and sometimes with reincarnation. Finally, this new perspective minimizes the importance of rationality and objectivity and relies heavily on subjective inner experiences as sources of ultimate truth.

Some Manifestations of the Shift

The cultural shift that is now under way has several outward manifestations. First, there appears to be a growing dissatisfaction with the status quo and with traditional belief systems like Christianity, Judaism and materialism, which have dominated Western thinking for centuries. Secular materialism, which has long been promoted by scholars and scientists in our colleges and universities, is losing its popular appeal. Its insistence that humans are only physical—that they came into being through chance evolutionary forces and that they perish forever when they die—seems too mechanistic, narrow and hopeless. People are not as impressed by such statements as they used to be, for they are aware of the failures of science and technology as well as their successes, and they realize that scientists do not have all the answers. They recognize that the rational, scientific approach has its limits, especially when applied to philosophical or theological issues.

And to those with a contemporary mindset, many aspects of Christianity aren't particularly appealing either. Churches may seem ineffective and irrelevant, and the Christian message too restrictive and demeaning. According to Christian doctrine, God is a personal being who has definite requirements and holds everyone accountable for their choices. Christians are called to live a life of selflessness, characterized by obedience to God, humility, service to others and self-sacrifice. Christian theology speaks of humans as unregenerate sinners, in desperate need of repentance and forgiveness, who cannot earn their way into heaven with good works but must depend on God's grace through the sacrificial death of Jesus Christ. For those who prefer to believe that they are inherently good, that they can control their own destiny, or who place great value on self-esteem, self-fulfillment and the pursuit of pleasure, such restraints seem totally unacceptable.

A second manifestation of the collective shift toward mysticism in broad segments of our population (including Christians) is a renewed appreciation for the spiritual side of human nature and a growing hunger for spiritually meaningful experiences. This collective yearning stems partly from a legitimate desire to verify that life has meaning and purpose, to know that death is not the end of our existence and to be reassured that we are not alone in this vast universe with our crushing problems. But many of today's spiritual seekers also have other goals in mind. They are apt to think of spiritual practices as methods for making contact with a deeper part of themselves, developing spiritual and mental prowess, and inducing emotional highs or unusual experiences rather than as means of making more meaningful contact with God. Many of these seekers are taking an activist approach to spirituality. They want to take charge of their own spiritual destiny and to experience whatever spiritual realities there are at first hand, even if this means that they have to use some very unconventional methods.

According to Donald Bloesch, professor of systematic theology at Dubuque Theological Seminary, the same desire for "deeper spirituality" that is sweeping through our secular culture is burgeoning among liberal and conservative Protestants. Seminaries are reflecting this new interest by placing high priority on the "spiritual development" of their graduates.

According to Bloesch, more conservative Christians are generally confining their search for deeper wisdom and spiritual techniques to the fathers and doctors of the church and the writings of ancient Christian mystics like Bernard of Clairvaux, John of the Cross and Teresa of Ávila. Many nominal believers and liberals, however, are sidestepping Christianity altogether, delving eagerly into New Age/New Consciousness teachings, Eastern traditions and paganism in their search for new heights of spiritual experience.[1]

A third indicator of the collective shift toward a new kind of mysticism can be seen in our growing and largely uncritical acceptance of esoteric phenomena that would have probably seemed very questionable to most Westerners just a few decades ago. This is evident in some national surveys. For example, in a 1990 Gallup poll 36 percent of a random sample of American adults said they believed in mental telepathy, 26 percent believed in clairvoyance, 25 percent said they believed in ghosts, and 18 percent thought it was possible to make contact with spirits of the dead. Gallup also discovered that 25 percent of his sample believed in astrology and read their horoscopes at least once a week, and 14 percent had consulted psychics or fortunetellers about their futures. In the same study, 21 percent said they believed in reincarnation, while another 22 percent marked "not sure" on this item, indicating that they were not willing to rule it out.[2] Since the early 1970s, polls have consistently shown that about half of all American adults believe in UFOs. In a 1990 survey Jon Miller found that 54 percent of his sample believed that "some of the reported unidentified flying objects are really space vehicles from other civilizations."[3]

A fourth indicator of the changing perspective is our willingness to experiment with all kinds of mystically tinged, nontraditional treatments for medical and psychological disorders. Some of these alternative medical treatments include biofeedback (which does have a scientific rationale for its use), hypnosis (which is widely used but still not satisfactorily explained), and acupuncture, acupressure and chiropractic (which were originally explained as methods of manipulating and normalizing spiritual or psychic energy, but which may also be partially explainable in terms of physiological principles). Many other alternative treatments simply cannot be reconciled with scientific knowledge or physiology, except, perhaps, in their ability to evoke a placebo response.[4] Four of the many examples that could be cited here include reflexology (in which the therapist massages different parts of the foot to alleviate problems in other parts of the body), bioenergetics (a type of "psychic" healing in which healing energy is presumably exchanged between the healer and patient), crystal healing (in which quartz and other crystallized minerals are placed on various parts of the body) and color healing (where the therapist shines lights of different colors on the body to alter its "vibrations" or "aura").

According to recent surveys, the use of nontraditional medicine is now widespread in the United States and other Western nations. In a 1991 poll for *Time* magazine, 33 percent of the respondents said they had tried nontraditional treatments of one type or another. In addition, 62 percent said they would definitely consider seeking medical help from an alternative practitioner if conventional medicine didn't work, and 84 percent of those who had already sought treatments from nontraditional practitioners said they would be willing to return to them for help.[5]

A recent report in the *New England Journal of Medicine* reveals even more surprising figures, with researchers finding that 34 percent of their sample had utilized alternative treatments during the previous year (1990). The authors estimate that this subgroup of Americans made some 425 million visits to providers of unconventional therapy during that year and paid approximately 13.7 billion dollars for their services, most of it out-of-pocket. This exceeds the estimated 388 million visits Americans made to traditional primary-care physicians and the 12.8 billion dollars they spent for traditional medical expenses during the same period. (Interestingly, nontraditional treatments were more often sought by Caucasians between the ages of twenty-five and forty-nine, with relatively more education and higher incomes, than by other socioeconomic groups.[6])

The same shift in perspectives that is evident in the area of medical treatment is also appearing in psychotherapy and counseling. A number of therapists have turned toward biofeedback, hypnosis, deep relaxation, guided imagery and Eastern-style meditation as treatments for stress and anxiety. In recent years a fair number of people have also attended dangerous, cultlike training seminars like Scientology, est (Erhard Seminars Training) and Lifespring to try to enhance their personal growth and development.[7]

The degree to which individual Westerners are adopting alternative mystical practices and perspectives obviously varies from one person to the next. At one end of the spectrum are people who have jettisoned traditional Western beliefs altogether and have embraced a worldview that incorporates Eastern religious teachings, paganism, occultism, the paranormal and/or elements of humanistic and transpersonal psychology. In its purest form this amalgam of beliefs has come to be known as "New Age" or, in some circles, "New Consciousness" thought. The number of people who have completely converted to such beliefs (or at least were willing to tell a pollster that their religion was "New Age") is actually small (probably less than 1 percent of the adult U.S. population, for example[8]), but it seems that many more people are sympathetic with important New Age concepts. In fact, according to the opinion polls cited earlier, substantial numbers of people are endorsing beliefs that are actually more compatible with New Age thought (or New Mysticism) than with Christianity or materialism.

Why the Shift?
Undoubtedly many factors are at work. Much general restlessness and openness to change is probably being fueled by uncertainties about the future, a genuine desire for greater meaning and purpose in life, and the erosion of confidence in traditional solutions or belief systems. Some people may be embracing the new perspectives because they offer empowerment and a measure of control over one's life. Others may simply be using today's permissive climate as an excuse to dabble in esoteric practices that were once considered out of bounds, or to satisfy curiosity, or simply to relieve boredom. Still others seem to be withdrawing into subjectivism and fantasy to escape from real and seemingly intractable social and personal problems.

Yet over and above these broad reasons for change, two highly significant developments are contributing to the growth of contemporary mysticism. One is an apparent explosion of extraordinary mystical experiences (most of which are very questionable from a biblical perspective), and the second is a rapidly evolving belief system that makes these experiences seem extremely positive and desirable.

The extraordinary experiences that are currently being reported come in an astonishing variety. A distinct "inner voice" is heard from time to time, giving the listener advice and counsel. People suddenly see a strange light emanating from an inspired religious teacher or find themselves "bathed in light" or "lifted out of themselves," apparently by some spiritual force they cannot explain.

Some long-time practitioners of Eastern meditation have reportedly been gripped by visions and powerful feelings of ecstasy mingled with intense flows of energy that coursed powerfully and painfully through their bodies intermittently over weeks or months, threatening their very sanity. A number of people who have had a close brush with death, or who have entered an altered state of consciousness, say they have been transported into realms of incredible beauty and have interacted with numinous beings of light. Other people have ostensibly learned how to rise out of their bodies in spirit form or to act as channels for powerful spiritual beings. And quite a few people are reporting that they have had visits from loved ones who have died, while still others say they have entered the nether realms through frightening encounters with UFOs.

According to surveys, some of these extraordinary events (particularly the near-death and out-of-body experiences, UFO encounters and meditation-induced experiences) may be followed by strange and unsettling aftereffects, such as recurrent episodes of ESP, visions, inner voices, power to disrupt the operation of electronic devices[9] or apparent visits from spirits.[10] Not surprisingly, experiencers often find it difficult to assimilate such phenomena, and some have turned to mental-health professionals for help. Counselors with traditional training and a materialistic worldview, however, are likely to interpret such reports as signs of mental illness.

In order to address this problem and help experiencers find "beneficial" counsel, a group of mental-health workers with New Age sympathies have formed a large international association known as the Spiritual Emergence Network.[11] Network counselors believe the current crop of extraordinary experiences is actually being initiated by higher spiritual beings or by spiritual forces within the experiencers, to push them toward a new level of spiritual growth and development. Thus their counsel is aimed at helping these clients cooperate with their experiences so they can "emerge spiritually."

Some U.S. polling results suggest that extraordinary experiences have been occurring with greater frequency in recent years. (We need to interpret these results conservatively, however, because they do not tell us how much of the apparent increase is real and how much of it is due to an increased willingness to report such events.) In 1973 Andrew Greeley found that 8 percent of his respondents claimed to have had unusual visions, 58 percent reported episodes of ESP, and 24 percent said they had had clairvoyant episodes. By 1984 the percentages reporting visions, ESP or clairvoyance had risen to 29 percent, 67 percent and 31 percent, respectively.

In the same survey Greeley asked, "Have you ever felt very close to a powerful spiritual force that seemed to lift you out of yourself?" In his 1973 survey 35 percent of respondents said this had happened to them at least once, and one-seventh of this group (5 percent of the total sample) reported full mystical experiences such as being bathed in light or actually leaving their physical bodies, experiences they said had profoundly affected the rest of their lives.[12] In Greeley's 1984 survey the percentage of people who said they had been "lifted" by a powerful spiritual force had risen to 47 percent, with 15 percent of this group reporting several such encounters and 8 percent saying that it happened to them often.[13] Greeley also included the question "Do you believe that you have ever been in contact with someone who has died?" In 1973, 27 percent of the respondents said yes, and by 1984 the percentage was up to 42 percent (a 25 percent increase).[14] Among widows and widowers the percentage was 51 percent in 1973 and moved up to 67 percent by 1984.[15]

More recent statistics generally support Greeley's contentions that unusual, mystically tinged experiences are now fairly common. In a 1990 poll 25 percent of Gallup's respondents said they had had telepathic experiences, and another 25 percent said they had healed their own body using just the power of their mind. In addition, 14 percent of the sample claimed they had been in a house that was haunted, 9 percent said they had seen or had been in the presence of a ghost, 14 percent reported they had seen UFOs, and 17 percent claimed they had been in touch with someone who had died.[16] According to other sources, approximately 5 percent of the U.S. population have had near-death experiences,[17] while another 10-14 percent say they have had "out-of-body" experiences not connected with death.[18]

New Experiences, New Explanations

The varied mystical experiences that are being reported do have some important commonalities. Quite a few of them occur while the experiencer is in an altered state of consciousness—usually precipitated by drugs, hypnosis, sensory deprivation, Eastern-style meditation or sleep. In other cases, experiencers have been actively engaged in "spiritual" experimentation (such as some form of divination, attempting to leave one's body or channeling) before their experience took place. But in many other instances the experiences have apparently just come out of the blue, unbidden and unexpected.

From a psychological point of view, two of the most striking features of these experiences are their subjective reality (which experiencers describe in very emphatic terms) and their effect on beliefs. The experiences are so incongruous with ordinary reality that they force people to question their basic assumptions about life. The experiences seem so real, so positive and so important that experiencers find that they cannot just dismiss them as a quirk and put them out of their minds. Yet they do not square well with everyday reality or with Western orthodoxy. From a Christian or materialistic perspective, such experiences might be explained as products of an overactive imagination, an extravagant flight of fancy brought on by being in an altered state of consciousness, or perhaps demonic deception. But experiencers are unwilling to conclude that these events were either imaginary or negative. So they generally resolve the issue by *modifying their beliefs* rather than questioning the validity of their experience.

According to experiencers, the most significant aspect of their encounters is their spiritual meaning. They serve to authenticate the reality of the spiritual realm and to convey the message that there is more to life than mere physical existence. Many experiencers believe that their encounters were deliberately initiated by spiritual forces, and they feel very privileged to have had such an experience. Most are also left with the impression that they now are responsible to share the spiritual truths they have learned with others.

The recent profusion of extraordinary mystical experiences is a noteworthy turn of events in and of itself. Yet the parallel development of a system of beliefs that effectively explain and interpret these experiences (and do so in a way that can appeal to a broad cross-section of Westerners) makes this turn of events even more significant, because in several quarters the new belief system is evolving into a close counterfeit of Christianity.

I had the opportunity to observe this emerging belief system at close range at an international conference on near-death experiences (NDEs) in St. Louis, Missouri.[19] Those in attendance ranged from professionals with M.D.s and Ph.D.s who were interested in researching NDEs to people who had had such experiences and wanted to understand them. As the conference wore on it became obvious that most of the speakers and attenders endorsed universalism (everyone goes to "heaven" when they die, regardless of their beliefs) along with assorted New Age and spiritualistic beliefs. Yet many of them were well-grounded folks who knew their Bible and wanted to reconcile their new beliefs with a biblical perspective wherever possible.

This strange amalgam of ideas created a very upbeat and seductive system of beliefs. This system incorporated the concept of a personal Creator God, but he was also portrayed as a God of unconditional love and acceptance who is apparently indifferent about "sins." (This contrasts markedly with the Christian God, who hates sin and demands justice, but who loves sinners so much that he paid the price for sin himself on the cross so that those who would turn to him in repentance can be saved.) Jesus plays an important role in the new system, but he is portrayed as a great teacher and leader rather than our Savior and Redeemer.

In the emerging system, humans are depicted as spiritual beings whose life continues in heaven after death and whose major purposes on earth are to love other people, to grow spiritually and to develop their spiritual abilities. The new system acknowledges the existence of other spirit beings (departed human spirits, angels and others) and tacitly assumes that these beings are good and have our best interests at heart. In strong contradiction to the Bible (see Deut 18:9-13), it assumes that contacting these spirits, interacting with them and heeding their advice is a beneficial thing to do.

Most of the attenders at the conference shared the view that their mystical NDEs had more than just a personal meaning. They were taken as evidence that a new program of spiritual growth, presumably mandated from on high, was now in progress.

The belief system on display at this conference was also notable for the items that were left out or minimized. The problem of evil and human sin was minimized, with sins characterized as mistakes that can ultimately be used for growth. It largely ignored the question of justice and the severe consequences that sinful acts can inflict on other people. It also denied or minimized concepts like hell, Satan and demons. Most important, it left out the very crux of the Christian message: that human beings are weak and sinful by nature and that we are not going to get to heaven by our own merits. If we are to get there, it must be through the means that God himself provided. We must believe that Jesus is the Son of God and that his death on the cross served as payment for our sins; as we confess our sins and turn away from them, we must accept Jesus Christ as Savior and Lord (see Jn 3:16-21; 5:24-30; 14:6).

The Need to Stay Informed

The new developments on the mystical scene bear watching, for they could be very significant. The religious system that is taking shape within New Mysticism looks like Christianity and sounds like Christianity, but leaves out the heart of the Christian message. It encourages spiritualistic and occult practices that are strongly condemned in the Bible. When paired with the extraordinary experiences that are now in evidence, the system could be described as a "new and improved" version of Christianity, complete with "signs and wonders."

If mystical experiences continue at their present rate and maintain their popular credibility, and if the accompanying religious beliefs start catching on, the combination could become a very effective means of deflecting the unsaved from the truth and pulling in unwary and nominal Christians alike.

This new turn of events clearly demands that we pay heed. We need to stay informed of the extraordinary experiences that are occurring and the religious beliefs that are evolving to explain them. We also need to evaluate these developments and try to understand what they mean. It is for these purposes, and in the spirit of such an inquiry, that I have written this book.

The experiences themselves raise a number of crucial questions. Are they really new, or are they just new to us? Have they occurred in the past, perhaps in different forms or with different names? Is the rate of occurrence at some all-time high, or have such experiences also occurred as frequently at other times in the past? *Are* these phenomena actually occurring as frequently as it seems, or is their apparent frequency being exaggerated by selective media attention? Are people just more willing to report such experiences now than they would have been fifteen or twenty years ago?

Another vital issue is the identity of the persons who are having these experiences and the circumstances leading up to them. For instance, it would be very helpful to know whether the experiences are occurring primarily among nonbelievers or whether they are also occurring with some frequency among Christians or nominal Christians, or even whether these groups might differ with respect to the types of experiences they are encountering. Unfortunately, it is not possible to answer this latter question at present, because we simply do not have usable, applicable data.[20] There are some anecdotal accounts of NDEs, inner voices, light experiences and encounters with angels among professed Christians, but we cannot tell from these how frequently such events are occurring or even whether the experiencer is truly a Christian in the strictest sense of the word.[21]

In the absence of concrete information, I will generally assume throughout this book that most of the experiences I am dealing with (particularly those that involve divination, spiritualism, paganism or occult practices) are relatively uncommon among true Christians—not only because Christians are unlikely to engage in such practices but also because much of the available data comes from groups that include few if any Christians. If subsequent research should reveal that similar experiences are cropping up among Christians, these too will need to be examined critically.

As will shortly be evident, it is not wise to assume that all unusual experiences are from God just because they feel "wonderful" or "spiritual." John's warning to the first-century Christians, in 1 John 4:1-3, that they should "test the spirits to see whether they are from God" is surely as applicable today as it was when he penned it.

A further question that needs to be answered is where these extraordinary experiences are coming from. Are their causes natural (explainable in physical or human terms) or supernatural (from God or from Satan)? Determining this is not as simple or straightforward as it might seem, because some highly unusual experiences can be have completely natural causes. And even when an encounter is initiated supernaturally, our experience— that is, the way we perceive and respond to the situation—will be tempered by physical and psychological factors, because we are complex beings composed of both body and spirit.

Fortunately, a fair amount of scholarly and scientific evidence is available to help us understand these phenomena. Believers and skeptics in a number of disciplines have been investigating subconscious activities, hypnosis, paranormal abilities, channeling and near-death experiences for years. In addition, brain scientists (from areas like neuroscience, medicine and biopsychology) continue to advance our understanding of mind-brain relationships and the physical aspects of certain altered states of consciousness. Considered prayerfully alongside biblical principles, this research offers some valuable insights into current mystical experiences.

The belief system within New Mysticism draws its fundamental assumptions from several sources. It incorporates elements of Christianity and New Age thought along with some popular concepts from psychology, like the beliefs that humans have a separate, subconscious mind and that we may have latent paranormal abilities (ESP and abilities to foretell the future and to heal) which are, perhaps, talents of the subconscious mind. I will address these issues, along with the question of altered states, before describing the experiences themselves, because research in this area provides important background information.

2

New Age Thought & Its Contributions to the New Mysticism

The New Age movement has contributed substantially to the emerging mystical orientation in Western countries. It is has helped to popularize the extraordinary experiences that have captured public attention and interest, and it explains these experiences in an intriguing and appealing way. In fact, as you will see, some of the popular beliefs that are cropping up in New Mysticism have been drawn directly or indirectly from New Age thought. So it is appropriate that we review some of the basic tenets of New Age thought.

Accommodating the Inexplicable

Western thinking has long been dominated by two major belief systems, Christianity and secular materialism. Both systems offer explanations for some basic questions about human nature, origins and final destiny. New Age thought is a third major system of beliefs that attempts to answer the same questions. By Western standards, some of its answers and many of its basic assumptions seem strange, unconventional and difficult to comprehend. Yet one of this system's strengths has been its ability incorporate events that seem bizarre, incomprehensible or even evil by conventional standards and make them seem normal, plausible and good within its own frame of reference. For instance, it accommodates the following incidents quite handily.

1. Psychiatrist Raymond Moody has been working with a surgeon from the East Coast, helping him prepare to try to contact his dead mother. They have spent the day walking in the woods, discussing this woman, looking at photos and mementos that evoke strong memories of her, and just relaxing. At dusk the surgeon enters a darkened chamber (which Moody refers to as a "psychomanteum"), relaxes in a low easy chair and gazes into a large mirror, thinking how much he would like to see his mother.

Time passes; nothing happens. He grows drowsy and almost falls asleep. Rousing himself somewhat, he glances again at the mirror and immediately becomes more alert when he notices that it looks clouded. As he watches, a smoky mist emerges from the glass and a figure begins forming in the mist. As the mist clears away, the doctor sees that the figure is his mother.

Amazed and startled, he gathers his wits and asks her how she is. Her lips do not move, but he receives a mental communication from her. She answers that she is fine and that she loves him. The doctor then asks if she felt any pain when she died. She answers, "None at all. The transition to death was easy."

A little more comfortable with this strange situation, the doctor asks other questions. "What do you think of the woman I plan to marry?"

"It will be a very good choice," she answers. "You should continue to work hard at the relationship and not be your old self. Try to be more understanding."

The conversation lasts for about ten minutes, and then the mother fades away. The surgeon is extremely moved. He is totally convinced that he saw his mother. He also leaves the psychomanteum convinced that there is life after death.[1]

2. The Virginia sun is warm and the breezes gentle, but the mood among participants at a weekend seminar at the Monroe Institute of Applied Sciences is anything but relaxed. The group is outdoors, taking a break

after two hours of lying in a darkened room listening to Robert Monroe's unique sound tapes. These tapes, which ostensibly produce an unusual state of coherence between the right and left hemispheres of the brain, have apparently induced some very strange experiences. The attenders listen, somewhat apprehensively, as their teacher tries to reassure them that their "out-of-body" experiences will eventually seem quite normal.

Aware that he is not succeeding, the teacher attempts to relieve the tension by relating an incident from the night before. Having apparently awakened in the middle of the night, he got up to use the bathroom, but then discovered, to his great surprise, that he couldn't open the bathroom door. His hand passed right through the doorknob. Then he realized that he had apparently slipped out of his body spontaneously while asleep and hadn't bothered to reengage before making the trip to the bathroom. The group laughed nervously when he remarked that he had to go back to bed to get his body before he could complete his intended mission.[2]

3. The date is January 14, 1988, and thousands of people are watching the *Oprah Winfrey Show* with great fascination. Penny Torres, a housewife turned channeler, is explaining how she periodically allows her body to be taken over by an otherworldly entity named Mafu so he can share his metaphysical knowledge with humans. Viewers' fascination quickly turns to incredulity as Torres describes her first encounter with Mafu. By her account, she and her former husband (a policeman) were sitting on their bed talking when Mafu manifested his presence by levitating their bed. When they tried to escape, Mafu materialized in the hallway and beckoned them to follow him to the living room. Torres's husband, badly frightened, beat a hasty retreat, but Torres stayed to listen. Mafu informed her that he wanted to use her as a channel, and Torres gave her consent.

A little later, at Winfrey's request, Torres prepares to let Mafu take over. She crosses her legs, closes her eyes, drops her head and appears to relax deeply for two or three minutes. Suddenly she begins to shudder, her neck stiffens, her face contorts, and Mafu emerges with a low, growling noise. After a few moments of apparent confusion, "Mafu" shifts around, affects an arrogant smile and condescending manner and prepares to interact with his audience.

Mafu takes questions from the audience but answers most of them in very obtuse, highly stylized English, exceptionally difficult to understand. When questioned about his manner of speech, Mafu deftly blames it on the "transmission problems" he encounters while trying to speak in English with Torres's vocal apparatus. Several questioners (who evidently suspect that he is not what he claims to be) ask him directly about his true origin and purposes. His answers are so convoluted that no one can be sure what he is saying. Yet on some issues his messages are remarkably lucid. He makes sure the audience understands that he is privy to important supernatural truths and that his mission is to help correct some of their mistaken beliefs about God. His principal message comes through loud and clear: "That which you humans call God is really within each one of you."

Winfrey had invited two critics to attend the show, and one of them openly accuses Torres of "faking it." Mafu remains unperturbed and aloof in the face of these charges and at one point turns the tables on his accuser by suggesting that his accusations come from defensiveness and fear. Many in the audience are clearly delighted by this exchange.

Extraordinary events like these are now being taken quite seriously by quite a few Americans, thanks in part to the explanatory power of New Age thought. Raymond Moody and three of his successful psychomanteum clients appeared on the popular *Oprah Winfrey Show* in December 1993 to discuss Moody's experiments and to encourage others to try his techniques. Moody especially recommended the technique to anyone who was grieving the loss of a loved one. His book on this topic, *Reunions,* soared onto bestseller lists across the United States.

Robert Monroe's contributions to the New Age and more general mystic causes have also been substantial. For more than twenty years his research institute has been sponsoring seminars and perfecting techniques to teach people how to "get out of their bodies" and explore the spirit realm. Monroe's trainers have conducted workshops in virtually every major city in the United States, and he has also developed manuals and tapes that people can use at home to accomplish the same feats.[3]

Public interest in channeling and in channeled materials also appears to be extensive.[4] In his book on this phenomenon, John Klimo has estimated that there are thousands of channelers in the United States and tens of thousands throughout the world.[5] Whatever the actual count, it is likely that the numbers are increasing because media coverage has been positive and many self-help books available in reputable bookstores encourage novice channelers and give them step-by-step instructions for getting started.

The Basic Tenets of New Age Thought

New Age thought is like a patchwork quilt that has been assembled from a good many odds and ends but forms a surprisingly coherent pattern when all the pieces are stitched together. The beliefs that have been pieced together to create this system come from a variety of disparate sources. The major contributor is Hinduism, but significant elements have also been snipped from paganism, transpersonal and humanistic psychology, and various occult, spiritistic and shamanistic traditions. At first glance it is difficult to see how these could all fit together harmoniously, but they manifest some broad, central themes that are actually surprisingly compatible. One such theme is a common belief in a realm of spirits (shared by all but humanism), while another is that humans have great untapped spiritual potential.

The New Age/New Consciousness belief system is not static, but is continually shifting and evolving. At a distance its overall pattern is clear enough, but close up, on the level of specific beliefs and practices, its appearance is more chaotic. Those who embrace New Age thought often have very different backgrounds and interests, and they continue to disagree vigorously over specific issues.

New Age Perspectives on God, Reality and Human Nature

The New Age/New Consciousness view of the cosmos contrasts markedly with that of Christians and materialists. Materialists believe that reality is basically physical, composed of matter or energy; Christians accept the fundamental reality of both the physical and spiritual realms; but the advocates of New Age thought insist that everything is fundamentally spiritual. In their way of thinking, everything—be it a rock, plant or person—is actually composed of the same basic substance, a kind of universal spiritual energy that merely takes on a different form from one physical entity to the next.

Many New Agers take the idea of universal spiritual energy even further, insisting that all physical elements (objects, plants, animals, human bodies), which naturally seem so real and solid to human eyes, are actually plastic and impermanent and that the differences and distinctions we perceive among them are illusions. In reality they are all composed of the same substance, and even the boundaries between them are artificial. In Eastern terminology, "they are all one." The fact that physical things seem quite real and separate from one another is ostensibly an illusion created by our minds.

Universal spiritual energy (which in New Age thinking is roughly equivalent to "God") also has two other pertinent characteristics. It manifests definite qualities of consciousness at higher levels of organization (particularly in humans and other spirit beings) and, paradoxically, can itself be altered and shaped by conscious thought.

The "God" of New Age thought is not the personal Creator God of the Bible but rather an impersonal force, variously described as a "life force," "pure undifferentiated energy" or "pure consciousness." This "God" actually consists of the primal spiritual stuff out of which everything else has come into being. New Age beliefs about the formation of the physical universe and human origins have not yet been articulated, but adherents would probably go along with one Hindu explanation: God brought the physical realm into existence by accident while playfully (or malevolently) visualizing and imagining the existence of separate physical things. His thoughts were sufficient to alter reality, causing part of the universal energy to break away from its sublime spiritual state and assume the various physical forms (both animate and inanimate) that exist today.

In New Age thinking the status of human beings is paradoxical. On the positive side, we are composed of the very same universal energy as "God" and are therefore spiritual beings who have inherent godlike qualities. But on the negative side, we are born with a physical nature that limits our comprehension and stifles our ability to develop the spiritual attributes and powers that are rightfully ours. Therefore life is perceived as a struggle to overcome our physical limitations, recognize our true spiritual nature and develop our full spiritual potential.

Like Hindus and Buddhists, most New Age advocates assume that death is not an annihilation but a transition. They believe that the human spirit survives death and reincarnates from time to time in different physical bodies. But New Age versions of reincarnation are often considerably more purposeful and upbeat than the pessimistic fatalism of the East.[6] Many New Agers believe that people have some input into their own incarnations and that between lives they can help choose a life that will strengthen and accelerate their spiritual development.[7] As in Buddhism and Hinduism, the goal is to reach spiritual maturity and thereby escape the pains and burdens of physical existence. However, unlike their Eastern counterparts, many apparently expect to continue on as distinct spiritual entities ("gods") in the spiritual state rather than dissolving into undifferentiated universal energy and disappearing into the "Universal Consciousness."

The concepts of spiritual diversity and spiritual evolution are also important elements in the New Age worldview (and to a lesser extent in New Mysticism). New Age adherents believe that a variety of spiritual beings populate the cosmos. These include living humans, human spirits awaiting their next incarnation, advanced human spirits that can now forgo further incarnations (sometimes called Ascended Masters), and a great variety of spirit beings that have never inhabited physical bodies. Many New Agers believe that humans and the other spirit beings are jointly engaged in a continuing process of growth and evolution.

The appearance of profound mystical experiences and new "powers of mind"—mental telepathy, clairvoyance, the ability to contact and converse with spirits or to temporarily leave one's body—are taken as signs of spiritual growth. Advocates believe that human spiritual advancement is now accelerating, in part because of the assistance of "benevolent" and "more advanced" beings (spirit guides) who are acting as mentors. New Agers are excited about the future because their guides have been predicting that an era of unprecedented human growth and change lies just ahead.

New Age Views on the Mind and Consciousness

New Age perspectives on the mind and consciousness, which are also in evidence in New Mysticism, have been heavily influenced by Eastern beliefs. In the Eastern way of thinking, humans are equipped with two minds: the conscious, rational mind, which is basically physical and is closely tied to the body, and a superior, intuitive mind that flows from the spirit. The conscious mind is obviously necessary, because it accomplishes all the tasks that enable people to function as physical beings, but it is thought to be limited because it can perceive events only from a physical perspective.

The physical mind, being limited, cannot comprehend the unconventional insights or experiences that flow from the spiritual mind, so it blocks them, keeping them from entering conscious awareness. The spiritual mind is thus forced to operate at a subconscious level. This is not good, for it prevents people from recognizing that they are spiritual beings and slows their spiritual growth. In the Eastern view, the only way to break this impasse is to temporarily block or confuse the conscious mind. Techniques of meditation were designed specifically for this purpose.

Advocates of New Age thought generally accept the Eastern portrayal of the mind but have extended it, reinforcing and blending it with some contemporary ideas from psychology and the brain sciences, which make it seem more plausible. Coincidentally, while New Agers were struggling to formulate their ideas about human consciousness, Roger Sperry, a respected brain scientist, proposed that the right and left hemispheres of the brain might actually function as two separate brains, each giving rise to a separate mind.

Sperry based this hypothesis on his research with some "split-brain" patients. As a last-ditch effort to control their epileptic seizures, these patients had undergone an operation that severed the corpus callosum, a brain structure that serves as the major connecting link between the two cerebral hemispheres. In Sperry's testing situation the patients did act as though they had two minds—one a verbal, self-conscious mind and a second that appeared to act intelligently at a nonverbal, subconscious level. (See chapter three for a more complete discussion of this phenomenon.)

Although such was not his intention, Sperry's hypothesis proved very helpful to New Agers, who quickly drew a parallel between the "physical" mind of the East and the verbal, self-conscious mind that Sperry associated with the left (language) hemisphere of the brain. The "spiritual mind" also seemed to fit very well with the nonverbal subconscious mind, which was presumably housed in the right hemisphere.[8] Advocates who suggested this link drew upon a large body of psychological literature on subconscious processes to flesh out some of the likely functions of the "spiritual mind."

The "spiritual mind" is now more commonly referred to as the "Higher Self," a term that implies each person's inherent divinity. In New Age thinking, the Higher Self is literally considered a part of "God" within us. Curiously, the Higher Self can seem like a separate, even alien entity, especially on first acquaintance. New Agers tend to brush off the possible implications of this fact (that perhaps it *is* an alien entity) and generally attribute its strangeness to the autonomy of the Higher Self: it has its own, very different mental life, and it is usually completely hidden from conscious awareness by the physical mind.

In general, New Agers believe that it is good to make contact with the Higher Self, to search out its advice, absorb its wisdom and bring one's conscious thoughts into line with it as much as possible. But since input from the Higher Self (which presumably operates through the subconscious) is often opposed by the rational, conscious mind, this is not easy to accomplish. Seekers are generally advised that their best strategy for making contact is to temporarily disable the conscious mind through altered states of consciousness, which can be produced by mind-altering drugs, hypnosis, sensory deprivation or techniques of Eastern meditation. Engaging in various "spiritual" practices—reading Tarot cards, crystal gazing, channeling and the like—is thought to augment this process.

In addition to its own considerable resources, the Higher Self presumably has access to an incredible reservoir of wisdom and information that is available only to spirits. It is generally assumed that spirit beings of all types communicate with one another via mental telepathy. This implies that what one being knows can in principle also be known by all the others. This "collective consciousness" at the spiritual level ostensibly provides the Higher Self with vast spiritual resources.

The New Age View of Reality and Truth

There are some very crucial differences between the ways New Age advocates and traditional Westerners view the world about them. Some of the Western beliefs that are challenged by New Age thought are so fundamental and so widely accepted that most people wouldn't even think of questioning them. For example, virtually all Westerners, regardless of their religious stance, assume that the information their senses and minds are giving them about the world is basically accurate. They also assume that the physical universe is objectively real, that it runs by well-established, predictable laws and that its operations are basically independent of human actions or thought. As they see it, the universe was set in motion before humans came on the scene and would continue to function in the same manner even if all people were suddenly removed from it. In addition, Westerners tacitly agree that the conscious mind, with its capacity for language, problem solving and rational thought, is a fundamental component of the self. It is considered our most reliable means of finding truth.

In contrast, New Age advocates argue that the physical universe is not what it appears to be. They contend that it seems so fundamental, predictable and immutable only because our conscious mind and senses are physical and have been programmed to perceive it that way. When the spiritual mind takes over, as in altered states of consciousness, it reveals that there are many different ways to perceive reality and that one's perceptions can in fact be changed more or less at will. Many take this to mean that reality is actually plastic, taking on whatever forms our minds suggest. Of course, if this is true, it implies that human beings create their own reality with their minds, and this means that reality is different for every person. This line of thought leads to the conclusion that reality must be relative rather than absolute.

Westerners who adopt such views may suddenly find themselves adrift in a sea of confusion, with no fundamental or objective truths to serve as anchors. Here there are only subjective "truths" and vague inner feelings or experiences to guide one's steps. Moreover, the "truths" one has can change with the vagaries of one's inner thoughts and wishes, and they are valid only for the person experiencing them.

Individuals with this mindset can be extremely resistant to arguments that their assumptions about reality are wrong. Since they assume that each person's reality is different, they can easily dismiss another person's objections to their own beliefs on the grounds that the objections are "just a reflection of the other person's reality" and therefore are not relevant. This manner of thinking is completely circular and can seriously impair one's powers of reasoning.

I witnessed a striking example of this while attending a one-day conference on the New Age movement sponsored by the Committee for the Scientific Investigation of Claims of the Paranormal (CSICOP).[9] The audience was primarily composed of scientists and professors who were strongly committed to materialism and atheism. The speakers' explanations of New Age beliefs and their descriptions of the way these ideas were spreading on college campuses left the members of the audience visibly shaken.

After one of the scheduled sessions, while the conference attenders were engaged in an intense question-and-answer session, a young, confident, clean-cut New Ager stepped out from the audience and took his turn at the mike. He explained that he was actually a computer specialist attending a business conference down the hall. In passing he had overheard one of the speakers talking about the New Age movement and had slipped in to hear what he was saying. He had obviously heard the searching, logically devastating presentations on New Age philosophy and the incredulous, cynical comments made by members of the audience, but he seemed completely oblivious to all of this. He explained who he was and confidently defended his beliefs on the grounds that his reality was different from that of the scientists and professors who were present, and they had no right to criticize it because they didn't understand it. He then admonished his audience, suggesting in a rather patronizing tone of voice that good scientists should be more open-minded. Finally he parried a few questions and excused himself.

The audience was obviously stunned, not only by his audacity but also by his complete invulnerability. The irony and timing of his appearance were striking. His comments had provided a remarkably forceful demonstration of the very point that the conference speakers had been trying to make.

New Age Thought as an Alternative Religion

As other writers have noted, New Age thought probably qualifies as an alternate religion.[10] It attempts to explain God, reality, and human origins and destiny. It has mobilized a sizable group of believers who are enthusiastic about its answers to their questions, its promises for their future, and the meaning and purpose it provides for their lives.

New Agers maintain a sense of expectancy and excitement because they believe the entire human race is on the brink of great change and rapid development. And they are convinced that their beliefs will be an instrument of that change, replacing the outmoded systems of belief (mainly Christianity and Judaism) that they blame for the present state of our planet. They are hopeful that as larger numbers of people convert to this new way of thinking and discover their inherent powers, humankind will finally be able to solve the problems of hunger, war, poverty, disease and pollution.[11]

The movement's overt spiritual connections also qualify it as a new religion. Adherents not only contend that their belief system brings an entirely new spiritual dimension to life but are also convinced that their movement is somehow being organized and propelled by benevolent spiritual forces.[12]

Thinking about New Age beliefs and activities as components of a religious movement can help us understand the reasons for the movement's existence and its potential dangers. As a religion, it directly opposes Christianity—most of its underlying assumptions are totally incompatible with basic Christian doctrines. The Christian God is holy, loving, sovereign and personal. He does not tolerate evil or sin, and he holds people accountable for their actions. In New Age thought God is reduced to an impersonal, impotent force that embraces all the characteristics of both good and evil. New Age explanations that take an Eastern slant demean God's extraordinary and benevolent acts of creation, depicting the creation of the physical universe and human life as an unfortunate or even malicious accident. Furthermore, this perspective encourages many practices, like divination, spiritism and mediumship, that the Bible strongly condemns.

Even the two religions' views of human purpose and destiny appear to be at loggerheads. In the New Age system, spiritual advancement comes by deifying the self—recognizing one's status as a "god" and developing the spiritual (paranormal) powers inherent in one's being. It is not achieved through "demeaning" activities like confession, repentance and reliance on God's grace and strength. Likewise, one's basic purpose in life is self-fulfillment—doing whatever is pleasurable or promotes one's own development (in some cases even if that means dropping important responsibilities to a spouse or children). This path leads in an entirely different direction from the route of self-sacrifice and service marked out for Christians.

When New Age thought is cast as an alternate religion, it becomes clear that it is both seductive and dangerous. Yet in terms of numbers of converts it has apparently not been terribly successful. Estimates vary, but polls indicate that under 1 percent of the U.S. population, for example, identify their religion as "New Age."[13] Yet one thing the New Age movement has accomplished—and this very effectively—is to help set the stage for a broader emergence of mysticism. From the very beginning the New Age movement has succeeded in popularizing extraordinary experiences, and some of its perspectives along with them. The movement attracted media attention early on because it provided sensational copy. Interestingly, in recent years media coverage of New Age affairs has dropped, yet anomalous experiences still receive ample attention.

Television is a powerful communicator, and live televised discussions and demonstrations of esoteric practices such as channeling, along with programs that claim to document all manner of extraordinary experiences, have definitely raised public awareness and interest in this area. Undoubtedly such coverage has helped to convince people that such things really happen, raising important questions in their minds and whetting their appetites for more. This exposure has apparently not persuaded many people to accept the more radical New Age beliefs, but it has opened the door for moderate views that seem compatible with popular Western thinking.

3

The "Higher Self" & Subconscious Processes

The concepts of the "Higher Self," alternate minds and subconscious processes are critical elements in New Age thought because they help to rationalize the movement's heavy reliance on unusual experiences and subjective inner feelings as primary sources of truth. Modified versions of these views are working their way into popular thinking, providing support for New Mysticism as well. Because of their central role in both systems, it is vital that we examine these beliefs more closely.

Two Minds

From the New Age perspective, humans are complex beings with two minds. One of these is the physical, conscious mind, which we naturally perceive as an integral part of the self, and the other is the spiritual mind, more commonly known as the Higher Self. The Higher Self is presumably vastly superior to the conscious mind and operates autonomously, functioning somewhat like an alter ego. The Higher Self is thought to be the true self, the part of one's being that keeps its identity from one incarnation to the next.

In contrast to the Higher Self, the conscious mind and personality are strongly shaped by the particular brain and body that one is born with and are therefore considered transitory and impermanent. This implies that human life is terribly ironic, since most people live out their days identifying with the conscious mind and never suspecting the presence (or guidance) of the Higher Self. This presumably occurs because the physical mind, dominant in our embodied state, cannot grasp the spiritual truths and experiences that flow from the Higher Self, so it forces the Higher Self to function at a subconscious level.

According to New Age thought, messages from the Higher Self can still break through into normal consciousness from time to time. When they do they are ostensibly nonverbal and come as sudden intuitions, insights, profound feelings of knowing or unusual experiences. They do not come through logic or reasoning, because these functions are ostensibly controlled by the conscious mind. Advocates believe that the Higher Self can manifest itself more clearly during altered states of consciousness, including sleep, which temporarily disable the physical mind. (This helps to explain why many New Agers take their dreams quite seriously.)

It is easy to see how these beliefs legitimize a heavy dependence on unexplained mystical feelings and nonrational, subjective inner experiences. When such experiences occur, adherents usually attribute them to the Higher Self and assume that they are important. These assumptions also encourage adherents to engage in meditation, seek other altered states and pursue "spiritual" practices that presumably make such experiences more likely.

At the popular level, "the subconscious" appears to be taking on many of the characteristics that New Agers ascribe to the Higher Self. Freud popularized the idea of "the subconscious" in the early 1900s, and the concept has been expanded periodically in discussions of subliminal perception, hypnosis and multiple personality as well as popular accounts of "right-brain" versus "left-brain" capabilities. In fact, in popular thinking, the subconscious is now often associated with the "right brain," so that many presumed right-brained capabilities—artistic ability, creativity, "holistic" thinking, intuition, the ability to assess deeper meanings and so on—are ascribed to it.

The notion that humans have great untapped inner potential and/or latent paranormal powers has been brewing in Western culture for a number of years. Since these presumed capabilities remain mysterious and hard to access, it is natural to speculate that they lie hidden in the subconscious. Combining all these concepts yields a "subconscious mind" with great untapped potentials and powers, which probably imparts its wisdom through unusual feelings, intuitions and experiences, and which may communicate more freely in dreams or other altered states. The resemblance between this popular version of the "subconscious mind" and the New Age Higher Self are unmistakable.

A second way New Agers have used the Higher Self concept is to rationalize unusual experiences that might otherwise seem inexplicable or even dangerous. This concept is especially useful for explaining the appearance of "inner guides." Those desiring to make contact with inner guides are usually advised to choose some person, historical figure or even mythological character with whom they could feel comfortable, and then to practice visualizing this being until his or her image becomes very clear in the mind. (This can take quite a bit of practice.) Once this is achieved, they can begin asking this entity for advice. Adherents assume that the use of imagination and visualization simply provides a clearer channel of communication for the Higher Self.

Yet people who have contacted "guides" in this manner sometimes discover that they can become surprisingly autonomous, offering advice that contradicts one's better judgement. This should at least raise some suspicions about the guide's true identity, but it usually doesn't, because New Agers can always fall back on the Higher Self concept. The contradictions do not bother them very much, because they believe the Higher Self is fairly autonomous and operates on its own set of goals and values. They are also reassured that since the Higher Self is just another part of themselves, it is highly unlikely to be offering them advice with malevolent intent. Ironically, many New Agers do believe that there are real spiritual agents who can also act as guides, but in practice the distinctions between imaginary inner guides, the Higher Self and separate spiritual agents acting as guides tend to get very blurred.

Some of the general New Age concepts about inner guides and the Higher Self have been catching on in popular thinking. The idea that one can contact the "subconscious mind" for advice by vividly imagining a specific guide has become fairly popular and has sometimes been used in psychotherapy. Personally, I think we need to be wary of such techniques because they are based on questionable assumptions. While we know that our brains do carry out some sophisticated subconscious operations, the idea that we have a separate subconscious "mind" that is capable of imparting great wisdom is still an unproved assumption. If there is no such mind, the guides and their messages are at best purely imaginary and thus may or may not prove helpful. And, in the worst case, it is possible that some of the autonomous guides are demons in disguise.

Examining the Evidence for Two Minds

The concepts of the Higher Self and the subconscious mind rest on the twin assumptions that *humans have two minds* and that *one of these operates on the subconscious level.* New Agers have garnered support for these ideas by linking them with two related concepts that are widely accepted in Western culture. One of these is the "two-minds, two-brains" hypothesis, which in its original form was based on early data from "split-brain" patients, and the second is a belief in "the subconscious" that has existed within psychological and psychiatric circles for years.

Current evidence suggests, however, that these two concepts and the links that have been made between them and the Higher Self are probably inaccurate. This evidence cannot disprove the existence of a Higher Self (or a "subconscious mind," for that matter), but it certainly weakens the popular case that has been made for both of them.

Evidence for the "Two-Brains, Two-Minds" Hypothesis

Stated simply, the "two-brains, two-minds" proposal suggests that the right and left cerebral hemispheres of the brain function like two separate brains and that each gives rise to a separate mind. The investigators who put forth qualified versions of this hypothesis in the 1970s—Roger Sperry,[1] Joseph Bogen[2] and Robert Ornstein[3]—all based their propositions on neurological data available at that time from split-brain patients and from patients with damage to either the right or the left side of the brain.

Before summarizing this evidence, I need to digress slightly and comment on the assertion that "the mind arises from the brain." This belief is based on the materialistic assumption (favored by most brain scientists) that humans are just physical beings with no separate soul or spirit. According to this view, all of the characteristics of human mindedness, including personality, our sense of self and all our other capabilities, are somehow created by the brain alone. This perspective suggests that there is an equivalence between mind and brain, so scientists often use these words interchangeably. As a Christian and a teacher of neuroscience, I take the position that humans are both physical and spiritual beings and that the unique qualities of human mindedness (language capability, self-awareness, creativity and so forth) are due to the effects of the spirit (or soul) and the brain working together as a unit. I use *mind* in this latter sense throughout this book.

Based on well-known information about the brain, as well as their observations of split-brain patients, Sperry and the other researchers began speculating that the cerebral hemispheres might function like separate brains. For instance, deficits created by injuries to the right and left hemispheres suggested that the two halves might be specialized to accomplish different things. Serious damage to the left hemisphere often produces some loss of language ability (speaking, comprehending speech, reading or writing), whereas comparable damage to the right hemisphere is more likely to create deficits in spatial skills (drawing, copying simple figures, interpreting or drawing maps, finding one's way about in buildings, recognizing faces and so on).[4]

Sperry and the other investigators were also aware that the hemispheres could function independently, if necessary, because they knew of patients who were getting along remarkably well with just one intact hemisphere. The first known case of a missing hemisphere was reported in 1844 by A. L. Wigan, who had witnessed an autopsy of a fifty-year-old man in whom one hemisphere was entirely missing. (Glial cells in the brain can engulf and remove dead neurons, filling the spaces they occupied with scar tissue. Cerebrospinal fluid can also fill in vacant spaces.) In his report Wigan marveled that this man had conversed rationally and even written verses within a few days of his death.[5]

The case of Bruce Lipstadt is even more remarkable. Lipstadt had suffered from very severe, uncontrollable epileptic seizures as a child, and when he was five and a half his doctors performed a left hemispherectomy in a last-ditch effort to save his life. (Hemispherectomies remove most or all of a cerebral hemisphere but leave vital underlying brain structures intact on both sides.) The boy's doctors were pessimistic, expecting him to be severely paralyzed on his right side and unable to talk. But they were proved wrong. The young Lipstadt was eventually able to recover the use of everything but his right hand, and he soon learned to run, bike and swim. Equally remarkable was the gradual increase in his intelligence. When he was tested at the age of nine his IQ was in the dull-normal range, by the age of twenty-one it had risen to 113, and by the time he was twenty-six it had climbed to a superior 126. Lipstadt was working and completing a bachelor's degree in sociology at the time his case was reported.[6] Given his initial handicap, his accomplishments are truly surprising.

Lipstadt's recovery not only demonstrates that one hemisphere can function fairly well without the other but also raises some other pertinent issues. The left hemisphere isn't always the dominant, language hemisphere (although it *is* dominant in approximately 95 percent of right-handed and 75 percent of left-handed people). We could speculate that Lipstadt was one of the few persons who are born with a dominant (verbal) right hemisphere, but there is another plausible explanation for his recovery. If the left hemisphere is injured early in life, usually before the age of five, many of its language functions can apparently develop in the right hemisphere, although not perfectly. Since Lipstadt's seizures started when he was about four, it is possible that his right hemisphere started developing language capability at that time and that this early switch-over was what helped him recover so well. At any rate, data like this helped to convince Sperry, Bogen and others that the hemispheres might operate independently in normal brains.

The most persuasive evidence for the two-minds hypothesis came from the split-brain patients themselves. These patients had undergone callosal section in order to alleviate epileptic seizures that could not be controlled by medication.

The brain's control of voluntary movements is primarily crossed. That is, the left hemisphere controls the movements on the right side of the body, while the right hemisphere controls the movements on the left side of the body. (This is why Lipstadt's doctors anticipated that removing his left hemisphere would produce considerable paralysis on his right side.) Crossed control is especially pronounced in the hands, arms and legs and is less extensive in the muscles of the trunk, which receive input from both sides of the brain. Vision, hearing and kinesthesia (touch, muscle stretch, joint position and the like) are also crossed. Thus information coming from one side of the body travels first to the hemisphere on the opposite side, but then transfers rapidly to the hemisphere on the same side via a broad band of some 200 million neuronal fibers known as the corpus callosum. When the callosum is intact, both hemispheres can receive input from, and control, both sides of the body.

In the split-brain operation, neurosurgeons sever part or all of the corpus callosum. They do this because the callosum can act as a thoroughfare for the abnormal neuronal electrical activity that sweeps through the brain during seizures. This activity often originates in a specific area of the brain that has been injured and has formed scar tissue (focal epilepsy). As long as the abnormal activity is confined to a small area of the brain, it may not even be noticed. However, if and when it spreads across both hemispheres, it produces seizures and unconsciousness. When the callosum is cut, the abnormal brain activity cannot spread across both hemispheres, and this keeps the patient from losing consciousness.

The operation destroys the neurons that are cut, so it is not done often. Yet in spite of its apparent physical severity, it produces surprisingly few negative aftereffects, especially once the patients have had a few weeks to recover.[7] In fact, only in specially designed experiments have some of the more striking and permanent effects of cutting the callosum become evident.

In some of these experiments, patients were seated in front of a small screen and asked to look at a dot in the middle of the screen while the experimenter projected a word or picture to the right or left of the dot. The images appeared for only about one-tenth of a second, so patients would not have time to move their eyes. When a word was flashed to the right of the dot, the image was sent to the left (language) hemisphere, and the patient consciously saw the word, naming it easily. If a word was flashed to the left of the dot (to the right hemisphere), the patients were not aware of having seen anything. In this case, if the patients were asked to use their left hand (controlled by the right hemisphere) to reach behind a screen to identify the object named by touch, some patients could do this. If they were asked to *name* the object they were holding in their left hand, however, they could not do so.[8]

In these patients the right hemisphere had apparently recognized the word and identified the correct object by touch, but the patient was not aware of the word or the sensory information from the left hand because his or her callosum was cut and the crucial sensory information remained isolated in the right hemisphere. The effect was striking because it indicated that under some circumstances the nondominant hemisphere has the ability to direct intelligent action without one's awareness or conscious authorization to do so. The results also suggest that the left, or language, hemisphere plays a critical role in conscious awareness.

Sperry and his coworkers conducted many other interesting tests on this select group of patients. Eran Zaidel invented a tiny optical device that could be worn like a contact lens, which allowed him to test the right hemisphere more thoroughly. Patients wore this device on their right eye, with their left eye patched. The device shifted the visual image onto the right or temporal half of the retina, which projects only to the right hemisphere. In the patients he was able to test, Zaidel found that the reading comprehension of the right hemisphere was very limited. It could respond to nouns but not to other parts of speech, and did not comprehend the simplest of sentences.[9] However, the right hemisphere could apparently direct the left hand to identify pictures of the patient, family members and friends, or pets and belongings when these were scattered among similar but unfamiliar pictures.[10] Sperry interpreted this to mean that the right hemisphere knew, on its own, that the people and items in the pictures were personally significant, and he took this as evidence for a second mind.

Michael Gazzaniga's findings could also have been interpreted as evidence for the two-minds segment of the hypothesis, although Gazzaniga himself vigorously opposed this view. Gazzaniga was originally one of Sperry's graduate assistants and has probably tested more split-brain patients than anyone else in the United States. In the course of his testing he found two patients, a teenager named Paul and a young woman known as V. P., who had considerable language capability in their right as well as their dominant left hemisphere. They were unique among split-brain patients because their left hands (controlled by the right hemisphere) were able to spell out answers to Gazzaniga's questions with Scrabble letters.

On one occasion Gazzaniga flashed a picture of a playing card to Paul's right hemisphere, and Paul's left hand started spelling out the word *card*. The left hand had just finished assembling the letters *C A R* when Gazzaniga asked Paul what he had seen. Paul looked at the letters and said, "Car." Just as he was saying this, however, his left hand completed the word with the letter *D*. Paul then said, "Oh, it was a card," and smiled as if apologizing for his inconsistency.[11]

Another time Gazzaniga flashed two different scenes on the screen: a picture of a chicken claw that went to Paul's left hemisphere and a picture of a snow scene that went to his right hemisphere. Then Paul was shown four pictures and asked to point to the one that related to what he had seen. Simultaneously his right hand pointed to a chicken and his left hand pointed to a shovel. When Paul was asked why he chose what he did, he immediately responded, "Oh, that's easy. The chicken claw goes with the chicken and you need a shovel to clean out a chicken shed."

Paul was evidently not consciously aware of having seen the snow scene, but his right hemisphere apparently *was* aware and had directed his left hand to point to the shovel. Curiously, the discrepancy between his hands didn't seem to bother Paul. He could easily explain his right hand's response because he was fully aware of having seen the chicken claw. Yet he also came up with a reasonable explanation for the response made by his left hand with no hesitation. And even though Paul could only guess at the reasons for choosing the two pictures, he did not state his reasons as if he were guessing.[12]

On a number of occasions Gazzaniga tried flashing commands, like "Walk," to Paul and V. P.'s right hemispheres. When he did so, they usually responded by getting up and walking away from the testing area. When asked where they were going, they would reply something like, "Oh, just going into my house to get a Coke." Faced with the fact that they were walking away from the experiment, they surmised consciously that they must be doing so for a reason, but the reason that came to mind was different from the one that had actually prompted the action.[13]

Gazzaniga observed the same phenomenon on many different occasions. After the right hemisphere initiated an appropriate action based on its own information, Paul and V. P. would casually and effortlessly come up with rational, but incorrect, reasons to explain their actions.

As he pondered this, Gazzaniga began to suspect that their actions were not all that surprising. On occasion people with normal brains find themselves taking actions that are hard to explain (say, putting the salt shaker in the refrigerator) or that seem inconsistent with their conscious intentions. In Gazzaniga's view, such actions are too limited to come from some second "mind." He believes it is more likely they are initiated by subconscious brain mechanisms or "brain modules" that have a limited set of functions but may be able to initiate some highly circumscribed actions on their own.[14] Actions of this sort were presumably just more noticeable in Paul and V. P. because it was possible to communicate directly with their right hemisphere with simple verbal commands, bypassing normal conscious control.

Developing and Popularizing the "Two-Minds" Hypothesis

As Sperry and his younger colleagues continued their work and their confidence in the two-minds hypothesis increased, they cautiously attributed other mindlike qualities to the operations of the hemispheres. The operations of the left hemisphere were characterized as "logical," "analytical" and "rational," and those of the right hemisphere as "Gestalt" (able to see a pattern from many parts), "synthetic" (able to put disparate parts into a meaningful whole) and intuitive.[15]

Robert Ornstein, a psychologist who had studied hemisphere differences (EEGs) in normal subjects, generalized these ideas still further. He argued that the two hemispheres are specialized for different modes of thought, the left for logical, rational, analytic thought and the right for endeavors that are more intuitive, synthetic, artistic or creative.[16] He also proposed that we may use the hemispheres alternately, depending on the task at hand, and that while one hemisphere is busy, the other is probably idling on standby.[17]

From his writing and his appearances on the New Age speaking circuits in the 1970s and early 1980s, it is evident that Ornstein was sympathetic with New Age thought, and this undoubtedly influenced his views of mind and brain.[18] His popular book *The Psychology of Consciousness* added much to the movement's credibility. At the same time, however, Ornstein has sought to be a voice of reason and moderation and has debunked many of the movement's excesses.[19]

Many of Ornstein's generalizations went far beyond the data, and other researchers did not agree with him,[20] but his ideas had enormous popular appeal and were eagerly picked up and expanded by writers for journals and magazines. The ensuing popularization of right-left dichotomies has created something of a cultural myth. Some of its elements include the idea that we can be typed by our preferred mode of thinking. We are either "right-brained" (artistic, intuitive, holistic, in tune with Eastern culture and so forth) or "left-brained" (logical, verbal, mathematical, in tune with Western culture).[21] In addition, it has been suggested that the right hemisphere, and the mind associated with it, has all sorts of romantic and even mystical properties. The evidence currently available casts doubt on all these generalizations.

The Hypothesis in Light of Recent Evidence

The two-brains, two-minds hypothesis was intended to help explain the functions of the right and left hemispheres in normal brains. However, it is no longer taken seriously in the scientific community because it is inconsistent with new data and was based on an unreliable sample. One of the problems with using data from split-brain patients to infer the functions of normal nondominant hemispheres is that one cannot be sure that the patients' right hemispheres are like those in normal brains. Their brains have typically sustained serious injuries, in the accidents that precipitated their seizures and in the split-brain operation itself. Drawing inferences about normal brains from damaged brains is always risky because the brain can compensate for injuries, particularly if these occur early in life (as in the case of Bruce Lipstadt).

This difficulty is compounded by the fact that most of the reports of right-hemisphere abilities that were published in the 1970s and early 1980s were based on a very small subset of patients (according to Gazzaniga, two of the fifteen studied by Sperry and his colleagues on the West Coast and three of twenty-eight East Coast patients tested by Gazzaniga).[22] These five patients were different from all the other patients in a very significant way. Their right (nondominant) hemispheres could initiate intelligent left-handed responses when words or pictures were flashed exclusively to them, but the nondominant hemispheres of the other thirty-eight patients apparently could not do this. In fact, according to Gazzaniga these other patients' right hemispheres didn't respond independently to much of anything, so they were dropped from further testing.[23] In some of this latter group the lack of responsiveness may have been due to previous, extensive damage to the right hemisphere, but that probably cannot account for the lack of responsiveness seen in all of them.[24]

Gazzaniga points out that the five well-studied patients all had a certain amount of language ability in the right hemisphere. He believes that this probably was so because each had sustained some *early* damage to the left hemisphere. He also speculates that their right hemisphere's apparent ability to act with a certain degree of awareness and independence might actually be related to the unusual language capabilities they developed rather than some intrinsic capability for "mindedness" in the right hemisphere itself.[25]

Recent research into the activities of the right and left hemispheres in *normal* brains has also discredited the idea that the hemispheres function like separate brains. With more extensive investigation, the distinctive features of the right and left hemispheres have blurred, and it has become clear that they work together in close cooperation rather than by taking turns.[26] It is now evident that both right and left hemispheres have spatial and artistic capabilities, although these may be of different types in the different hemispheres. Many artists who have sustained fairly severe damage to their right hemisphere are still able to produce paintings and drawings at the highest level of creative expression.[27]

In the case of language, the left hemisphere is definitely dominant over the right in the production of speech and in many aspects of language perception. But the right hemisphere may be able to recognize words using a different mode of· perception,[28] and it definitely plays a role in both recognizing and expressing the emotional, nonverbal aspects of speech.[29] In general, contemporary investigators have concluded that it is more helpful to assign the various brain capabilities they are studying to "brain modules" (portions of the brain that have specific and limited functions) rather than to the right or left hemisphere as a whole because human (and primate) brains are evidently extremely variable with respect to the location of many of these modules.

New, nonintrusive recording techniques that allow researchers to observe the moment-by-moment activity of various parts of the brain reveal that the two hemispheres cooperate extensively. Researchers can now use delicate sensors to detect the amount of blood flowing to various parts of the brain. They can use this information to tell which areas of the brain are more active at any given time, because as activity increases, so does the blood flow. Studies of this type have shown that the similarities in the activation patterns of the two hemispheres are more striking than their differences, even when a person is engaged in an activity that is presumably highly lateralized, like speech. In one test, for instance, the blood flow was only 3 percent greater in the left hemisphere than in the right for a verbal analogies test and only about 3 percent greater in the right than the left for a picture-completion task.[30]

In view of the serious limitations of the split-brain data, and given mounting evidence that normal hemispheres work closely together rather than as separate brains, the "two-brains" portion of the two-minds hypothesis is no longer tenable, and most experts, including Roger Sperry himself,[31] have abandoned it.[32] Without the two-brains portion of the hypothesis, it is much more difficult to conceive of a physiological substrate for a separate subconscious mind, so this weakens the popular case for it. This does not necessarily discredit the Higher Self, because it is thought to be spiritual. Yet these findings do make it more difficult to see how the Higher Self is interrelated with the person.

In Search of Subconscious Minds

Thanks to the persuasive writings of Sigmund Freud, Carl Jung and others who have followed in their tradition, the concept of "the subconscious" is very familiar in Western culture. Yet there is much confusion and disagreement among various authorities and the public at large over what this term actually means. This confusion has helped obscure the fact that the New Age version of the subconscious lies at one extreme of an entire spectrum of beliefs. Many New Agers believe that the subconscious represents a separate, autonomous mind that is not only equivalent to the conscious mind but vastly superior to it.

Those who study subconscious activities (in cognitive psychology and neuroscience) are much more conservative, usually taking "the subconscious" to refer to subconscious *processes*—covert operations originating in the brain that can exert some independent influence upon our wants, moods and actions but that are also basically subordinate to our conscious desires and commands.

To bring some clarity out of the confusion, we need to address two questions. First, are there processes in our bodies and minds that are definitely carried out on a subconscious level, without our conscious awareness or intention? Second, if such processes exist, what is their probable source? Are they originating in our brain, or from some second mind?

A Survey of Subconscious Processes

The most rudimentary subconscious processes carried out by our bodies and brains are those that are aimed at keeping us alive. Certain parts of the brain monitor and control automatic processes like breathing, digestion, temperature regulation and blood circulation which keep the body functioning. Other brain mechanisms warn us when we need to eat, drink, sleep or rest, or to avoid potential dangers. In order to motivate us to meet these needs, these mechanisms can initiate a variety of sensations: hunger, thirst, tiredness, pain, sleepiness and fear, which incite us to take action, while feelings of gratification, restedness and physical well-being reinforce our efforts to meet our physical needs. Other parts of the brain mediate certain aspects of sexual desire and gratification. Since feelings of physical gratification and need are often integrated with emotional responses, it is likely that the brain mechanisms that initiate feelings of need can also induce, or at least influence, some of our emotional states.

Another major function of the brain is to enable us to use our bodies to move about and to interact with the physical world. Physically speaking, activities like reaching out to pick up an object, walking, biking, typing or driving a car are incredibly complex and sophisticated, yet the innumerable mechanical components of these actions usually proceed quite smoothly, well below the level of our conscious awareness. Such skilled activities do require a great deal of conscious effort and practice while they are being learned, but once they are programmed in the brain, they seem so easy and natural that we usually take them very much for granted. We probably shouldn't. Skilled motor behaviors of this type require the coordinated action of hundreds of muscles, all contracting with just the right strength at just the right time. In addition, these movements have to be integrated with a daunting, ever-changing flow of visual, kinesthetic and tactile information that is constantly streaming into the brain from the eyes, muscles, joints and skin.

Intriguingly, our brains appear to manage all this information and activity with a certain level of awareness and purposiveness of their own. One way to appreciate this is to think about our usual mental activities while we are engaged in a routine but skilled behavior such as driving. It is possible to get from point A to point B, ten miles down the road, with very minimal conscious awareness of driving. In fact, we are very likely to be consciously absorbed in an interesting radio program or in thinking about the day's events. Yet *something* has to remain alert to crucial roadway information and respond to it correctly, or we wouldn't stay on the road for very long. It is evidently the brain that directs our eyes to keep looking at the road and that processes the ever-changing visual information coming from them, using it to direct the movements of our hands on the steering wheel and the movements of our feet on the accelerator or brake. It even appears to act as a kind of sentinel, breaking into our reverie immediately if an unusual or dangerous situation starts to develop. (How many times have you found that your foot was moving toward the brake even before you became fully aware of a dangerous situation ahead?)

It is the brain's ability to execute fairly complex sequences of motor activities on its own that probably gives rise to the subconscious, automatic activities that occur during sleep—sleepwalking, sitting up in bed and "looking around." These activities are usually simple, short-lived and aimless. Researchers still do not know what initiates them, but it is apparently not our dreams, because in the dream state (REM sleep) our voluntary muscles are essentially paralyzed to prevent us from acting out our dreams. But these behaviors are very similar to the actions that can be carried out with little conscious effort while we are awake.

The automatic behaviors that occur during sleep are also similar to the "automatisms" that can sometimes be seen in patients with an unusual type of petit mal epilepsy. Oddly, their seizures disrupt their conscious awareness but still allow certain motor areas of the brain to function normally. As a consequence these patients may act like automatons during their seizures. They may wander about, confused and aimless, engage in some low-level stereotyped behavior or persist with the activities they were engaged in when the attack began. People who have received a severe blow to the head can also act like this for a time.

Neurosurgeon Wilder Penfield had three patients who displayed high-level functioning during their attacks. One was a pianist whose seizures would sometimes occur while he was practicing. When an attack began, he would pause briefly but would then resume playing and continue to play with great dexterity until he regained consciousness. Interestingly, his mother was apparently able to tell when he was in the midst of an attack, because she noticed a different quality in his music. Another patient sometimes had attacks while walking home from work, but he still managed to negotiate busy streets and stay on the correct route during these episodes. A third patient would sometimes lose consciousness while driving. He would continue to drive, but he apparently had a penchant for driving through red lights when he was in this state.[33]

It is relatively easy to identify examples of subconscious *motor* activities, but it is more difficult to find unambiguous examples of higher cognitive activities that are definitely initiated and carried out without any conscious input. Some experts believe that hypnotically induced activities may occur subconsciously, because people who are hypnotized may act and feel as if their consciousness has been altered and will not usually remember the episode unless the hypnotist tells them they will. But the question whether hypnotic activities are truly subconscious is still very controversial. Many authorities believe that hypnosis represents a kind of voluntary role-playing, others think it is an altered or trance state, but no one knows for sure.

One state that does incorporate subconscious mental activities is dreaming. In some dreams we appear to be thinking or working on problems. A few of these dreams may even eventuate in exciting "insights" or "solutions" (although their meaning and significance often evaporates in the clear light of morning). We also experience vivid narrative dreams, which range from the slightly unrealistic to the totally bizarre. In fact, if one were to characterize dreams using psychological criteria, they would be called hallucinatory (the events portrayed only occur in the mind), delusional (dreams create false beliefs while they are in progress) and cognitively abnormal (they involve illogical or impossible situations, distortions and absurdities). They also exaggerate emotions, especially fear, anger and surprise, and are exceptionally difficult to remember.[34]

Researchers do not yet know why dreaming occurs, but several are following leads that suggest they are somehow related to memory processing in the brain. J. Allan Hobson and R. W. McCarley have suggested that dreams may be produced when the mind/brain system tries to make sense of random memories, images or experiences that are stimulated accidentally by neuronal signals emanating from the brain stem during REM sleep.[35] F. Crick and G. Mitchison propose that senseless or bizarre dreams are produced incidentally while the brain is purging spurious or useless information from its memory banks.[36] As a third possibility, Jonathan Winson argues that dreams may be produced while the brain is reprocessing and storing memories acquired during the previous day.[37]

To make a long story short, at this point we still do not know where dreams come from or why they come. Some may impart insights into the way we process information, or perhaps into the things we think are important, although even these sorts of inferences may be a bit of a stretch. At this point there is little evidence to suggest that dreams emanate from a separate, subconscious mind. And even if they do, they cannot give us much assurance about that mind's ability to dispense wisdom and guidance (or even its state of mental health, for that matter).

One process that may seem subconscious, but actually isn't, is *nonverbal* problem solving. One example might be mentally mapping out an alternate route while driving, in order to get around a heavy pocket of traffic. Another might be mentally reviewing the shapes of various tools one has on hand in order to find one that could substitute for a tool that's missing. A third example might be visualizing how a finished flower arrangement should look in order to guide the process of assembling it. The mental processes involved in these efforts are difficult to label or describe, but they are still occurring as a direct result of conscious effort, so it would be inappropriate to say they are subconscious.

The evidence that helped convince Freud and other therapists that human beings might have a subconscious mind was their patients' hidden, inner conflicts that kept surfacing during counseling sessions and needed to be resolved. To explain these, Freud conjectured that there were three separate parts of the personality, the id, ego and superego, which operated in different modes, possessed different values and goals, and frequently acted in opposition to one another. And, partly because his patients seemed to lack real insight into their conflicts, he surmised that the id and superego must be operating subconsciously.

In the beginning Freud may have meant for the id, ego and superego to be used primarily as explanatory *constructs*. However, as he developed his theory and worked out the dynamic interrelationships between these parts of personality, these constructs began to acquire a life of their own. And as the id, ego and superego began to seem more real and lifelike, so did the subconscious mind.

The crucial question in this case is whether we need the concept of a subconscious mind to explain the deep inner conflicts that are sometimes uncovered in therapy. In my opinion we don't. By itself, the presence of inner conflict does not demand a separate mind, because we can as easily demonstrate conflicts within one mind as between two (for example, "Shall I buy the Ford or the Toyota?"). In fact, there are many ways to create serious conflicts within one mind. This can happen whenever we have to make decisions that carry the possibility of serious gains *and* losses. It can also happen when our personal goals and wants clash with the external demands placed on us by situations or by other people.

The fact that psychotherapeutic clients sometimes seem unaware of the nature of their inner conflicts can be explained in other ways as well. Perhaps some haven't really examined their reasons for feeling the way they do. People sometimes suppress conflicts and avoid thinking about issues because they cause deep pain and because the solutions that do come to mind promise to be even more painful if carried out. At times people suppress conflicts because they don't want to take responsibility for the decisions that need to be made.

It's possible that some aspects of these conflicts do lie buried in sub-conscious processes—in the brain, the spirit or the interactions between them—that we simply do not comprehend. Human mindedness is still very much a mystery. But whatever the source, it still does not appear that we need to invoke a subconscious "mind" to explain them.

Are Subconscious Activities Initiated by a Separate Mind?

The answer to this question depends heavily on one's definition of a mind. At its most fundamental level, mindedness includes the ability to be aware of events, to respond to them appropriately, to learn, to remember, to work out simple physical problems and to respond with appropriate emotion. If these are our criteria for mindedness, then we could conclude that some of our subconscious activities are being directed by a separate mind. (Interestingly, all these characteristics of mindedness can be seen in animals as well as humans.)

But human mindedness entails much more than this. It includes a sense of self, the ability to use language, logic and abstract reasoning, to appreciate meaning and humor, to make inferences, to create, to produce and appreciate art and music, to define goals and purposes, and much, much more. Above all, it includes conscious awareness, the ability to know that we know, to reflect on our existence and even to reflect on and make judgments about the various things we are aware of. There is no experimental evidence for a subconscious mind that can do any of these things on its own. In fact, by definition, a *subconscious* mind cannot contribute to either awareness or self-awareness, yet these are generally considered the hallmarks of human mindedness.

How are we to explain the impressive subconscious processes detailed in this chapter if we do not resort to a subconscious mind? I would argue that these processes originate from the brain, which manages the incredibly complex operations of the body for us, freeing the conscious aspect of our being for more productive and interesting endeavors. We do not yet comprehend how these subconscious operations of the brain influence our conscious life, but from what we do know about them, we can say that they do not appear to be coming from a second, subconscious "mind."

4

Altered States & Extraordinary Experiences

Altered states of consciousness have contributed to the development of the New Age movement and New Mysticism in several important ways, but most notably through their connections with the extraordinary experiences that seem to be occurring in great abundance. Those who investigate such experiences have discovered that most of them are occurring while experiencers are in altered states of consciousness—produced by sleep, hypnosis, mind-altering drugs or Eastern meditation. These experiences can assume many forms, but some of the more persuasive include visits to spectacular, otherworldly places, feelings of transcending space and time or of merging with the elemental forces of the universe, apparent journeys out of the body and contacts with awesome spiritual beings.

From a traditional Western perspective, the relationship between altered states and extraordinary experiences is fascinating but enigmatic. Here New Agers are a jump ahead of the rest of us, because they do have a ready explanation for the connection. Altered states presumably facilitate unusual experiences because they block the conscious mind, providing access to the Higher Self and the spiritual insights and experiences that flow through it. For those of us who do not subscribe to New Age thought, there are two other possibilities. One is that these experiences are provoked by altered states, and their cause is primarily physical or psychological. The second is that some of the experiences are initiated by real contacts with spirits, but that these are somehow enhanced or made easier when one is in an altered state.

Whatever the actual nature of this relationship or the reasons for it, it is important that we understand it, because it can provide some crucial insights into the experiences and the impact they are having on people's lives and beliefs. Fortunately, there is quite a bit of objective evidence related to altered states which we can draw upon in our search for an explanation.

General Characteristics of Altered States

Many important attributes of ordinary consciousness are missing in altered states of consciousness. Ordinarily we can control our thoughts and actions and are consciously aware of events within and around us. Our mode of thinking may be active (planning, solving problems, making decisions, evaluating and so forth) or passive (letting thoughts wander or simply taking in sensory information), but in both modes it is predictable and experienced similarly by other people. In ordinary consciousness our sensory and perceptual systems also function accurately, emotions are maintained within normal bounds, and memory is intact and functional.

In altered states all these essential functions can be lost or severely limited. These losses can be seen in sleep, an altered state that is familiar to everyone. When we sleep we lose all awareness of our surroundings and are only dimly aware of our thoughts and dreams unless we happen to awaken while they are in progress. We are also unable to control our thought processes or the movements of our body. In fact, our voluntary muscles are virtually paralyzed while we dream (evidently to prevent us from acting out our dreams), and mental events become highly improbable and surrealistic. In our dreams we may encounter persons we have never met, fly, leap over tall buildings, float down the stairs or find ourselves acting and thinking in ways that seem completely foreign and out of character.

Memory is also greatly impaired during sleep. Most adults dream for about an hour and a half each night in regular dream periods, which recur about every ninety minutes and are controlled by the brain. Yet by morning virtually all of this vivid mental activity has disappeared. When we do awaken with a dream in progress, the details of the event slip away even as we are struggling to recall them. In fact, the loss of dream material is so rapid and so insistent that it almost seems we are programmed to forget it.

The term *altered states* can mean different things to different people, but here I will use it in a fairly restricted manner. It is important to distinguish between true altered states and minor alterations in ordinary consciousness. Daydreaming or deep absorption in a novel, a movie or even prayer may sometimes seem like being in an altered state, but these conditions still have much more in common with ordinary consciousness than they do with true altered states. (One can still differentiate between what is real and unreal, think clearly, control thoughts and actions, and so on.) I will use *altered states* to refer to sleep, moderate to deep hypnosis, and drug, trance and meditative states that interfere significantly with important volitional, cognitive and perceptual functions.

Sensory Deprivation

There are many ways to induce altered states. Four techniques that have been popular in New Age/New Consciousness circles include sensory deprivation, hypnosis, psychedelic (mind-altering) drugs and Eastern meditation. Meditation is currently a very popular method, but I am not including it here because it is treated in detail in chapter six. All these techniques produce some similar effects on consciousness.

For reasons that scientists do not yet understand, drastically reducing the normal flow of sensory information into the brain from the five senses, or simply making it very monotonous and uniform, can create fairly profound alterations in consciousness. This was discovered accidentally in the early 1950s by some young researchers at McGill University in Montreal, Canada, working under the supervision of Donald Hebb. These investigators were interested in studying the effects of the "brainwashing" techniques that were then being used on American prisoners by Korean communists.[1] For the experiment, student volunteers were asked to lie in bed in a small soundproof room, wearing translucent goggles that prevented them from seeing anything but diffuse white light. Earphones delivered a monotonous humming sound; to minimize the sense of touch, hands were covered with soft cotton gloves, and cardboard tubes lined with cotton were placed over arms and legs. The students could sleep as much as they wanted and were allowed brief timeouts to go to the restroom or eat meals (although they had to keep their goggles on). Each volunteer was offered twenty dollars a day for every day he could stay in this strange environment. (Twenty dollars was a large incentive at the time.)

Many students volunteered, but despite the potential financial rewards, half quit before forty-eight hours, and only a few stayed longer than four days. Most of the students found the situation very stressful and unpleasant. At first they spent a good deal of time sleeping, but as time wore on they slept less and became extremely bored and restless. Most experienced major mood swings, periods of confusion in which they could not think clearly or control their thoughts, and feelings of mild nausea and fatigue. Many of them also reported hallucinations and unusual perceptual distortions.

Most of the hallucinations were visual, but others were auditory or even tactile. Interestingly, the visual hallucinations typically followed a progression from simple to more complex. Participants would first notice a lightening or brightening in some portion of the uniform white field produced by the goggles. This was followed by simple geometric patterns like those that can be seen at the beginning of a migraine headache or certain types of epileptic seizures, then by cartoonlike figures (for example, "eyeglasses everywhere" or "an endless line of squirrel-like figures with sacks over their backs marching over a hill"), and finally progressed to more complex and realistic scenes (people, bizarre architecture and other images).

The images, which seemed to be external rather than internal, moved and changed fairly rapidly, and scanning the drifting scenes caused eyestrain and nausea. At first the subjects thought this imagery was interesting and amusing, but later it became irritating because it interfered with their sleep. The imagery would generally disappear during cognitive activities that required conscious effort, such as doing mental arithmetic, but it was not disrupted by physical exercise or conversation.[2]

A few of the students also experienced very unusual disturbances in body image. One reported feeling as if he was twins, two bodies overlapping one another. Several people reported feelings of floating, and one person felt that his mind had left his body and was floating around the room.

Later studies generally confirmed the results obtained at McGill, although the frequency and extent of hallucinatory activity varied from study to study. Other investigations have also shown that prolonged sensory deprivation (over weeks) can even alter the physical activity of the brain, substantially slowing normal brain-wave activity.[3]

One investigator who eventually developed strong New Age leanings in connection with his sensory-deprivation research was psychiatrist John Lilly. He developed a water-tank technique that drastically reduced all forms of sensory input. Volunteers were suspended vertically in the middle of a deep tank, in water maintained at skin temperature, wearing a lightweight diving helmet that allowed them to breathe. The water reduced their sense of touch and their ability to sense the pull of gravity. The tank was in a dark, soundproof room.[4] This severely restricted environment produced dramatic results, including deep relaxation and novel mental imagery, within two or three hours.[5]

Lilly experimented extensively on himself, experiencing waking dreams, trancelike states and even mystical (spiritually significant) encounters in this setting.[6] When he took LSD before entering the tank,[7] he discovered that he could apparently leave his body and travel to other realms at will. Earlier in his life Lilly had encountered two spirit guides during an out-of-body experience after an injury that had left him comatose and very close to death. On one of his excursions from the tank, he decided he would try to visit those guides. He "found" them (by willing to go to them), but they weren't pleased. By Lilly's account, the guides admitted that his visit demonstrated spiritual progress, but they advised him that there were better ways of reaching them. He was instructed to go back and work with techniques like deep hypnosis or meditation which would allow him to contact them without leaving his body. After refining these techniques, he was to teach them to others.[8] Lilly's subsequent research and writing were dedicated to this cause.

I attended one of Lilly's seminars at a professional symposium in Chicago in 1981 entitled "The Healing Potential of the Human Brain: Exploration of a New Frontier"[9]—a gathering that turned out to be an early teaching forum for some of the important leaders in the New Age movement. The first part of Lilly's seminar dealt with his research on bottlenose dolphins, but in the second half of the presentation he described his latest spiritual adventures. By his own account, he had become an unwilling agent for an extraterrestrial group known as ECHO, who were carrying out a plan to take greater control of the earth. He described how these beings would take over his body and use it to communicate with other people when it suited their purposes, and how they had roughed him up quite a bit when he didn't want to join their cause.

In a book written in 1972 Lilly had been very enthusiastic about his spiritual adventures, but at the conference nine years later he seemed disillusioned, mechanical and devoid of any hope or joy. He commented ruefully that many times he could no longer tell whether he was really in control of his body and mind or not. My impression was that he had either slipped over the edge psychologically or completely surrendered to demonic control. Whatever the case, the other professionals in attendance did not seem shocked or incredulous. Judging by their comments, they were taking what he had to say quite seriously.

Hypnosis

People have been trying to explain hypnosis ever since the Viennese physician Franz Anton Mesmer (1734-1815) brought it to public attention with his controversial demonstrations of "mesmerism" in the latter half of the eighteenth century. In spite of many valiant efforts, however, hypnosis is still almost as mysterious and controversial as it was in Mesmer's time. Authorities still disagree over what it is. Most, like Earnest Hilgard, a well-respected investigator who has conducted many scientific studies of the phenomenon, think it is essentially an altered state because of its unusual effects, especially in people who are moderately to deeply hypnotizable.[10] (There are wide differences in hypnotic susceptibility. Only about 5 percent of the population can be deeply hypnotized; another 20 percent or so can scarcely be hypnotized at all. Everyone else falls somewhere between these two extremes.)

People who are moderately hypnotized feel as if they are in a different state and can sense definite changes in consciousness when the trance is deepened. Sometimes they experience dizziness or feel as if they are blacking out, floating or spinning around.[11] The focus of their awareness and their behavior also changes. They become less aware of external events and less willing to think, plan or take any initiative without instructions from the hypnotist. Their passivity and dependence can be considerable. One of Hilgard's subjects described it this way: "At one point I was trying to decide if my legs were crossed, but I couldn't tell, and didn't quite have the initiative to move to find out."[12]

Hypnosis produces marked changes in mental activity. It enhances imagination, fantasy and visual images and may increase one's access to visual memories from the past. These memories can seem very vivid and realistic. At the hypnotist's suggestion, subjects can relive childhood memories or even dream, with the dream beginning and ending on a prearranged signal from the hypnotist. In very deep states of hypnosis, subjects can have full-blown mystical experiences in which they seem to leave their bodies to travel in mysterious spiritual realms or reach a new sense of oneness with the universe.

The enhanced capacity for imagination and fantasy that occurs in hypnotic states does come at a price, because it is accompanied by increased suggestibility and a considerable loss of reality testing. These qualities allow susceptible individuals to accept all kinds of strange distortions. If the hypnotist suggests that the number of people seated at the table will double or that people walking around the room have no heads or feet, deeply hypnotizable subjects will actually see this happen. The hypnotist's suggestions literally shape the subjects' reality when they are in this state.

For a fair number of people, hypnotic suggestion is powerful enough to reduce or eliminate physical pain. Although not widely used for these purposes, hypnosis has been employed to reduce pain in childbirth, in surgery of various types and in dental work.[13]

Hypnosis has some significant effects on memory. Hypnotic subjects have difficulty remembering what transpired during hypnosis (this is called posthypnotic amnesia) unless the hypnotist tells them they will remember. Hypnosis makes visual memories seem more vivid but decreases the accuracy of recall. It is very easy to interweave fantasy with real memories or to create entirely fictitious episodes in this state.[14]

Psychotherapists and law-enforcement officials have sometimes used hypnosis to help people recall repressed or forgotten memories. This practice is risky, however, because it is easy to confabulate memories that conform to one's inner wishes or the hypnotist's suggestions. Once the new "memory" is created, it replaces the original and is retained as a "true" memory after the hypnotic session is over. Courts of law recognize these dangers, and most will not accept testimony obtained under hypnosis[15] or from witnesses who have previously been hypnotized.

Psychotherapists need to be especially careful with hypnosis, or they can create false memories, as in the case of "false memory syndrome." These can seriously mislead the therapists and their clients. In a typical case of this sort, adult clients (usually women) come for therapy for some common problem (such as recurrent headaches, anxiety, depression or an eating disorder), but over the course of therapy they "recall" bits and pieces of incidents that suggest they were sexually abused by parents or relatives while they were young.

There is well-documented evidence of childhood sexual abuse and incest in America, and this is a real problem. However, in cases of false memory syndrome, the only indications of wrongdoing are "repressed memories" that were totally unknown to the clients at the beginning of therapy but come out bit by bit as clients are urged to recall while in deep relaxation or a hypnotic state. The parents of these clients are typically horrified by the accusations and deny them absolutely. The parents' statements and their character are supported by the testimony of siblings, other family members and close friends. The situation that ensues can be totally devastating. Families split into warring camps. Devoted parents are charged with terrible crimes against their children (or even their grandchildren) and then left alone to deal with ostracism, lawsuits or even jail sentences. Sometimes their marriage breaks under the strain.[16]

What is creating this problem? According to statistics compiled by the False Memory Syndrome Foundation (formed by a distinguished group of psychologists and psychiatrists to combat this problem), the origin is a subgroup of psychotherapists who call themselves "traumatists." These therapists share the conviction that childhood sexual abuse is very common. They believe that the memories of such events get repressed into "the subconscious," where they cause all sorts of problems until they are consciously recalled and dealt with.[17] These therapists assume that the offending memories can be dislodged from "the subconscious" through hypnosis, dream interpretation, sodium amytal, trance writing, reading self-help books, participating in "survivor" groups or massage. Yet there is no scientific evidence to support their assumption that these techniques produce accurate memory recall.[18] In fact, the evidence points strongly in the other direction.

The problem is not that the therapists are uncaring but rather that they are operating on questionable assumptions. Many seem to have latched onto some of Freud's early ideas without attending to the fact that he reversed his opinions on these issues later on. Early in his career Freud made extensive use of hypnosis, and he was amazed at the number of hypnotized women who would recall being raped by their fathers. At that time he assumed that the memories were true, that they had been repressed into the subconscious and that hypnosis was a valid way of bringing them out into the open. With time, however, Freud and other analysts and psychiatrists began to doubt the truthfulness of these memories, and they dropped the use of hypnosis.[19]

Another of the traumatists' assumptions that is now being questioned is whether childhood memories of traumatic incidents are actually forgotten.[20] In many cases victims of incest remember the incidents all too clearly and wish they could forget them. One final observation about the traumatists' techniques, which should have made them question their methods immediately, is the fact that *they are just as likely to produce "memories" of abuse by space aliens, of Satanic ritual abuse or of being someone else in a "past life" as they are to produce memories of incest.*[21]

Another therapy situation in which hypnosis may be creating problems is in the treatment of "multiple personality disorder." Some therapists commonly use hypnosis to uncover covert personalities and to reintegrate them with the main personality. In most cases, however, new "personalities" apparently do not manifest themselves in normal consciousness unless they have first made an appearance in the hypnotic state, while the therapist is actively searching for them. This, along with the fact that people with multiple personality disorder are often deeply hypnotizable and suggestible, raises the disturbing possibility that therapists are unwittingly creating many of these personalities with their own suggestions.[22]

Psychedelic Drugs
Historically, the psychedelic or hallucinogenic drugs, such as mescaline and LSD (lysergic acid diethylamide), have played a very important role in the New Age movement. Their widespread use throughout the 1960s and early 1970s created a flood of unusual, mystically tinged experiences that set people searching among assorted gurus and Eastern religions to try to explain what was happening to them. Drug experiences are still attracting people to mysticism; however, experienced seekers prefer meditation to drugs because the experiences it offers are very similar but are less hazardous and easier to control. Still, it is instructive to take a brief

look at these two drugs, their uses and their unusual effects.

Mescaline comes from the peyote cactus, which grows in the arid region between the Rio Grande and central Mexico. Indian shamans (medicine men) in the region have used it for many years to aid them in curing, divination and communing with supernatural powers. It has been used legally by members of the Native American Church to create or enhance religious experiences.[23] LSD is a derivative of ergot, a fungus that grows on old rye or wheat. It is odorless, tasteless and extremely powerful. It was first synthesized in 1943 by Albert Hoffman, who learned about its conscious-altering properties firsthand when he accidentally got a tiny bit of it in his mouth.

Both of these drugs can produce very positive or very negative effects, depending in part on the setting and the user's frame of mind and expectations. Both drugs affect the user's ability to perceive space and light. During positive experiences, colors become more vivid, surface details and contours of nearby objects seem sharper and more defined, and physical surroundings can seem very beautiful. Objects may take on a strange luminescent quality, as if illuminated from within. When users close their eyes, they see a visual display that constantly moves and changes. What they see varies greatly, but can include brightly colored, abstract patterns, dramatic scenes, people, animals, scenes from exotic places or ancient times, and mythical or religious figures.

Both drugs can also produce very ugly, frightening experiences. These may include being caught in impenetrable darkness, being overwhelmed by gloom and isolation, seeing garish distortions of natural colors, or experiencing terrifying distortions of the body in which one's arms or legs seem to be misshapen, detached or decaying. Experiences like these are so vivid and disturbing that they can create fear and depression that lasts for several days or weeks.[24]

The effects of LSD are generally more profound and longer-lasting than those produced by mescaline. LSD can disrupt normal consciousness so completely that users can no longer tell whether the things they are experiencing are real or imaginary. It also creates powerful visual distortions.

Objects and people can change their shape, color or character (for example, at one moment a woman may seem exceedingly beautiful, but a few seconds later she may look like a grotesque monster), and walls or other surfaces may appear to move, bulge or undulate in waves.

Users are also subject to incredible emotional extremes and profound disturbances in body image. They may lose their ability to sense the boundaries of their own body and feel as if they are dissipating or merging with other people or objects in the vicinity. Out-of-body experiences are fairly common. These drugs can produce mystical visions in which users are transported to higher realms and commune with various spiritual beings. Early proponents were convinced that the use of these drugs allowed people to achieve a degree of personal insight and spiritual awareness that they could not obtain in any other way.[25]

But LSD has perilous side effects. During intoxication, users can experience a loss of muscle coordination, spastic paralysis and elevated heart rate, blood pressure and blood sugar. They can have "bad trips" that are psychologically harrowing and traumatic. They may risk serious injury, because they can become convinced that they can fly, walk on water or accomplish other impossible feats. LSD can create profound depression and anxiety, increasing the likelihood of suicide. Users are also subject to unexplained flashbacks that occur weeks or months after taking the drug. These sudden, involuntary recurrences of the altered state, with all of its distortions and hallucinations, create panic and confusion because they cannot be controlled and are totally unexpected.[26]

The Defining Characteristics of Altered States

The specific experiences induced by altered states can vary in many different ways. Yet altered states also have important commonalities. They can all impair one's ability to test reality, to think critically and logically or to remember. They create a passive state in which mental events seem to develop on their own and are simply experienced rather than being controlled. Many also weaken emotional restraints, allowing moods to swing from wild jubilation to deep fear and depression. In addition, they can all create perceptual distortions and hallucinations and precipitate unusual bodily sensations like numbness, dizziness, tingling or rushes of energy. At deeper levels they are often accompanied by unusual disturbances in body image, which may include the loss of a sense of body boundaries and the impression of leaving the body and viewing it from outside.[27] Altered states can induce some unusual psychological changes too. They can make people hypersuggestible, so they are open to many strange beliefs and are easily influenced by the suggestions of other people. Altered states have the singular ability to make all kinds of improbable events seem exceptionally real and significant. Under their influence, people may suddenly "know" that they are receiving profound insights or that they are privy to ultimate truths. Remarkably, these very persuasive feelings may have no bearing on objective reality.

Researcher Arnold Ludwig describes one of his own experiences with LSD to illustrate this point. Once while under the influence, he went into a public restroom. There he noticed a sign above the urinal that read, "Please Flush After Using." As he thought about these words, he suddenly realized that they had profound meaning. Thrilled by this startling revelation, he rushed back to his companion to share his discovery. However, as Ludwig relates it, tongue in cheek, "Unfortunately, being a mere mortal he could not appreciate the world-shaking import of my communication and responded by laughing."[28]

One final effect of altered states is their apparent ability to facilitate or enhance mystical experiences (experiences that seem supernatural or spiritually significant). Profound mystical experiences are apparently not that common relative to all the other effects that altered states can produce. But when they do occur, they can make a big impact, whether they are out-of-body experiences, journeys to otherworldly places, encounters with spirit beings, or simply perceiving some ordinary object in an extraordinary way. One woman reportedly had a mystical encounter with a peach that was ripening in her kitchen while she was under the influence of LSD. As she looked at the peach, it suddenly began to glow, radiating a mysterious, otherworldly beauty. Suddenly she was overcome with feelings of great reverence and awe and fell on her knees, worshiping the peach. After she regained normal consciousness, she realized that the incident was absurd, but she was still left with the definite impression that something very significant had happened.

Physiological Factors

Although New Agers assume that many of the experiences they are encountering in altered states are spiritually significant, our current knowledge of the brain suggests that many are due to more mundane causes. Many of the unusual visual events in altered states are undoubtedly illusions or hallucinations caused by disruptions in the normal cognitive and perceptual operations of the brain. Others may be due to an abnormal activation of brain mechanisms that are responsible for dreaming.

Disturbances in sensory or perceptual processing can probably account for a number of the simpler experiences. To illustrate, when we glance at a clock to check the time, the light reflected from its surface enters our eyes and stimulates an array of sensitive cells (rods and cones) on our retinas. These receptors excite an army of connected nerve cells (neurons), which send complex patterns of nerve impulses to visual receiving areas in the back of the brain. These patterns are somehow translated into the subjective images that we see.

Scientists do not yet understand this translation process, but they are fairly confident that what we see depends on the particular *pattern* of neural impulses that manifests itself in the visual areas of the brain. If this pattern is altered or disrupted by some unrelated physical event, the image perceived will also be inaccurate or distorted. In the case of the clock, random alterations in visual patterns might make the clock appear to blur, move, change its shape or radiate particles of light from the highlights on its surface.

All our senses apparently follow the same general rules of operation. Specialized sense organs respond to physical information (light, auditory signals, heat, pressure and so on) and activate connected neurons. Intricate patterns of impulses are sent to different receiving areas of the brain and are translated into our sensory experiences. Normally sensory transmission is very accurate, but certain agents, including the psychedelic drugs, can interfere with this process by disrupting neuronal communication.

Neurons communicate with one another through numerous interconnections known as synapses. Neuronal messages (impulses) from one neuron are carried across its synapses to connected neurons by means of specific chemical transmitter substances. There are many different types of transmitters in our bodies. These transmitters are released in carefully controlled quantities, because the amount of transmitter determines how vigorously the receiving neurons will respond. If too much transmitter is released, receiving neurons will respond too strongly and add extra impulses to the signal stream. If too little is released, the signal stream will be diminished.

Some of the chemicals that can interfere with transmission exert their effect by slowing or blocking transmitter release, while others make synapses release too much transmitter or even create extraneous signals of their own. Virtually all the drugs that affect people psychologically (LSD, mescaline, cocaine, antidepressive drugs and others) exert their effects by altering neuronal transmission at specific synapses. Sensory deprivation and Eastern meditation can also affect the operation of neurons to a certain extent, because both states can apparently alter the electrical patterns (EEGs) that emanate from the brain.[29]

There are several phenomena that might be created through interference with the neuronal operations that underlie perception. Drug-induced visual distortions in which colors are altered or inanimate objects appear to move or change shapes (like walls that bulge at the corners or appear to breathe) could probably be explained this way. It is also possible that some of the simpler hallucinatory episodes are created by extraneous stimulation that artificially activates neurons in sensory areas in the brain.

This possibility is supported by the findings of Wilder Penfield, a neurosurgeon who discovered that he could create false sensory experiences in conscious surgical patients by gently stimulating their brains with an electric probe. The electrical pulses from the probe artificially activated groups of neurons, causing them to respond somewhat as they might if stimulated by normal neuronal input. Penfield could infer the normal functions of an area of the brain by observing the reactions of his patients and asking them what they experienced each time he activated the probe.

Penfield used this technique right before surgery to give him more information about areas that might have to be removed. The procedure was not painful, because the brain doesn't have a sense of pain and scalp pain was eliminated with a local anesthetic. Over his long career Penfield applied this procedure to over one thousand patients, keeping careful notes of the results. His studies were carried out some time ago, but they still constitute one of the most thorough investigations of the human cortex in conscious humans that have ever been undertaken.

Penfield discovered that stimulating the visual areas on the cerebral cortex caused his patients to see colors, lights and shadows that assumed crude shapes and moved around. Stimulating auditory areas caused them to hear ringing, hissing or thumping sounds, while stimulating areas that receive tactile or stretch information from muscles and skin made them feel tingling sensations or illusory movements in various parts of the body.[30] If the artificial stimulation provided by Penfield's probe could produce such experiences, it is possible that artificial stimulation by other agents, such as drugs, could produce similar effects.

Unusual feelings like numbness, tingling or "electrical" phenomena can be duplicated by other physical manipulations such as bumping the "crazy bone" in the elbow (actually a sensory nerve that supplies the arm and hand, which apparently misfires as a result of the jolt) or accidentally cutting off blood circulation in an arm or leg, causing it to "fall asleep." Cutting off the oxygen supply to sensory neurons will definitely alter their signaling patterns. Feelings of dizziness, floating or spinning may also have physical origins, because similar sensations occur with inner-ear infections. This latter condition probably alters the neuronal messages coming from the vestibular apparatus, a delicately tuned organ of balance that is part of the inner ear.

Artificially stimulating or interfering with the brain mechanisms that take part in emotional and cognitive processes can generate even more complex psychological experiences. Penfield discovered one area of the brain (which he named the "interpretive cortex") that could initiate complex hallucinatory/memory episodes when it was stimulated. One woman heard an orchestra playing a popular song every time he stimulated a particular spot in this area. The music started when stimulation started and stopped when the current was discontinued. Remarkably, she could hum along with the song and was convinced that it was coming from the operating room rather than her own head.

Another of Penfield's patients cried out in astonishment when Penfield stimulated this area of the cortex: he suddenly heard himself laughing with friends in South Africa although he knew he was actually on an operating table in Montreal. On another occasion Penfield's probe caused a young boy to hear his mother talking on the telephone. When Penfield immediately reapplied stimulation to the same place, the boy heard the same conversation again. But when he restimulated after an interval of time, the boy had an entirely different experience. This time he heard his mother tell his younger brother that he had put his coat on backwards, an event that had transpired shortly before the family had left for the hospital.

In most cases Penfield's stimulations of the interpretive cortex produced no noticeable effects, but in some cases it seemed to change the way the patients interpreted their situation. Sometimes it made their present situation suddenly seem very familiar (similar to feelings of déjà-vu) or very strange. Sometimes it made sights and sounds seem distant and small, sometimes large and close. On rare occasions it created feelings of dread or made people feel that they were observing themselves from a distance.[31] Stimulation made one patient feel as if he was actually leaving his body.[32]

Epileptic seizures, which are episodes of abnormal neuronal activity, can also create extraneous neuronal stimulation and often give rise to a wide variety of false subjective experiences. Seizures that occur in the temporal lobe of the brain (which includes Penfield's interpretive cortex) or in the underlying structures of the limbic system can stimulate unwarranted feelings of terror, sadness, fear, anger, depression and foreboding, or feelings of reality or unreality. Sometimes temporal-lobe patients experience mystical or psychic episodes alongside their seizures. Intriguingly, these decrease in frequency or stop when the seizures are controlled with anticonvulsive medication.[33] The fact that epileptic seizures or electrical stimulation of the brain can initiate such complex yet obviously unrealistic responses lends credence to the hypothesis that some of the more complex psychological responses observed in altered states may also be set off by abnormal neuronal conditions in the brain.

Another mind/brain mechanism that may be artificially activated during altered states is the system that creates our dreams. Although human beings vary in their ability to produce fantasy and mental imagery while they are awake, research indicates that virtually everyone experiences vivid imagery and complex fantasies while dreaming. This plus other observable characteristics of the dream state suggest that we must have some type of built-in brain mechanism that can create new images, or pull up and modify old ones from memory, and then shape these into incidents or stories without our conscious instruction. Since this mechanism can operate in one altered state (while we are asleep), perhaps it can also operate in the others, particularly at deeper levels of those states, when conscious awareness is greatly diminished.

This hypothesis is supported by studies of hypnogogic hallucinations—brief episodes of dreaming (usually less than three minutes) that some people experience when they are fully conscious. These occur when the dream process gets slightly out of sync with sleep, usually at the very beginning or end of a sleep period. Many of the subjective characteristics of these episodes seem similar to those encountered in altered states. Hypnogogic hallucinations are primarily visual, although they can occur in any sensory mode, and often have amazing clarity, detail and vivid color. Objects and people often have an unusual luminous quality and seem to be real and external rather than vague and internal as they are in ordinary mental images. In this state it is also possible to see objects or scenes from odd angles—from below (for example, looking upward into tree roots) or from above (as if the observer were floating). Auditory hallucinations, including crashing noises, music, or hearing one's name or remarks directed toward oneself, can also be quite vivid.[34]

Hallucinations of various types appear to have physiological origins because they can be triggered by a wide variety of agents that affect the brain, including drugs, fever, epileptic seizures, advanced syphilis, insulin-induced hypoglycemia, psychotic episodes and migraine headaches. Hallucinations initiated by these agents come in great variety and are often quite complex, but may still have some predictable characteristics.

The hallucinations induced by psychedelic drugs, which develop in two stages, illustrate this point. In the first stage users see four basic form constants that are repeated over and over with various alterations and embellishments: (1) a lattice, grating or filigree pattern, (2) cobwebs, (3) tunnels or cones and (4) spirals. In addition to the repeating form constants, these hallucinations are characterized by vivid colors, intense brightness and light (particularly in the center of the image), symmetry, and explosive or rotational movement. These images apparently develop on their own and cannot be consciously controlled.[35] More realistic images of every conceivable type can appear in the second stage. These are likely to incorporate childhood and emotionally charged memories, elaborated into fantastic scenes that go far beyond the original experience. With milder doses of psychedelic drugs, people seem to be watching their activities through the eyes of an outside observer (which they may do from above, as if floating above the scene), but with larger doses the events seem real, and people describe them as if participating in them. With even higher levels of intoxication, it is not uncommon for people to feel as if they have separated from their body.[36]

It is conceivable that the complex hallucinations that appear in this second stage are actually being created by an artificial activation of the dreaming process, although much more research is needed before we can say this for sure. The physiological effects of LSD provide some support for this hypothesis. LSD interferes with the transmission of neuronal impulses in a collection of neurons that use serotonin as a transmitter. Some of these neurons are apparently responsible for inhibiting dreaming and are active periodically throughout the night and consistently during the day. LSD can block the inhibitory effects of these neurons and may allow the hallucinatory images of dreams to invade the waking state.[37]

Possible Spiritual Dimensions of Altered States

From New Age and mystical perspectives, one of the most valued characteristics of altered states is their presumed ability to make the spiritual realm more visible and accessible. At this point we need to ask whether, or under what circumstances, this might be true.

New Agers support this belief with reference to the many diverse cultural groups that have used altered states to facilitate spiritual contacts throughout recorded history. The ancient Egyptians and Greeks apparently used sleep temples, and perhaps a form of hypnosis, to facilitate contact with spiritual beings.[38] Shamans or witch doctors in tribal groups throughout the world have entered trances by ingesting mind-altering potions, drumming incessantly, dancing or twirling in circles, to enable them to contact and then appease the spirits that are troubling their patients. In Eastern religious traditions, adherents engage in meditative techniques that are specifically designed to alter consciousness and thereby facilitate spiritual contact. As it stands, this evidence is suggestive, but it is certainly not conclusive.

The Bible does not clearly state whether altered states facilitate contact with the spiritual realm. Scripture includes records of God or an angel communicating with human beings while they were asleep. In the New Testament, Joseph was contacted by an angel four different times in dreams, once to let him know that he should take Mary as his wife (Mt 1:20) and the other times in connection with their escape to Egypt and return to Israel.

At other times God communicated through visions that were apparently accompanied by alterations in consciousness. In Acts 10:9-16 Peter fell into a trance when God sent a vision in which various animals were lowered from heaven in a large sheet. The purpose of the vision was to let Peter know that the Gentiles as well as the Jews were to receive the good news of salvation. But the Holy Spirit waited until the vision and the trance were over to help him understand the vision and to tell him not to hesitate to go with Cornelius's servant.

In a few biblical cases, contact with spiritual beings had such a profound impact that it apparently *induced* an altered state. In one of Daniel's visions (Dan 10:9) he saw an angel, and the experience was so powerful that he fell into a "deep sleep, [his] face to the ground." Interestingly, the angel did not try to communicate with Daniel when he was in that state. He awakened him and told him to stand up and listen carefully to the message so he could record it accurately.

In the case of prophecies, we do not know very much about the mental state of the prophets while God was communicating with them. It is not likely that they were in an altered state of the type described in this chapter, however, because their memories and their ability to think were apparently fully operational. In fact, they had to *remember* God's messages in detail and deliver them accurately, because any sign of falsehood, false imaginings or inaccuracy would have identified them as false prophets.[39]

Tangible encounters with the living God, like those the prophets experienced, must create a state of consciousness that seems quite different, opening up an entirely different perspective on reality and evoking very powerful feelings and emotions. Yet unlike the altered states produced by drugs, hypnosis or Eastern meditation, these encounters do not appear to interfere with memory or the workings of the mind.

In most other types of supernatural contact recorded in the Bible, God or his angels apparently interacted with people while they were in a very normal state of consciousness. In fact, in many of these cases God seems to have taken precautions, such as acting before multiple witnesses or supplying tangible evidence, to ensure that his people would know these experiences were real and not just products of their imagination. After Abraham and Sarah were visited by the angels who told them that they would have a son (Gen 18:1-15), Sarah's pregnancy provided concrete proof that the visit was real. All the public supernatural events that transpired while the Israelites were preparing to leave Egypt, the various miracles that attended their entrance into the Promised Land, virtually all of Jesus' miracles, and Paul's encounter on the road to Damascus were accompanied by witnesses and/or concrete evidence. In the case of biblical prophecies, the confirmation appeared later rather than immediately, but there *was* confirmation.

It is clear, then, that God has interacted with people who were in an altered state (usually sleep), but he has also interacted with many more who are not. So it is certainly not necessary to be in an altered state to receive such contacts. And there are no intimations in Scripture that people should enter trances or altered states so they can draw closer to God. In fact, we are explicitly instructed in 1 Peter 4:7 to be "clear minded and self-controlled" so we can pray. There are great mysteries in our faith, and there is definitely a place for fasting, setting aside time to listen to God, meditating on scriptural truth[40] and praying fervently, but in my own opinion these are surely not meant to put us into altered states of consciousness.

The biblical evidence does not tell us whether altered states facilitate spiritual contacts, either from God or from the forces of evil. However, it is obvious that such states could certainly magnify any influence that these spirits might exert on the human mind. In fact, Satan and his forces could hardly find a more opportune situation in which to deceive or mislead people. If this seems like too strong a statement, stop and review the various characteristics of altered states.

In altered states people are subject to vivid imagery, unconstrained imaginative processes that resist conscious control, and intense emotions. Having largely set aside their ability to think rationally and critically or to exercise their will, they have become hypersuggestible, which means that they are likely to accept any "spiritual truth" that enters their minds. Even more remarkably, they seemed to be primed for mystical experiences and may attach great spiritual significance to virtually any event or thought, no matter how mundane or outlandish. Seeking mystical experiences through altered states, as defined here, looks like an open invitation for deception.

5

Near-Death & Out-of-Body Experiences

Nine-year-old Nina was undergoing surgery for appendicitis. The operation was proceeding routinely until her heart stopped beating, prompting emergency resuscitation procedures. Nina, who was anesthetized and unconscious, with her eyes closed, suddenly found herself watching all this urgent activity from a vantage point above her body. Later she described her experience this way:

I heard them say my heart had stopped but I was up at the ceiling watching. I could see everything from up there. I was floating close to the ceiling, so when I saw my body I didn't know it was me. Then I knew because I recognized it. I went out in the hall and I saw my mother crying. I asked her why she was crying but she couldn't hear me. The doctors thought I was dead.

Then a pretty lady came up and helped me because she knew I was scared. We went through a tunnel and went into heaven. There are beautiful flowers there. I was with God and Jesus. They said I had to go back to be with my mother because she was upset. They said I had to finish my life. So I went back and woke up.

> The tunnel I went through was long and very dark. I went through it real fast. There was light at the end. When we saw the light I was very happy. I wanted to go back for a long time. I still want to go back to the light when I die. The light was very bright.[1]

Cory, an attractive, middle-aged counselor with advanced training in social work, shifted nervously in her chair as she talked with me, describing how she occasionally floated out of her body while praying or meditating. These excursions had started while she was practicing transcendental meditation and had persisted even though she had dropped TM and was attending an evangelical church. Noticing my questioning look, she assured me that the experiences were real, not imaginary or dreamlike. Cory was ambivalent about these excursions. On the one hand she welcomed them because they seemed spiritually significant, yet they worried her, partly because they didn't fit very well with Christianity and partly because she was afraid that one day she might drift too far from her body (although she had discovered that physically touching the floor with her hand seemed to keep her from drifting out of the room).[2]

Nina's and Cory's strange adventures are examples of what are now called "near-death" and "out-of-body" experiences (NDEs and OBEs). Both types of experience appear to be occurring fairly frequently in the United States and other Western countries. Random surveys from the United States, England and Iceland indicate that 10-14 percent of the respondents have had OBEs (although the reported incidence can be as high as 25 percent among college students in these nations and Australia[3]). Surveys also indicate that about 5 percent of American adults have had NDEs.[4] New Agers and "New Mystics" value these experiences very highly because they validate their views of death and human nature.

The current interest in NDEs was initiated in 1975 by Raymond Moody's book *Life After Life,* which rapidly became an international bestseller.[5] In this book Moody summarized the experiences of 150 people who were clinically dead and resuscitated, who had come very close to death, or who had died but related their experiences to others in the process. Moody discovered that these people were encountering some very similar and remarkable experiences. His findings, which were primarily descriptive, were later substantiated in more thorough studies carried out by Kenneth Ring,[6] a psychologist, and Michael Sabom, a cardiologist.[7] Elisabeth Kübler-Ross, a psychiatrist known for her work on death and dying, has also helped to popularize NDEs in books and lectures detailing her patients' experiences and her own views of life after death.

Out-of-body experiences, which are not associated with death, are less familiar to Westerners than NDEs, but they are not a new phenomenon. In Eastern, occult and spiritualistic traditions they are called "astral projections" and are often prized as spiritual achievements. Since OBEs are very similar to NDEs, it is appropriate to discuss these experiences together.

Characteristics of NDEs and OBEs

Near-death experiences may vary a great deal from one person to the next, but they do have meaningful commonalities. Most consist of one or both of two phases, which Sabom has labeled "autoscopic" and "transcendental."

The autoscopic phase begins when NDErs recognize (or hear) that they are dead and perceive that they have left their bodies. Often they see their bodies below them, as if watching from a vantage point near the ceiling. NDErs do not seem to be greatly perturbed by this and say that they feel very much at peace. They are free from pain, in spite of the fact that their bodies are obviously in distress (unanesthetized and often being subjected to painful resuscitation procedures). NDErs watch the frantic efforts to save them with a surprising amount of detachment, although some see the grief of loved ones and attempt, unsuccessfully, to reassure them. For about one-third of the NDErs, the experience ends at this point, and they are abruptly pulled back into their body.

NDErs who go through both phases usually shift into the transcendental phase by entering a dark space or tunnel, through which they move rapidly toward a distant source of light. During this transition they may hear "whooshing" noises, "electrical" humming, music or other sounds. Many sense that they are being guided through this space by some kind of spirit. They emerge into a beautiful, brilliantly lit, otherworldly environment and are typically met by luminescent spirit beings who radiate love, joy and acceptance. In American, Australian and English NDEs, these spirits are usually identified as friends and relatives who have died. The surroundings vary a great deal from one report to another but are often described as pastoral scenes or beautiful cities.

A few NDErs meet an extraordinary "Being of Light" whom they intuitively identify as God, Jesus, an angel, Buddha or Allah, depending on their religious background. The being apparently does not identify itself. Reportedly this being radiates total love and acceptance and is never judgmental, regardless of the way the NDEr has lived or his or her beliefs. A few of the NDErs who meet the being are given a quick life review, ostensibly to help them see what they need to change. Some are given a choice whether they will return to life, but others are simply told that they must return because it is not their time to die. NDErs who do not meet the being are usually told by a relative or friend that they must return and are rapidly returned to their body.

In the "typical" NDE, sketched by Moody and Ring, NDErs start with the out-of-body phase and then move into the transcendental phase if they are not resuscitated fairly soon. But in his systematic study, Sabom discovered that most NDEs do not follow this pattern. Only one-fifth of the NDErs in his sample went through both phases. One-third experienced only the autoscopic phase, and *half* experienced only the transcendental phase, skipping the autoscopic phase altogether.[8]

Popular portrayals of NDEs are based almost entirely on positive experiences, but there are some reports of negative NDEs. These generally include a sense of being out of the body, feelings of extreme fear or panic, entering a black void, sensing the presence of evil and entering a hellish setting.[9] Negative NDEs are uncommon, however, accounting for 1 percent or less of the reported cases, so in early reports they were often ignored or treated as anomalies.

Out-of-body experiences, like Cory's, which occur in situations that have nothing to do with death, are very similar to the autoscopic phase in NDEs. During these experiences OBErs seem independent of their bodies and can see them from the outside. They discover that they can breeze through solid walls and fly to remote places by simply willing it to happen. According to researchers, OBEs can occur spontaneously or can be induced (although not easily or reliably). People who report frequent OBEs say they learn to manage them, but few claim to be able to initiate them totally at will. Several organizations with New Age connections, like the Eckankar Foundation, Silva Mind Control and the Monroe Institute of Applied Science, claim that they have developed techniques that can produce OBEs,[10] but they do not publish their success rates.

Investigators have identified four types of OBEs. The "simple" type occurs spontaneously and has no special significance, aside from leaving the definite impression that the spirit can separate from the body. The "ecstatic" OBE incorporates additional mystical and religious elements, conveying a sense of transcendence and great meaning. In the "esoteric" OBE the experiencer appears to travel to other planes of existence and to receive information and advice from spiritual guides. This type of OBE appears to be more common among experienced OBErs with occult worldviews and among shamans. Finally, there are also infrequent, negative OBEs. These are spontaneous and terrifying, and they appear to be controlled by powerful, malevolent forces.[11]

Challenges Created by These Experiences
Since New Mystics and New Agers are convinced that NDEs are valid, these experiences are having a profound impact on their beliefs. Since most reported NDEs are sublime and uplifting and there are few "hellish" NDEs, they conclude that virtually everyone goes to "heaven" and that hell probably doesn't exist. They also assume that the "Being of Light" encountered in NDEs is God, but since he seems relatively unconcerned about their sins or feelings of remorse and doesn't chastise anyone, they assume that he must accept everyone unconditionally without judging or condemning. His apparent lack of concern makes sins seem more like "mistakes" that can be corrected and used for growth, rather than disobedience that requires God's forgiveness and Christ's supernatural atonement. NDEs make it seem

that the only "judgement" humans will face are the feelings of sorrow and remorse that arise from their own conscience. With these assumptions there is no need for a redeemer, so Jesus is stripped of much of his supernatural power and considered a great human teacher like Buddha or Muhammad.

Reports of NDEs and OBEs and the way they are being interpreted by principal investigators (most of whom are not Christian[12]) are helping to create a belief system that opposes the fundamental tenets of Christianity. This poses a challenge that we cannot afford to ignore. A first step toward meeting this challenge is to gain a more thorough understanding of NDEs and OBEs.

NDEs and OBEs in Biblical Perspective

One way to evaluate OBEs and NDEs is to ask whether they are plausible in light of Scripture or Christian doctrine. In the case of NDEs, however, this approach does not yield decisive answers. It is possible to argue for or against the legitimacy of NDEs from a biblical perspective. On the positive side, NDEs sound plausible because Christians have traditionally assumed that body and spirit do separate at death (see Eccles 12:7; Mt 10:28).[13] Moreover, NDEs have been reported by respected Christians through the centuries. In fact, NDEs that included extended visits to heaven and hell were popular among Christians in antiquity and during the Middle Ages. At that time they were used to convert the unsaved and to warn believers to stay on the narrow path. NDEs were reported less frequently during the Reformation but have reappeared from time to time since then.[14] There are also modern examples of Christian NDEs. But these need to be considered with discernment, because the authenticity of at least one of the book-length accounts is very questionable.[15]

On the negative side, aspects of many reported NDEs seem inconsistent with the scriptural view of God and of death. In addition to the inconsistencies already discussed, current NDEs give the impression that the death process is being handled rather carelessly. If God determines the time of death, he obviously knows whether it is time for a person to die before an NDE gets under way. Why then would he allow a transition to begin, only to abort it a short time later, allowing NDErs to get some very misleading impressions in the process?

God could certainly use an NDE to teach or impart spiritual insights if he chose to, but there is no record in the Bible that he has ever done so. In a number of instances God enabled certain people to see spiritual realities that lie beyond the physical world (in prophetic visions, visits from angels and the like), but only one of these came just before the visionary died. Stephen was granted a vision of heaven before he was stoned to death, but this occurred before he was injured (Acts 7:54-57).

It is easier to get a biblical perspective on OBEs than on NDEs. True separations of body and spirit that are deliberately induced and have nothing to do with death simply do not fit with scriptural teachings. According to the Bible, the separation of body and spirit is synonymous with death (for instance, see 1 Kings 17:20-22; Eccles 12:7; Mt 10:28; Lk 8:53-55), and death is not a trivial event. It was ordained by God as a punishment for sin (Gen 3:17-19; Rom 5:12; 6:23), it occurs only once (except by divine intervention; Heb 9:27), and its timing is evidently controlled by God, not by our own choice. In this light, the claim that humans can learn to leave their bodies in spirit form more or less at will, imitating the process that occurs at death, is highly questionable. If my interpretation of Scripture is correct, only God, or his designated agents, could bring about a true temporary separation. Human beings surely do not have this power on their own.

Interestingly, an incident recorded in 2 Corinthians 12:1-4 might be interpreted as an OBE. Here Paul describes how he was caught up into paradise and was given a vision of the incredible things that are in store for Christians there. Of his state he says, "Whether it was in the body or out of the body I do not know—God knows." John's experience just before he received the visions in Revelation may have been similar (see Rev 4:1-2). Yet even though these instances may seem like OBEs, it is very doubtful that they were, because they are both described as visions. In the Bible, visions are incidents in which God enables people to see things that are normally hidden from human eyes or are meant to serve as a message.[16]

Biblical visions are probably more similar to contemporary "clairvoyant episodes" than they are to OBEs. Biblical visionaries were enabled to see different places, times and events as if they were there, but they did not have to leave the body to do so. In addition, there is no indication that John or Paul saw his body from an outside vantage point (one of the main aspects of current OBEs) or that their experiences were initiated by their own efforts. They were clearly initiated by God.

Scientific Perspectives on Spirit-Body Separation

Several investigators have tried to determine whether the spirit separates from the body during NDEs and OBEs. However, the extent to which scientific methods can be applied to this question is necessarily limited. For NDEs, about the only way to try to verify separation is to see if there are events that NDErs have witnessed while out of their bodies that they couldn't possibly have seen through their physical eyes. Yet even this type of evidence cannot prove conclusively that a true separation has occurred. It would only tell us that the NDErs were able to see events unfolding in a way that convinced them that they were outside the body. (One could argue that instead what they "saw" was imparted by a vision, or perhaps by an unusual "clairvoyant" episode.)

Some of the most intriguing evidence of this type was collected by Michael Sabom, a cardiologist who began his initial study as a skeptic but ended it believing that NDEs were more than just figments of the experiencers' imaginations.[17] Sabom asked NDErs who said they had watched their own resuscitations to describe the procedures they observed in as much detail as possible. He then compared their accounts with the medical records and his own medical knowledge. (This comparison was somewhat subjective, because the medical reports were brief and routine and the patients' descriptions were often very general.) Sabom found that there was quite a bit of consistency between the medical records and NDE accounts, and no obvious discrepancies.

Since many of Sabom's NDErs were heart patients, many of whom had undergone multiple resuscitations before their NDEs, he checked for the possibility that they were reconstructing their experiences from memory. He asked twenty-five patients who had had multiple resuscitations but *not* an NDE to imagine that they were watching a resuscitation attempt and describe what would happen. In this group, twenty-two of the twenty-five made at least one major error in their descriptions, and the three who didn't make errors gave only very general accounts. By way of contrast, twenty-six out of thirty-two NDErs gave general visual impressions with no errors, while six gave unique, specific details that could be verified by medical records.[18] Sabom also studied thirteen surgical patients who had had NDEs and found that many of these patients were also able to furnish impressive visual details of their surgeries that they probably should not have known.[19]

Sabom's work does not prove that NDEs produce real separations of body and spirit, but it does strongly suggest that something unusual is happening. If his conclusions are correct, some of his patients did acquire accurate visual impressions of the medical procedures that were being used on them while, by all physical indications, they should have been completely unconscious.

John Palmer, a parapsychologist, devised a method of OBE induction that could be used in controlled experiments. He had previously studied OBE adepts and discovered that they prepared for their OBEs using similar methods. They would begin by relaxing very deeply. Then, when right on the verge of shifting from conscious awareness to sleep or a hypnoticlike state, they would attempt to launch themselves by intently willing, visualizing or imagining themselves leaving their bodies. Palmer used adaptations of these techniques in three experiments and found that between 40 and 50 percent of the students who participated reported OBEs.

Wisely, Palmer also included an objective test to determine whether the students had actually left their bodies. Before the experiment he took them into an adjacent room and told them that if they succeeded in getting out of their body they should enter this room and study a picture that he was going to place on the table. Quite a few of the students thought they had entered the room, but none of them could describe the picture with enough accuracy to convince Palmer that they had actually seen it.[20]

As they stand, Palmer's studies could be interpreted to mean that OBEs are nothing more than flights of imagination, similar to self-induced hypnotic experiences. Yet other parapsychologists would strongly disagree with this inference. H. J. Irwin utilized Palmer's OBE induction techniques and found that the OBEs produced were very weak and unrealistic when compared to spontaneous OBEs. In Irwin's opinion they often consisted of little more than a vague feeling of dissociation.[21] If this is true, Palmer's techniques may not provide an adequate test of the separation hypothesis.

Other researchers have studied OBE adepts to see if they were actually leaving their bodies during OBEs. For instance, psychologist Charles Tart conducted a series of nine tests on Robert Monroe (founder of the Monroe Institute, mentioned earlier) in which he was to exit his body in one room, then float into a locked equipment room next door and read a five-digit number that had been placed there on a very high shelf. Monroe could never get the correct number—he claimed that he had difficulty getting out of his body in the laboratory setting; on one occasion, however, he did correctly describe an incident that occurred in the hall during one of his OBEs.[22]

Monroe was also tested at a Veterans Administration hospital by Stuart Twemlow and Fowler Jones, who were interested in the physiological correlates of OBEs. Monroe was hooked up to recording equipment in the psychophysiology laboratory, with both Twemlow and Jones observing him from a separate room. Just as a technician entered the room to tell them that Monroe's brain-wave pattern was changing, both men observed what looked like a heat-wave distortion around the upper half of Monroe's body; the distortion obscured their vision, even though the lower half of his body was clearly visible. The distortion lasted for approximately two minutes and coincided with a self-reported OBE and observable changes in his brain waves.[23] In this case something unusual was clearly taking place, but what was observed still did not prove that Monroe had departed from his body.

Up to now, experimental attempts to validate the separation hypothesis for OBEs have been negative or inconclusive.[24] Moreover, some researchers have uncovered disconfirming evidence. Sometimes OBErs encounter small but significant discrepancies between what they see in their OBEs and what actually exists. One woman thought she was out of her body in her own bedroom, viewing her body from above, until she realized that the wallpaper pattern in the room wasn't quite right. In another case a man who thought he was out of his body in front of his house noticed that the bricks in the street were running the wrong way. Another man noticed a laundry basket in his bedroom during his OBE which wasn't there when he "got back."

Many parapsychologists interpret these inconsistencies to mean that people are not actually viewing their physical surroundings during OBEs, but rather a mental representation of them.[25] This suggests that OBErs are experiencing hallucinatory or dreamlike episodes within themselves or seeing visions that seem real but are somehow less than perfect.

Death and the Afterlife
Several lines of evidence indicate that NDEs are probably not an accurate source for information about death and the afterlife. In the first place, many NDEs seem to contradict Christian doctrines. In the second, none of the unusual features of NDEs are uniquely associated with death. These features have also turned up in OBEs. For example, OBErs have occasionally entered dark spaces or tunnels, met spirits of the dead or encountered spirit guides or "beings of light." OBE adepts have even entered heavenly or hellish planes of existence during their travels.[26] Such incidents are more common in NDEs than in OBEs, but the fact that they can occur in OBEs weakens the argument that NDEs are unique glimpses of the afterlife, afforded only to those who have been miraculously snatched back from the jaws of death.

The inconsistencies among various NDE accounts also raise questions about their applicability to the afterlife. While it is natural to expect some variations among accounts, there should also be a certain amount of consensus if NDErs are actually making a transition to the same place. Many investigators have minimized the inconsistencies between NDEs by concentrating on the features that NDEs have in common, but a few, like Phyllis Atwater, have detailed some of the striking differences. Among Atwater's NDErs, one woman left her body encased in a "blue bubble," a man saw himself being held by a giant hand, a young woman "straddled a beam of light and toured the universe," and another man saw nothing at all but heard a thundering voice giving him instructions for a job he was to do after he returned to life. Descriptions of the afterlife and the beings encountered there were especially variable. Some of these beings seemed human, others angelic, while others were described as "globular," "cylindrical" or simply "a glowing mass."[27] The enigmatic "Being of Light" has also been identified in many different ways, as God, some higher being, a religious figure (whether Jesus, Buddha or Muhammad), an angel or even the Higher Self.[28]

NDEs from other cultures reveal even greater inconsistencies. Satwant Pasricha and Ian Stevenson found that the NDEs from India were quite different from American NDEs. None of the Indians in their sample went through the out-of-body phase (which is experienced by at least 33 percent of American NDErs), and all were transported to the netherworld by messengers. After they arrived they were taken before a kind of gatekeeper, who consulted a book or papers. These consultations invariably revealed that the messenger had made a mistake and had seized the wrong party. These mistakes seemed reasonable to the Indian NDErs because they expect to be taken away by couriers of death (the *Yamdoots*) and because their names were very similar to the names of the intended parties. After discovering their mistake, the messengers unceremoniously returned the shaken NDErs to their bodies. Pasricha and Stevenson point out that in no known example of Western NDEs was a person ostensibly returned to life because of a supernatural foul-up.[29] Findings of this type suggest that the content of NDEs may tell us more about the NDEr's cultural and religious expectations than about the afterlife.

The strange distribution of negative or hellish NDEs also raises questions about the authenticity of NDEs. From a Christian point of view, one of the puzzling attributes of negative NDEs is their scarcity. If people are actually dying during their NDE and have these experiences en route to their eternal destination, shouldn't there be more hellish accounts than there are?

Maurice Rawlings, a Christian cardiologist, offers one possible answer to this question. He claims to have found about as many negative as positive NDEs and suggests that other researchers have missed many negative accounts because they could not question NDErs immediately after the incident. (Almost all of the NDE accounts in the literature have been collected months or years after their occurrence.) Rawlings came to this conclusion through his experience with one cardiac patient who kept slipping in and out of clinical death during a long and difficult resuscitation. Every time the patient regained consciousness, he was absolutely terrified and begged Rawlings to keep him alive because he was slipping into hell. The patient was finally stabilized, but when Rawlings went to question him about these experiences, just two days later, the patient couldn't remember any hellish incidents at all. (He did, however, remember watching the resuscitation from outside his body on one occasion.) Rawlings believes that people either become reluctant to talk about negative NDEs or repress them shortly after they occur because they are too horrifying to assimilate.[30]

Even though Rawlings's discoveries might help explain the scarcity of negative NDEs, some of his other findings raise questions of their own. He found that heavenly and hellish experiences were distributed rather indiscriminately among believers and nonbelievers, and that individuals with multiple NDEs could have heavenly or hellish experiences on different occasions. One staunch Christian whom Rawlings treated had three NDEs in separate episodes of clinical death. His first was a horrific episode in which he narrowly escaped from the gates of hell. His second NDE was the classic positive experience, complete with out-of-body and transcendental components. His third NDE was simply positive and transcendental.[31]

Possible Physiological Variables

A number of the researchers studying NDEs and OBEs think they may be generated physiologically. According to one popular hypothesis, many of the features of NDEs are created by abnormal neuronal activity in the temporal lobes of the brain. This abnormal activity is presumably stimulated by the physical and chemical changes that accompany death.[32]

Researchers do have good reason to suspect some kind of temporal-lobe involvement in NDEs. Both epileptic seizures and electrical stimulation in that region can induce components of NDEs, including buzzing or ringing sounds, music, ineffable feelings, hallucinations of supernatural or "mythological" beings and sensations of brightness, rising, sinking or even in a few cases separating from the body.[33] Michael A. Persinger has reproduced these and other components of NDEs by using a magnetic-field source to induce unusual electrical activity in the temporal lobes.[34] In addition, some doctors have noticed that patients with temporal-lobe epilepsy are prone to paranormal experiences of many types, including OBEs. Intriguingly, the frequency of these experiences apparently varies with seizure activity. When seizure activity is controlled with medication, the paranormal experiences also tend to subside.[35]

The temporal-lobe hypothesis is appealingly simple. Yet there are some important facts that it cannot account for. Temporal-lobe seizures are generally unpleasant and distressing, not positive and uplifting like NDEs.[36] They are also accompanied by a wide and unpredictable array of other experiences that do not occur in NDEs (lip smacking, nausea, distorted color perception, hallucinations of geometric patterns, pain, disorientation and so on). In addition, seizures or stimulation of the temporal lobes produce only isolated components of the experience, never the recognizable, coherent sequence of events seen in NDEs.

So far no one has demonstrated that the temporal lobes are unusually active during NDEs, but even if they did, this would not prove that temporal-lobe activation is the only element that needs to be present. Such activation could be a response to input from another part of the brain or some outside source rather than the ultimate cause of the NDE. Temporal-lobe activation may be a component of NDEs, but it is probably not sufficient to explain them.

A broader and probably more promising explanation for NDEs and OBEs assumes that both originate out of altered states of consciousness and that they are created or enhanced by the same brain mechanisms that produce dreams and hallucinations. In the case of NDEs, the altered state is presumably generated by physiological changes in the brain that take place at death, such as lowered levels of oxygen and a buildup of carbon dioxide in the blood.

Increased blood levels of carbon dioxide can trigger altered states that exhibit some of the features of NDEs.[37] Psychiatrist L. J. Meduna used carbon-dioxide inhalation as a therapy in the 1940s and 1950s and found that it sometimes produced sensations of light and brightness, a sense of bodily detachment, the revival of past memories, a sense of communicating telepathically with a religious or spiritual presence, and feelings of great spiritual ecstasy and significance.[38] Like the temporal-lobe effects, however, these components were usually brief and were mixed unpredictably with many other experiences not found in NDEs. Thus carbon-dioxide buildup is probably not sufficient by itself to explain NDEs. But it may induce an altered state that then sets the stage for such an experience. It may also set off abnormal activity in the temporal lobes of the brain.[39]

There are some very obvious links between OBEs and altered states that would support an altered-states hypothesis. OBEs have occurred in every type of altered state, including meditation, sensory deprivation, sleep, hypnosis and drug intoxication (see chapter four). And OBEs rarely occur unless the experiencer is in some type of altered state or a borderline condition like deep relaxation or great physical or psychological stress.[40]

The relationship between OBEs and sleep is particularly intriguing. People who have spontaneous OBEs usually have their first one while falling asleep or just upon awakening. Many of the techniques devised to induce OBEs instruct people to try to leave their body during the twilight state right between wakefulness and sleep.

There are also marked similarities between OBEs and an uncommon state of sleep called lucid dreaming. In this state sleepers apparently become conscious while they are dreaming and can exercise considerable control over their dreams. A few people can even use distinctive eye movements to signal to outside observers that they are lucid.[41] Both OBEs and lucid-dream periods may start or end with feelings of numbness, paralysis, bodily vibration or shock. Both also commonly include feelings of flying or floating and the peculiar sense that surrounding objects are illuminated from within. OBEs and lucid dreams can incorporate similar distortions or simplifications of the real world, and both can be changed simply when one imagines or suggests that the desired change will take place.

The obvious similarities between the two states have led some authorities to conclude that OBEs are lucid dreams. Others disagree, however, because there are also important differences. Lucid dreamers are aware that they are dreaming and know that their experiences are completely fanciful, but OBErs are sure they are awake and are equally convinced that their experiences were genuine.[42]

Possible Psychological/Sociological Variables
Investigations of the social and psychological dimensions of NDEs and OBEs have turned up a few clues. In general, people who have NDEs or OBEs do not appear to differ from those who do not in terms of age, sex, socioeconomic status, years of education, religious background or frequency of church attendance.[43] Studies using various psychological tests have shown that OBErs are at least as psychologically healthy as non-OBErs and that they have similar personality profiles.[44] As a group, OBErs do have higher scores on traits like "absorption" (the ability to become very deeply involved in a novel or movie), fantasy proneness[45] and dissociation,[46] which suggests that they may be fairly susceptible to altered states like hypnosis. The link with hypnotic susceptibility is also supported by a study done by S. Wilson and T. Barber, who asked a group of twenty-seven excellent and twenty-five poor hypnotic subjects whether they had had OBEs. The differences in the way the two groups responded was striking. Fully 88 percent of the highly susceptible group said they had experienced OBEs, compared to only 8 percent of the group with low susceptibility.[47]

One recent study has shown that NDErs have apparently had different childhood experiences from non-NDErs. NDErs are more likely than non-NDErs to report that they were aware of psychic abilities and supernatural events while they were children. They also report more childhood abuse (physical, psychological and sexual) and a more negative home life than non-NDErs.[48]

Possible Supernatural Influence

Scientific investigations of OBEs make them seem almost natural, even possibly explainable in simple physical or psychological terms. Yet viewing them from the context of their history or through the eyes of OBE adepts reveals that they have other, more disturbing dimensions. There are indications that some OBEs may involve demonic activity.

OBEs have actually been around for a long time. Before parapsychologists changed their name to disassociate them from their spiritualistic roots, OBEs were commonly known as "astral projections" (the projection of the "astral" or spiritual body from the physical body). Shamans and holy men in various cultures have employed astral projection to demonstrate their spiritual prowess and to ascend to the spirit world to negotiate on behalf of others. Astral projection has been a valued spiritual achievement in pantheistic Eastern religious traditions for centuries. Taoism, Tibetan Buddhism, Hinduism (yoga) and even Cabalism (a mystical Hebrew sect) provide instructions and techniques for leaving the physical body.[49] Astral projection has also had its periods of popularity in America and Europe over the last 150 years, primarily through its connection with spiritualism (a religion that promotes contact with the dead and other spirit beings). Throughout this period self-proclaimed OBE adepts like Hugh Calloway (alias Oliver Fox), Sylvan Muldoon and, more recently, Robert Monroe have written popular books describing their astral travels and the spirits they have met in their journeys.

The personal accounts of people who have had multiple OBEs also show that many of them were deliberately or inadvertently involved in occult or spiritistic practices before the experiences began. In several cases the adept's first OBE occurred fairly early in life and appeared to be assisted by some kind of guide or spirit.

Parapsychologist D. Scott Rogo writes that he started having OBEs when he was between four and five. He would awaken in the night, float above his bed, travel down the hall in his house and then return to his room. He usually sensed that some kind of guide was present and that this being wanted to teach him something.

Later, as a teenager, Rogo tried to produce OBEs on his own. He delved into spiritualistic teachings on the subject and experimented diligently for several months without success. Then, about a month after he had stopped trying, OBEs started occurring spontaneously while he was asleep. On one of these occasions he awoke with fearsome gushing noises in his ears and felt as if he was being pulled out of his body through his head. Frightened, he tried to abort the experience. As he did so, however, he suddenly saw three grotesque, "positively menacing white faces" hovering above him. Rogo decided that he didn't want any more OBEs, but they kept occurring anyway. He eventually learned how to partially control them and went on to make OBE research the focus of his career.[50]

Some NDErs have also had occult or spiritualistic involvement before their NDEs. Phyllis Atwater certainly did. In her book *Coming Back to Life*, which is primarily a study of NDE aftereffects, she describes three dramatic NDEs of her own. As the book progresses, we learn that Atwater had been heavily involved in occult activities for at least ten years before her NDEs. She was a meditator and a teacher of Eastern meditation and by her own report had developed "considerable expertise" in other psychic pursuits, including trance mediumship, dehaunting houses and out-of-body travel.[51]

Three of the popularizers of NDEs and OBEs, Raymond Moody, Robert Monroe and Elisabeth Kübler-Ross, also have unusual spiritualistic affiliations. Besides promoting the same (New Age) messages about life and death, all three have had their own encounters with the spirit world.[52] Monroe's connections are probably the most obvious. According his *Journeys out of the Body*,[53] in various OBEs he has traveled to different realms, encountered a variety of spirit beings and received all sorts of metaphysical insights. He describes several "visits" to living people who could ostensibly verify that he was present. However, investigative reporter David Black and others, including Rogo, question the truthfulness of these accounts. Black could not locate any of the witnesses Monroe mentioned, and Monroe was evasive when Black questioned him about this.[54]

In the early 1970s Monroe founded the Monroe Institute of Applied Science, an organization that conducts research on OBEs and offers weekend seminars for people who would like to "explore new spiritual dimensions" and experience OBEs for themselves. One of the techniques offered is a program of taped sounds, heard through separate earphones, which ostensibly synchronizes the brain-wave patterns of the left and right hemispheres. Tal Brooke was a participant in some of Monroe's experiments while he was perfecting these tapes. According to Brooke, who later became a Christian, Monroe was learning how to make these tapes from the "beings of light" he conferred with during his own OBEs.[55]

Kübler-Ross apparently had her first direct encounter with spiritual forces in the 1960s, when she was seriously considering abandoning her work with the dying (primarily because of the stiff opposition she had received from other doctors). A woman appeared in her Chicago office, identifying herself as a patient who had died ten months earlier. The woman looked identical to the patient and had the same handwriting. She told Kübler-Ross not to give up with her work because "the time was not right." Later, in her speaking tours, Kübler-Ross revealed that she had acquired her own spirit guides.[56]

Moody's connections with the spirit world have been more subtle, at least until recently. Moody relates one incident that occurred on Halloween in 1975, when his wife was taking their children trick-or-treating. At one house the homeowners struck up a conversation and asked the children their names. When the oldest said, "Raymond Avery Moody, the third," the woman looked very startled and expressed a need to speak to the boy's father. When Moody contacted her, he learned that she had had an extensive NDE in 1971. Toward the end of this experience a spirit ostensibly showed her Moody's picture, gave his full name and then informed her that she should tell Moody her story "when the time was right." This incident occurred just a few months before his book *Life After Life* was published, so it was before his name became associated with NDEs.[57] Recently Moody has started promoting the use of the "psychomanteum," a darkened chamber with a mirror that has ostensibly enabled many people to make contact with the spirits of people who have died.[58]

The Aftereffects of NDEs

Researchers have uncovered two important types of NDE aftereffects: changes in certain attitudes and beliefs and the subsequent appearance of unusual abilities or experiences. Within the first category, NDErs frequently report that their attitudes toward other people have changed. They say they feel more tolerant, compassionate and loving and are less interested in personal gain or material possessions than they were before their NDEs. It is often assumed that these attitude changes are due to the NDEs, but they may simply result from narrowly escaping death. Kenneth Ring compared the attitude changes reported by his group of NDErs to the changes reported by a control group consisting of people who had nearly died but didn't have an NDE. He found that his control group reported as much attitude change in these areas as his NDErs.[59]

One of the most commonly reported, and superficially appealing, NDE aftereffects is the overwhelming sense of love that NDErs say they feel for other people. What is not so commonly known, however, is that these feelings do not necessarily translate into improved relationships. In fact, many NDErs find that their relationships become strained and difficult after their experiences. Many get divorced, quit their jobs and just drift for considerable periods of time.

Why does this happen? People who counsel NDErs and take a positive view of NDEs (like Moody) attribute these changes to the "readjustment problems" that experiencers face. They point out that individuals and their families can have a difficult time adjusting to any changes in personality or beliefs, even if those changes are for the better.[60]

Phyllis Atwater, who argues that NDE aftereffects can be negative, offers a different explanation. Based on her own difficult experiences and those of others in her study, she believes that NDErs get so caught up in their unusual, otherworldly feelings and become so disoriented and confused that they get totally wrapped up in themselves and can't respond to the needs of others. She suggests that the "love" NDErs bring back is a kind that interferes with their ability to personalize their emotions and feelings. In her words, "The kind of love encountered in dying is not emotional . . . not personal. It is a transcendental state. Love flows through you, not to or from you. It makes no demands and seeks no response. . . . It dissolves all emotion, feeling, and relationships."[61] If NDErs are applying this kind of "love" to family members and friends, it is not surprising that their relationships suffer.

NDEs can also have far-reaching effects on religious beliefs. Many studies indicate that NDErs lose their fear of death and become more confident in the existence of life after death. However, Ring found that these experiences did not strengthen NDErs' belief in God, even though NDErs did report more religious and ecstatic feelings after their NDEs. Most indicated that they were less interested in attending religious services, but more "privately religious and prayerful" than they had been before their experiences. Many shifted toward a universalist position, asserting that all religions accomplish the same ends. Quite a few indicated that reincarnation now seemed more plausible to them as well.[62]

Other researchers have replicated Ring's basic findings and added important discoveries of their own. Margot Grey found that 20 percent of her English NDErs shifted from orthodox Christianity to universalism after their NDEs, while an additional 27 percent converted to occult systems like spiritualism or theosophy. These people changed because they thought that their new belief system offered a better explanation of their experiences than traditional religions.[63] Atwater found that about one-third of her American NDErs remained in their church after their experience, with the aim of "working quietly from within to uplift and enrich its ministries." The other two-thirds either cast aside their religious affiliation or were never affiliated to begin with. Many in this latter group eventually joined "metaphysical," New Age or Eastern congregations.[64]

Cherie Sutherland, working with Australian NDErs, discovered equally dramatic shifts. Fifty-four percent of her NDErs were affiliated with Catholic or Protestant churches before their experiences, but only 14 percent continued any kind of affiliation with a traditional church afterward. Only two of the people who were not affiliated before their NDEs moved toward affiliation: one became a Catholic, the other a Buddhist. Sutherland also found that NDErs who were not affiliated with traditional congregations disdained established religion. Approximately 80 percent saw no value in organized religion and never attended church, yet this same group said that they often prayed, meditated and sought supernatural guidance. Many felt that they had a direct, ongoing contact with God or some Higher Power that went beyond the church and its doctrines.[65]

Alongside their changed religious beliefs, many NDErs report another set of aftereffects that are both surprising and disconcerting, especially to more scientifically minded NDE researchers. These include the appearance of various "psychic" abilities and apparent supernatural encounters. In fact, the list of aftereffects in this category is virtually identical to the roster of consequences that reportedly accompanies any spiritualistic or occult activity. It includes spontaneous OBEs, poltergeist activity, contacts with spirits of the dead or beings of light, seeing UFOs, receiving supernatural guidance and even experiencing supernatural rescue. Many NDErs report that they developed unusual powers like healing, precognition, clairvoyance, mental telepathy, automatic writing or channeling after their NDE.[66] Effects of this type strongly suggest demonic involvement.

Kenneth Ring and Christopher Rosing found that quite a few American NDErs (25-50 percent in their sample) reported highly unusual psychophysical symptoms following their NDEs. These included peculiar energy flows, ecstatic bodily sensations, feelings of excessive heat or cold, periods of mysterious and uncontrollable trembling and shaking, extreme mood swings, and episodes of "mind expansion" when spiritual insights seemed to come flooding in. Ring speculates that these events are indications of the arousal of the kundalini force, which he depicts as a subtle form of "bioenergy" that is released during the process of "psychospiritual trans-formation."[67] ("Psychospiritual transformation" is a name for the rapid spiritual evolution and development that is ostensibly now in progress, at least among the more "spiritually sensitive" among us.)

Ring's description of kundalini may sound fairly harmless, but it masks kundalini's occult roots and its likely connection with demonic activity.[68] The term *kundalini* actually comes from yoga, where it means "the serpent force." Hindus believe that this force is aroused when yogic adepts suc-cessfully "yoke" or join with the Hindu god Brahman, releasing supernat-ural powers which then manifest themselves in their bodies. Yogans who succeed in arousing kundalini exhibit the same physical and psychological perturbations that are reported by NDErs. However, the Hindus are acutely aware that kundalini can be very dangerous. This state can reportedly ebb and flow for months, and people who are caught up in it usually become very disturbed psychologically. Some make it through this crisis, ostensibly gaining greater powers and a closer communion with the spirit world as a reward, but others become seriously deranged. (See chapter six.)

Possible Explanations for OBEs and NDEs

Seven important conclusions about OBEs and NDEs can be drawn from the current literature, and all of them need to be taken into account if we are to explain these experiences adequately. These conclusions can be summarized as follows:

1. OBEs and NDEs are probably not real separations of body and spirit, even though they give the strong impression that they are.

2. NDEs may not tell us anything about death or the afterlife, because all the features of NDEs can also occur in OBEs that are not associated with death.

3. People from very different cultures can have very different NDEs. The content of NDEs seems to be related to the NDEr's cultural and religious expectations.

4. OBEs and NDEs probably have significant physiological components, because it is possible to elicit various elements of these experiences phys-

ically (through brain stimulation, epileptic seizures, CO_2 buildup and other means).

5. There appears to be a definite connection between OBEs, NDEs and altered states of consciousness.

6. The vast majority of NDEs and OBEs described in the current secular literature support occult, New Age and contemporary mystical beliefs about human nature, death and the afterlife.

7. There are strong intimations of demonic involvement in many current OBEs and NDEs.

If the first conclusion is correct and current NDEs and OBEs are not authentic separations of body and spirit, how are we to explain them? In my opinion the two most likely explanations are that they are self-generated (due to unusual events in the brain, being in an altered state, imagination, fabrication, faulty interpretation) or that they are visionary experiences that are initiated and/or shaped by spiritual forces. (In the incidents considered here, those forces are very likely demonic.) It is quite possible that both factors are operating. Some episodes (such as simple OBEs that apparently occur spontaneously during sleep) are probably self-generated, while others may be due to a mixture of internal and spiritual influences.

Physiologically based explanations can account for some of the features of NDEs and OBEs, but not all of them. Hypotheses that rely solely on physical events in the brain as an explanation are probably the least adequate, because they cannot explain the sequencing of events, their intense reality and spiritual significance, their unusual aftereffects or the belief changes that reportedly follow these events.

The altered-states hypothesis fares better and could account for a number of OBEs and/or NDEs, particularly the unsought, spontaneous types that are not followed by unusual aftereffects. These may simply be a peculiar type of hallucination or dream that can occur in an altered state. This hypothesis accounts for systematic cultural differences in NDEs, because hallucinations and dreams are influenced by memories and beliefs, and beliefs differ in systematic ways from culture to culture. The fact that these experiences are occurring during altered states could help explain why they often seem so real and spiritually meaningful.

On the negative side, the altered-states hypothesis by itself probably cannot explain the unusual aftereffects that apparently follow many NDEs (the appearance of psychic abilities and supernatural incidents), the strong support they provide for New Age and mystical worldviews or the apparent ability of some NDErs to view the details of their resuscitations, as if watching them in progress. Some parapsychologists have suggested that this latter phenomena may be due to ESP, but so far this is only conjecture. (See chapter seven for a discussion of ESP.)

Self-generation of a deliberate sort may be involved in some NDEs. It is possible that some NDE accounts are grossly exaggerated or are even outright fabrications, concocted for profit, publicity or attention. Currently there is a very strong market for book-length accounts of NDEs, and unfortunately many readers are willing to accept such accounts at face value. This creates a situation that is ripe for exploitation by unscrupulous storytellers.

The way NDEs are being studied and reported is also creating biases and inaccuracies in the current NDE literature. To start with, most NDE accounts are several years old by the time investigators get them. Human memory being what it is, this means the accounts have probably been altered or embellished before they are collected. In addition, virtually all the studies of NDEs in the current literature are based on questionnaire data, which is very likely to be influenced by the respondents' beliefs and what they think investigators are looking for. This difficulty is compounded by the fact that much of the published NDE research is drawn from a very limited pool of subjects. Almost invariably these are either members of the Association for Near-Death Studies (IANDS) or persons who have voluntarily contacted the organization to share their stories. Since many of these NDErs and the researchers share the same beliefs, including elements of the "New Mysticism" described in chapter one, it is very likely that the NDErs' responses and the researchers' interpretations of these responses are strongly biased in favor of New Mysticism.

As far as supernatural explanations are concerned, there appear to be three options. For one, it is possible that some of the NDEs reported by Christians, particularly those of a transcendental or visionary type, are allowed or initiated by God to encourage or instruct believers or warn them to take their faith seriously. In light of the scriptural considerations mentioned previously and Rawlings's observation that positive and negative NDEs seem to be distributed indiscriminately between believers and nonbelievers, this possibility does not seem very likely, but we cannot rule it out.

Theoretically at least, it is possible that some of the experiences reported by professed Christians are deceptive and are being initiated by Satan or his agents, possibly to mislead Christians or to try to keep everyone confused about where NDEs are coming from. (They might look suspicious if they only occurred among non-Christians.) It is difficult to evaluate this hypothesis, because God evidently protects believers from undue harassment (see Job 1:9-10; Jn 17:15), yet the Bible also warns us that we are engaged in spiritual warfare as long as we reside on this planet (Eph 6:10-18; 1 Pet 5:8-11). One could argue that the potential for deception extends to NDEs, since these events by definition take one near death but not through the final, irreversible event. In relation to NDEs, it is also striking that in 2 Corinthians 11:14 Paul warns Christians that "Satan himself masquerades as an angel of light."

A final possibility is that a number of current OBEs and NDEs are being initiated or shaped by demonic forces, particularly among people who have deliberately rejected the basic tenets of Christianity and are seeking other spiritual paths. In this case OBEs and NDEs may be *deceptive visions,* intended to convince the unsaved that they do not need Christ to get to heaven and to provide support for New Mysticism, a religious system that could become an effective alternative to biblical Christianity.

This hypothesis could account for the illusory, deceptive character of these experiences (such as the fact that they appear to be real separations of body and spirit but probably are not), their frequent association with spiritualistic, occult and paganistic practices, the support they provide for contemporary mystical belief systems, and their unusual aftereffects. Intelligent agents could vary the experiences to mesh effectively with different cultural and religious expectations; it is also likely that they would time them to coincide with altered states, whenever possible, to maximize their impact. All this is highly speculative, of course, but it is even possible that some of the special effects that accompany these experiences (music, humming or buzzing sounds, sensations of floating or vibrating, feelings of ecstasy, peace or painlessness) are being created by the judicious stimulation of certain brain areas.

Interestingly, even though this last hypothesis may seem far-fetched, it is actually quite compatible with the explanations for NDEs that prominent NDE researchers have offered. Both Kenneth Ring and Bruce Greyson (currently the director of research for IANDS) have concluded that NDEs are probably not related to death but are, rather, "seed experiences" that are being deliberately initiated and orchestrated by spiritual powers (presumably God, the Higher Self or spirit guides) and meant to serve as catalysts for spiritual awakening and development. The aftereffects, including changed religious beliefs, the appearance of psychic abilities and the more intimate relationship with the spirit realm, are interpreted as indications that the intended spiritual development is now well under way.[69]

Greyson adds some particularly insightful comments:

> The NDE itself, striking though it may be, does not sound to the investigator all that different from hallucinations or dissociative states. Its aftereffects, on the other hand, are uniquely profound, pervasive and permanent, totally unlike the aftereffects of any phenomenologically comparable experience. NDEs are seed experiences, and it is only by studying the fruits that eventually grow from those seeds that we can understand their full meaning.[70]

Jesus also reminded his followers that they could exercise discernment by studying certain "fruits" (Mt 7:15-20). I believe his advice is exceptionally relevant in the case of OBEs and NDEs.

6

Eastern Meditation & Mystical Experiences

No analysis of our present mystical climate would be complete without some discussion of Eastern religious beliefs and meditative practices, for both have played a crucial role in the development of contemporary secular mysticism. Eastern religious beliefs not only provided the foundation and framework for New Age/New Consciousness thought but have also influenced the broader contemporary climate in important ways. This entire system of beliefs is reinforced by the dramatic mystical experiences that Eastern meditation can produce. In New Age circles, Eastern meditation has long been considered the most effective way to alter consciousness and acquire fundamental spiritual insights. Those who were blitzed into "superconsciousness" in the late 1960s and early 1970s by psychedelic drugs quickly turned to Eastern meditation as the technique of choice when they discovered that it produced some of the same "mind-altering" effects as the drugs but in a safer, more controllable manner.

In recent years a much broader cross-section of the Western population has also experimented with Eastern meditation, not necessarily because they were interested in mystical experiences or in the New Age movement, but usually because they had read or heard that Eastern-style meditation could confer significant health benefits—lowering blood pressure and cholesterol or relieving pain, stress, anxiety and depression. It is difficult to know how many Americans and other Westerners have experimented with Eastern meditation for these purposes, but the numbers are fairly large and are apparently still growing.

Is this widespread experimentation with Eastern meditation a cause for concern? I believe it is. Although much of the casual, health-related experimentation may prove to be of minor consequence, there is still the nagging question whether it is ever possible to completely separate such practices from their spiritualistic and pantheistic underpinnings. According to the available evidence, when Eastern meditation is consistently and seriously exercised as a religious technique, it can bring about profound alterations in consciousness and activate extraordinary, self-validating experiences that appear to support key Eastern/New Age beliefs. Since many of these beliefs contradict Christian doctrines, we can only conclude that such experiences (or at least the way they are being interpreted) are deceptive.

Also, careful research on the effects of Eastern meditation has shown that it is not the health panacea it has been made to seem. There is a high drop-out rate among those who try it, not only because of its rigorous demands but also because it can aggravate or even *create* serious long-term problems including pain, anxiety and depression.

Eastern Traditions in Western Culture
The Eastern traditions that have become fairly common in Western countries have their roots in Hinduism (from India) and Buddhism (an ancient branch of Hinduism that spread through China, Tibet, Japan and other Eastern countries). Like Christianity, both Hinduism and Buddhism have numerous sects or subgroups that differ in some of their beliefs. But these subgroups still generally subscribe to spiritual monism, the idea that everything, living and nonliving, is composed of the same, all-pervading spiritual substance. They believe that humans are trapped in endless cycles of reincarnation unless, or until, they are able to reach spiritual perfection

through accumulated growth over many lifetimes. All these subgroups place a very high priority on the practice of meditation, for it is considered one of the most effective means of spiritual growth and advancement.

Some of the specific Eastern traditions that have become influential in the West include Hindu bhakti and yoga (hatha, raja and tantra) and Zen and Tibetan Buddhism. Bhakti, the predominant tradition within Hinduism, emphasizes complete devotion to a holy person or one of the Hindu deities as a means of spiritual advancement. The Hare Krishnas, who are easily identified by their Indian garb, shaved heads and frequent drumming and chanting, practice a form of bhakti. They are devoted to the god Krishna, and one of their ways of exercising that devotion is to continually chant his name.

Transcendental meditation (TM), founded in the United States by Maharishi Mahesh Yogi, also contains elements of bhakti. In TM adherents may be devoted to Maharishi, to Maharishi's dead master, Swami Saraswati, or to any of the various Hindu gods. TM has been presented to Westerners as a nonreligious, "scientific" technique that can be used to "improve perception, expand awareness, or reduce stress," but closer examination reveals that it is neither nonreligious nor particularly scientific. The mandatory rituals that accompany it indicate that it is actually classical Hindu mantra meditation.[1]

In order to become full-fledged TM meditators, aspirants must go through an initiation ritual in which they kneel before a picture of Saraswati, offering fruit, flowers and passive assent, while an initiator intones a lengthy Sanskrit hymn of worship and surrender to departed masters and Hindu gods. According to Maharishi, this hymn is specifically designed to attract the attention of higher spiritual beings, presumably to obtain their blessing and assistance in imparting the mantra.[2] After this ceremony, new meditators are given a mantra, often the name of one of the Hindu gods, which they are to repeat over and over in their meditations. The mantra presumably helps the meditator become "attuned to transcendent forces, which manifest as higher beings or gods."[3]

The practice of yoga can take many forms. In general, *yoga* (which literally means "to yoke") refers to any physical, mental or spiritual practice specifically intended to bring the participant into union with higher spiritual powers and/or "ultimate reality." Three forms of yoga that are known in the West are *hatha* (physical yoga), *raja* (royal yoga) and *tantra*, which is identified most clearly with Tibetan Buddhism. All three were designed to alter consciousness in a way that ultimately allows the seeker to experience a profound sense of unity with "God" or the entire universe. Hatha and raja yoga both make use of difficult physical postures that are meant to help free the subtle body (spirit) from the gross body (physical body). Many Americans have engaged in hatha yoga thinking that it is simply a strenuous type of physical conditioning. But they may be getting more than they bargained for, because even hatha was intentionally designed to alter consciousness and to begin the process of Eastern-style spiritual development.[4]

Tantra yoga can seem both baffling and bizarre to Westerners. (It also seems that way to many Hindus.) Tantric practices can range from the strange (assuming very difficult yogic postures) to the sublime to the horrible (sexual relations with a corpse). Adherents know, from the experiences of others, that they face great risks—possible insanity or even death—when they engage in some prescribed tantric practices. Yet aspirants still choose this path, because they see it as a shortcut to the state of spiritual perfection they are seeking. (Some believe they have to risk this shortcut because the time allotted for the reincarnative process is running out.)

Most traditions attempt to get disciples beyond their everyday "false" impressions of reality by teaching them to shut out the physical world and turn off the activities of the mind. However, tantra takes an entirely different approach. It encourages its adherents to interact fully, even shockingly, with the "illusory" physical world, in the belief that such interactions are the surest way to pierce physical illusions and reveal the unity and true spiritual nature of all things. In tantra, much effort is directed toward learning to control and manipulate one's body, whether through yogic postures, mantras, managed breathing, visual symbols or sexual arousal (*maithuna*).

In tantra, one of the definite signs of spiritual progress is the arousal of kundalini, or the "serpent force," which presumably lies coiled and dormant at the base of the spine. Once aroused, this force begins a process of "purification" which, if successfully resolved, presumably allows the disciple much closer contact with the spiritual realm. However, if the process goes awry, the experiencer can also become permanently psychotic. The kundalini process is accompanied by a host of extraordinary symptoms which are described in detail later in this chapter.

The Purposes of Eastern Meditation

In all Eastern traditions, meditation has three general purposes. It presumably enables meditators to recognize the true nature of the physical world (its impermanence and illusory nature), to sense their place in the scheme of things (to know that they are part of a spiritual reality that supersedes and transcends the physical world) and to progress spiritually (to overcome undesirable personal characteristics, advance their position in their next reincarnation, get in touch with and utilize spiritual power, and so on).

In our natural way of thinking, the world, the objects in it and the people around us all seem separate, independent, and tangibly and sensibly real. Eastern adepts mistrust these perceptions, partly because they have been taught to distrust them and partly because of their experiences in deep meditative states. In such states objects can appear to change their contours, become diaphanous, merge with other objects or even disappear. The boundaries between the meditator and other people or objects may appear to melt, producing a profound sense of unity or "at-oneness" with everything else. Because these experiences are often accompanied by a profound sense of realism, meditators usually assume that they are valid revelations of the true nature of things.

Individuals with a Western or scientific perspective of reality would very likely attribute such experiences to *faulty* perception, created by the disruption of normal perceptual processing. But to Easterners these experiences reinforce the belief that the common attributes of physical objects, like their apparent reality, solidness or separateness, are actually illusions imposed by the mind and senses. The stubborn pervasiveness of such "illusions" in normal consciousness assures them that the only way for human beings to comprehend the true nature of things is to experience it for themselves, through meditation or some other method that can block normal physical perception.

In most Eastern traditions the primary purpose of meditation is to re-train attention.[5] In fact, before meditators can attain significant experiences they must learn to attend continually to some very simple object or sound, and to do so with such single-mindedness that they can block out all other sights, sounds or thoughts for extended periods.[6] This can take months or years of regular, disciplined practice.

Aspiring meditators are encouraged to seek out a competent teacher or guru to guide them, because meditation can create deep altered states of consciousness[7] and generate experiences that are so unusual and poten-tially disorienting that novices can founder if left to navigate them by themselves. The teacher is there to help students interpret their experi-ences and to keep them moving along the right path. Teachers may also assist disciples by directly imparting some of their own acquired spiritual power to them, through touch or other means. The relationship between teacher and disciple can become a very subservient one, with novices agreeing to serve their teacher completely, surrendering every aspect of their lives to him or her for the sake of instruction. In many cases the teacher is even worshiped as a god.

Techniques of Meditation

Eastern meditative techniques vary widely, but most can be classified as either techniques of concentration or techniques of mindfulness.[8] Concen-tration techniques restrict attention to a single image or object, whereas mindfulness involves attending to all of one's mental experiences in a nonanalytic, nonjudgmental way. Most traditions make some use of both types of meditation.

In all forms of concentrative meditation, the immediate goal is to learn to attend to a single thing to the exclusion of everything else. But the ultimate goal is to use this ability to *shut down the mind* for indefinite periods of time, eliminating all images, thoughts or sensations. The objects of concentrative meditation vary greatly. Sometimes meditators attend only to their breath. In other cases the object of concentration is a mantra, a word that is repeated over and over, either aloud (chanting) or silently (meditation). While repeating the mantra, the meditator is to attend only to the sound of the word, not its meaning. With much practice, meditators are eventually able to shut out everything except a nonanalytic awareness of the sound of the word.

In yoga, objects of concentration are often visual—a candle flame, a vase, a waterfall or a mandala (a circular picture or design that has religious significance). In Zen Buddhism the student may be asked to concentrate on a koan, a riddle or paradox that cannot be solved by logical means (the most famous being "What is the sound of one hand clapping?"). The goal in this case is to frustrate the conscious mind, leading to a cessation of all verbal, logical thought.

Bhakti provides an informative example of concentrative meditation. Bhakti aspirants choose one of the Hindu gods and make this god (referred to as an "ishta") the central object of their thoughts and meditations. Devotees eventually spend many hours a day repeating the name of their ishta while working up intense feelings of love and devotion for this deity. According to adepts, this practice eventually brings about unusual "spiritual" experiences that include deep feelings of bliss and ecstasy and, eventually, episodes in which the devotee seems to merge more and more completely with the god he or she is worshiping.

The great truth that is finally experienced at the culmination of bhakti meditation is that the meditator's Higher Self and the deity being worshiped are actually one and the same. This means that the meditator is no longer constrained to worship the ishta but is now free to engage in unrestrained *self-worship*. All the feelings of devotion and love once directed toward the ishta can now be directed inward, with the same blissful and beneficial results. Bhakti's purpose is to reveal the unity of all things, the meditator's true inner self and that self's essential divinity.[9] From an experiential perspective, it apparently accomplishes this purpose quite effectively.

The techniques of mindfulness meditation are meant to enable meditators to grasp the true nature of their mental life and of the world around them. In this form of meditation, beginners are instructed not to initiate any mental activity but simply to observe passively as thoughts, sensations or impressions arise on their own. Meditators are simply to note each of these mental events as it occurs, without reacting to it, and then let it go as the next event arises. This noting of events is to be done with the same intensity of concentration attained in concentrative meditation; in this case, however, meditators also try to maintain full, nonanalytic awareness of *all* their mental activities instead of attending to just a single object or thought.[10]

Mindfulness meditation is particularly important in Buddhist traditions, and its continued practice brings about a series of experiences that appear to confirm the Buddhist view of reality. As meditators passively watch their own mental states come and go without trying to control them, these begin to fluctuate more and more rapidly and unpredictably. After a while this chaotic activity creates the strong impression that the mental events are springing into life on their own, from some separate source, rather than the observer's own mind. As meditators persist with this practice, they also notice that there is a definite separation between the mental events being observed and the mind that is doing the observing.

As meditation progresses still further, both the mental events and the observing mind begin to seem alien and impersonal, as if they do not really belong to the observer. At about this point the meditator's sense of "self" becomes confused and weakened, and finally it disappears entirely for brief periods of time. This experience of dissolution strongly reinforces the Buddhist notion that there actually is no such thing as an "I" or "myself"— that such concepts are actually false constructions of the mind.

At still deeper levels, meditators eventually reach a stage in which their awareness of events and the events themselves seem inextricably bound together and the whole scene churns in a wild state of flux. Ideas, images and thoughts seem to appear and then dissolve into nothingness with great rapidity. At this point every aspect of mental life (and the physical world itself) seems impermanent, transitory and alien, and disturbed meditators desperately want it all to stop. Relief finally comes when meditators break through to Nirvana, a state in which all awareness of physical and mental phenomena ceases, at least for a short time.

Reaching this stage ostensibly produces permanent changes in consciousness. Inner processes are set in motion which fill the meditator with equanimity and bliss. These presumably destroy defiling mental states like self-interest, ambition, greed and hatred, and ensure advanced placement in the next life. When interpreted through Eastern lenses, these experiences strongly reinforce the Buddhist belief that the physical universe, our concepts of self and even our inner mental life are only illusions.

Eastern Meditation as a Source of Truth

To Easterners, meditation is crucial because it is the only way to achieve clear spiritual insights and experience fundamental truths. At this point we need to pause and ask whether such techniques are reliable sources of truth. There are at least three compelling reasons to argue that they are not.

From a Christian perspective, the first and most obvious reason for questioning these experiences is that they appear to support false doctrines. The second (which I develop more fully later in this chapter) is that alternate and more plausible ways of explaining these experiences place them in quite a different light. For example, they may simply be unusual side effects created when one forces one's cognitive and perceptual systems to operate in restricted and unaccustomed ways. If this is true, it implies that the experiences are *misperceptions or illusions* rather than glimpses of some superordinate reality.

A third reason for mistrusting such "truths" is that they are being generated in altered states of consciousness. From the discussion in chapter four it is clear that many events can seem incredibly real and significant in altered states even though objectively they are patently false or trivial. Ironically, Easterners are clearly aware of this possibility, but they are curiously inconsistent in the way they react to this information. Teachers warn novice meditators that many of their early experiences (which can include feelings of great rapture and bliss, transcendent visions, extraordinary encounters with mythic beings and so on) are very deceptive and not to take them seriously; yet they believe that by going even deeper into altered states, with more disciplined meditation, they can finally reach levels of consciousness where their experiences are completely trustworthy. This assumption is obviously very questionable.

The Assumed Health Benefits of Eastern Meditation

Many Westerners who have tried Eastern meditation have done so because they had heard or read of its apparent health benefits. Keith Wallace and Herbert Benson of the Harvard Medical School carried out some of the first supportive research in this area. Their work suggested that meditation might relieve some of the physiological and psychological symptoms of stress. Benson began this research after a group of TM meditators convinced him that the area was definitely worth investigating.[11] As it turned out, this was a strategic move by the TM supporters, because the results looked positive and were published in prestigious medical journals. This gave TM a great deal of credibility.

In their studies Wallace and Benson measured heart rate, blood pressure, oxygen consumption and blood lactate levels before, during and after meditation in experienced TM meditators. They found that all these stress indicators decreased during and after meditation. In addition, they (and other researchers) discovered some intriguing changes in EEG patterns (brain waves). Meditation appeared to produce more slow-wave activity (which is more characteristic of sleep) and EEG synchrony (greater uniformity of brain-wave patterns over many parts of the brain) than is generally apparent during simple relaxation.[12] Findings of this type eventually prompted Wallace, himself a long-term meditator, to conclude that the meditators were actually entering a unique state of consciousness, a "wakeful, hypometabolic state" that differed from ordinary states of relaxation or sleep.[13] This implied that TM might be an even more effective stress reducer than standard relaxation techniques.

But these conclusions were soon challenged by other researchers, partly because Wallace and Benson did not include a control group of nonmeditators to see how they might respond under similar conditions, and partly because they did not compare the effects of meditation to those of standard relaxation techniques. Later experiments, which did take these variables into account, revealed that meditation *can* decrease the physiological components of tension and stress, but not any more effectively than mock meditation (employing meditation techniques without any religious elements), hypnosis, self-hypnosis, biofeedback or progressive muscle relaxation.[14]

In fact, David Holmes and others have shown that there are no significant differences in the physiological responses obtained by experienced meditators during meditation and those of control subjects who simply rested for the same amount of time. Holmes argues that the beneficial effects of meditation are primarily due to the fact that the meditators are resting.[15] Holmes's conclusions stirred up a storm of protests from meditators and health professionals who were convinced that meditation is a superior stress reduction technique.[16] However, they have not been able to refute either his data or his logic.

Time and additional research have also modified the notion that meditation produces a unique and beneficial state of consciousness. All the brain-wave changes that seemed exclusive to meditative states have now been observed in nonmeditative states like relaxation or sleep. It is also clear that increased EEG synchrony is not necessarily a sign of exceptional or even beneficial brain activity either, because synchrony can also be observed during epileptic seizures, comas and schizophrenic states.[17] It now seems likely that the increased EEG synchrony that occurs during meditation simply reflects the fact that normal information-processing activities, which desynchronize EEG patterns, are greatly reduced when experienced meditators meditate.

Some of the unusual EEG patterns that occur during meditation resemble those seen during drowsiness or sleep. These may actually be caused by brief sleep episodes, or they may indicate that meditators have learned to maintain a state of consciousness that lies somewhere between sleeping and waking. Meditators do occasionally fall asleep. In fact, Pagano and his colleagues discovered that one group of experienced TM meditators spent about 40 percent of their time asleep.[18] There are also episodes of sleeplike EEGs in meditators who are clearly awake. These are intriguing because there is a stage of sleep, which sometimes occurs at sleep onset, in which people can experience "hypnogogic hallucinations"—very brief, vivid and realistic visual experiences. Hypnogogic hallucinations are probably brief dream episodes that manifest themselves while the dreamer is still partly conscious. It is possible that meditators have learned to enter and prolong the hypnogogic state. If so, this may explain some of the vivid visual experiences they encounter.[19]

In addition to using meditation as a method of relaxation and stress reduction, some psychotherapists have used it to try to reduce anxiety and depression. But current research indicates that in most cases meditation is not an appropriate treatment for these conditions,[20] especially for individuals with moderate to severe difficulties. These clients have a very high drop-out rate and generally do not benefit from meditation.[21]

Significantly, there are also studies indicating that Eastern-style meditation can have adverse and long-lasting physical and psychological consequences. In one study Leon Otis randomly assigned sixty volunteers to four groups. The first group learned TM from regular TM instructors; the second engaged in mock meditation (their mantra was the phrase "I am a witness only"); the third group was told to relax in any way that suited them; and the fourth group did not change their lifestyle in any way. The three experimental groups were instructed to practice meditation or relaxation twice daily for fifteen to twenty minutes for three months.

Well before the three-month period was over, Otis started receiving complaints, especially from the two meditation groups. Quite a few were experiencing physical and mental distress (headaches, insomnia, anxiety, gastrointestinal upsets and the like). When he checked with officials at SIMS (the Student's International Meditation Society, which is the parent organization for TM), he discovered that such problems were common. In fact, TM teachers were routinely instructed to assure their students these were only harmless and transient side effects of "unstressing." In Otis's study, however, these side effects were not inconsequential. Two of the meditation control subjects and three of the TM subjects (out of fifteen in each group) actually had to drop out before the completion of the experiment because the meditation revived serious medical conditions that had been under control at the beginning of the experiment.[22]

In a second investigation, Otis sent surveys to every twentieth person on the SIMS 1971 mailing list (which included about forty thousand names) and found even more serious negative effects. Up to 48 percent of his respondents indicated that they had suffered at least one or two adverse effects from meditation; most important, the longer the respondents had persisted with TM, the more numerous and severe their problems. The persons whose difficulties were most severe were advanced TM trainers who had meditated for many years—*not* the people who had dropped out, as Otis had anticipated. The most commonly reported negative effects in this study were anxiety, depression, confusion, frustration, mental and physical tension, and inexplicable outbursts of antisocial behavior.[23]

Why did the meditators persist with TM in the face of such problems? Otis wasn't sure, but the unsolicited comments and letters he received from many disgruntled meditators indicated that they didn't think they had a choice. They wanted to stop but felt as if they were somehow being coerced to continue, because their symptoms would get even worse when they tried to stop. Many felt very trapped and frustrated. Among his conclusions, Otis says, "Our data raise serious doubts about the innocuous nature of TM. In fact, they suggest that TM may be hazardous to the mental health of a sizeable proportion of the people who take up TM."[24]

Psychotherapist Frederick Heide (and others[25]) has also documented some serious negative side effects associated with Eastern-style meditation. Among a group of Heide's clients who were using meditation to combat anxiety, a sizable number reported symptoms like agitation, stress, moderate to severe anxiety, fears of losing control, headaches and elevated heart rates. Heide also found that the clients who were experiencing greater anxiety after starting meditation also experienced floating sensations, feelings of heaviness, tingling, numbness, muscle spasms or shaking, excessive sadness or anger, or realistic, disturbing visions.[26]

Meditation and Mystical Experiences

Eastern meditation can bring about a variety of extraordinary experiences that appear exceptionally real and significant. Many could aptly be described as "mystical" in the sense that they appear to convey great meaning, insight or truth, involve highly unusual perceptions or reveal transcendent realms beyond mere physical existence. The types of things meditators experience depend on both their level of expertise and the specific methods of meditation they are using. Two highly valued experiences I have already described include "unity" (in bhakti), in which meditators experience a profound oneness with their god, and "dissolution" (in Buddhist traditions), in which everything, including the self, appears to dissolve away into nothingness. Two other important categories include "access experiences," which occur in the early stages of meditation, and "kundalini arousal," which can occur in advanced meditators, especially those engaging in tantra yoga.

Access experiences begin when meditators are just learning to exercise a significant amount of control over their attention. They may include rapturous feelings, electrifying thrills and chills that move through the body, sensations of tingling, prickling, intense heat or cold, or of bugs crawling on the skin. These sensations can be interspersed with pain or with unusual releases of physical energy, called *kriyas*. Kriyas may take the form of prolonged shaking or trembling, single involuntary movements (such as a writhing motion along the trunk) or more complex, longer-lasting actions.

Jack Kornfield, a Western psychologist in training to be a monk, described a meditation session in a Thai monastery in which his arms suddenly and involuntarily started flapping like chicken wings. They continued to flap like this for two days while he tried to sit calmly and contemplate the experience as his teacher instructed him to do.[27]

Other raptures are accompanied by the appearance of moving colored lights, intense white light, changes in body image (suddenly feeling very tall, short, heavy or light), feelings of floating and inner sounds like bells or music. Meditators can also have startling, realistic visions. Objects in the environment may suddenly start to sparkle, then dissolve into a swarm of tiny lights. Ethereal beings, hideous monsters or mythological creatures may suddenly appear. The visions may reveal other cultures and times, nuclear explosions or other catastrophes, or apparent scenes from one's "past lives."[28]

Even though access experiences seem extremely real and significant to novice meditators, their attainment is not an important goal of Eastern meditation. In fact, advanced meditators dismiss these experiences as inconsequential byproducts of the meditation process. They are viewed as a mixed achievement: they are positive in the sense that they indicate progress, but they can become an obstacle to further spiritual advancement. They frighten some meditators away and produce an unhealthy fascination in others. Without expert guidance, inexperienced meditators may want to stay at this level instead of moving forward to more meaningful experiences.[29]

Kundalini arousal is a second and potentially very dangerous set of experiences that can occur among advanced meditators. According to the tenets of tantra yoga, kundalini, or the "serpent force," is a type of dormant spiritual energy that lies coiled at the base of the spinal cord. If and when this energy is awakened through serious meditation or other "spiritual" practices, it moves upward along the spinal column through seven *chakras* (points at which the spiritual body is connected to the physical body) to the crown of the head. Its arrival at the head ostensibly gives rise to "bliss and enlightenment."[30]

According to tantric legend, this supreme state occurs when kundalini, the female polarity of the divine within human nature, unites in sexual embrace with Shiva, the Hindu god of death.[31] However, while kundalini is ostensibly blasting and burning its way through supposed "blockages" in the various chakras, it is anything but blissful. According to authorities it can produce an incredible array of painful, frightening and disruptive symptoms, and it may take weeks or months for the process to run its course. In tantric literature these symptoms are explained as the normal side effects of the "purification" process that kundalini sets in motion.

One of the prominent symptoms of kundalini arousal is pain. This pain can occur anywhere, but it often occurs around the eyes, in the head (where it produces viselike headaches) or along the spine. It can begin abruptly, without apparent cause, and vanish just as abruptly and mysteriously. The pain can be very severe and can last from seconds to days or even weeks at a time. In addition to pain, meditators may sense "energy flows" coursing through their bodies or feel tingling, tickling, itching or vibration in their skin. These sensations usually begin in the feet or pelvic area and move up the back and neck to the crown of the head, then down across the face and abdomen.

Meditators may experience extreme heat or cold and find their bodies making strange involuntary movements—muscle twitches, prolonged trembling or sinuous writhing. In some instances meditators have reportedly watched incredulously as their bodies spontaneously and automatically assumed difficult yoga postures. The automatic movements of the body may be accompanied by spontaneous crying, laughing, screaming or whistling.[32] Other common involuntary behaviors include speaking in tongues, chanting unknown songs and making a variety of animal sounds and movements.[33]

Besides these physical manifestations, kundalini arousal can produce profound psychological disturbances. There is a real danger of developing full-blown (and permanent) psychosis in this condition.[34] Emotions swing wildly from ecstasy, bliss and peace to intense fear, depression, anxiety and anger. Thoughts become strange and irrational, and experiencers may slip into dissociative or prolonged trance states. They may feel very alienated and confused and often seem to be watching the things that are happening to them as if they were outside observers.[35]

Not surprisingly, experiencers often fear that they are losing their minds.

Some people in the throes of kundalini have apparently been consigned to mental hospitals by psychiatrists who judged them psychotic.[36] Besides these psychological and physical aberrations, kundalini arousal may be accompanied by "out-of-body" experiences and psychic phenomena—clairvoyance, telepathy and so on.[37]

Kundalini symptoms have apparently occurred sporadically among Eastern meditators from different traditions over many centuries.[38] This syndrome also started cropping up in the United States and Western Europe during the 1970s, and although it is still relatively uncommon (at least in its classical, full-blown manifestation), it now appears to be occurring with increasing frequency in the West.[39] Most of the documented cases of classical kundalini arousal are still apparently confined to long-term meditators. The nonmeditators who have experienced it are usually described as having other unusual spiritual pursuits (channeling) or abilities (psychic talents) that ostensibly conditioned them for this experience. Very recently researchers Kenneth Ring and Bruce Greyson have discovered a significant number of isolated kundalini symptoms occurring as aftereffects among near-death experiencers. Because of this, both men now believe that NDEs and other mystical experiences are being deliberately initiated by spiritual powers for human instruction and that all such experiences are probably driven by the kundalini force.[40]

Kundalini symptoms and other extraordinary experiences—including "past-lives" regressions, communication with spirit guides, channeling, close encounters with UFOs, near-death experiences and spirit possession—can obviously be very unsettling, and experiencers sometimes turn to mental-health professionals for assistance. But since many counselors don't even believe in the existence of spiritual forces, they are usually ill-prepared to help. As already noted, they may suspect psychosis and have the client hospitalized.[41]

To counteract this problem, psychiatrist Stanislav Grof and his wife Christina Grof (who underwent a prolonged kundalini experience herself) founded the Spiritual Emergence Network in 1980. SEN is now an international network of some eleven hundred psychotherapists, psychiatrists,

M.D.s, social workers and spiritual leaders who deal specifically with such crises. They all subscribe to the idea that these experiences are crises of "spiritual opening"—that is, they are meant to shake up people's lives, force them to question their basic beliefs and open their minds to broader (Eastern or New Age) spiritual vistas.[42] SEN counselors believe that such experiences are positive, and they generally do not question their source, validity or purpose. With this perspective they can offer clients an upbeat, intriguing explanation of their experiences, reassure them about their mental health and encourage them to cooperate with whatever inner processes their experiences appear to have set in motion.

Possible Explanations

How are we to explain the unusual experiences of meditators? The Eastern perspective is that most are valid, hard-earned glimpses of a spiritual reality that lies beyond mere physical life, while adverse physical effects are simply reactions to the process of spiritual purification. But from a scientific or Christian perspective, there are plausible alternative explanations for these experiences which place them in an entirely different light. One of the more convincing is that meditative practices force the mind and brain to operate in very unaccustomed ways, and this creates misperceptions or misinterpretations of reality. These misperceptions seem very real and significant partly because they are occurring in altered states and partly because of the experiencer's prior expectations.

Psychologist Arthur Deikman was probably the first to suggest that this might be the case. In an experiment devoid of any religious overtones, he simply asked volunteers to contemplate a blue vase for twelve fifteen-to-thirty-minute sessions. This is not much practice by Eastern standards, but it was sufficient to produce some interesting effects. As the sessions progressed, the participants reported that the vase became more vivid, its color richer and its boundaries less stable. Sometimes its size and shape appeared to change, sometimes it appeared to move or undulate, and sometimes its edges blurred and disappeared. In a few cases the vase appeared to be luminous or animated, as if it had acquired a life of its own.

In one case it seemed to radiate particles of light out of highlights on its surface, which induced ecstasy and sexual arousal when they reached the meditator's body. All the participants were fascinated with their experiences.[43] Some even volunteered to extend their participation to forty sessions. Those who did reported occasional interludes of "unity" in which they lost the sense of their own body boundaries and felt as if they were merging with the vase. According to Deikman, these episodes grew longer and more profound as practice increased.[44]

Deikman believes that these effects occur because meditation "deautomatizes" underlying sensory and perceptual processes that are normally automatic and subconscious. By way of illustration, when I consciously decide to get a drink of water, the perceptual and motor processes controlled by my brain help me scan the glasses in my cabinet, select one, reach up and grasp it, locate the faucet, turn it on, check the temperature, fill the glass and so on. I am generally unaware of all the physical events that allow me to take these actions—my eye movements, the processing of visual and tactile information in my brain or the complex stream of orders and replies racing back and forth between my brain and the muscles in my hands and arms. All this activity proceeds very smoothly and automatically, always subject to the demands of higher brain centers or the conscious mind. Meditation apparently uncouples some of these automatic sensory processes from their service to the conscious mind, simultaneously allowing the meditator to become much more aware of their operations.

Eastern meditative techniques can force the perceptual system to operate in very unnatural ways. Deikman's meditators had to look steadily at the vase for at least fifteen minutes, passively attending to the resulting sensations without thinking about them analytically and without controlling or directing them in any way. In this mode, elementary visual sensations (colors, textures, shapes) will naturally become more salient because these are the only features the meditator is allowed to attend to. This could explain why the color and other sensory qualities of the vase seemed to intensify with practice.

Gazing steadily at the same object for fifteen minutes is also highly unnatural. Our visual systems are designed to process information that changes very rapidly from one glance to the next, and under normal circumstances our eyes are constantly moving. Our visual system is also "wired" to exaggerate the boundaries of objects that we see, and this undoubtedly contributes significantly to our perception that external objects are real and separate from us. Clear boundary perception depends partly on normal eye movements. In the case of Deikman's meditators, the fixed gaze and the resulting eye strain and faltering boundary perception probably all contributed to the vase's apparent movement, the illusory changes in its size and shape, and its disappearing boundaries.

The "unity" experience that is so important in many Eastern traditions may also be precipitated by highly disturbed boundary perceptions. In addition to the enhancement of boundaries in our visual systems, we have a built-in, highly developed tactile sense of the boundaries of our own body. This sense is apparently maintained by the continual flow of sensory information from the surface of our skin (feelings of touch, pressure, stretching of skin and muscles, and the like). If experiencers' awareness of the flow is significantly reduced, as it is during sensory deprivation and other altered states, they could easily conclude that their body boundaries were suddenly dissolving or that they were expanding or merging with other objects, even with God or the entire universe. Other features of the unity experience may be due to the fact that experiencers are in an altered state and realize that they have just reached a highly prized and hard-won goal. Acting together, these factors could produce profound feelings of reality, sacredness, ultimate meaning, bliss and ecstatic sensations throughout the body.

The "dissolution" experience, which forms the basis of important Buddhist beliefs, may also be prompted by a disruption of normal perceptual processes. In mindfulness meditation, meditators are not allowed to initiate any mental activities or to try to control the flow of events, but are simply to observe nonanalytically and nonjudgmentally as ideas, feelings, images and memory snatches come automatically to mind. With practice, these mental events begin occurring rapidly, popping up and disappearing in a disconnected, random manner. Easterners assume that these wild, random fluctuations reflect the true operations of the conscious (physical) mind, and this reinforces their conviction that the conscious mind is inferior. From a scientific perspective, however, it is just as plausible to argue that what meditators are observing in this state is *not* the activity of the conscious mind but rather the operations of automatic memory and perceptual processes that have been artificially disconnected from the control of the conscious mind by the rules of meditation.

Meditators notice that the mental events they are observing, and even the watching process, can begin to seem impersonal or alien. There are at least four elements that might contribute to this belief. In the first place, the mental events being observed are apparently not being initiated by conscious processes but by some hitherto-unrecognized subconscious source. In the second place, the rules of meditation prohibit meditators from exercising any personal, conscious control over the process. All they can do is passively observe what happens. A third factor that probably contributes to such feelings is the meditator's prior expectations of what should happen during meditation. These three elements, combined with the effects of being in an altered state, are probably sufficient to explain how meditators get the impression that their mental operations are impersonal and alien.

The experiences that kundalini unleashes are more difficult to explain from a strictly physical or psychological point of view. The pain, trembling, involuntary movements and extreme sensations of heat or cold are obviously mediated by the brain, but this does not tell us how the brain is being stimulated to produce them. In some cases, kundalinilike symptoms may be due to underlying pathology or epileptic seizures.[45] Since most experiencers appear to be in normal health before their symptoms begin and apparently return to a normal state after kundalini symptoms dissipate, however, this probably isn't an adequate explanation.

In the case of classical kundalini there are reasons to suspect that some of the symptoms result from demonic activity. Most of the individuals who develop this syndrome are serious, long-term meditators who are dedicated to the practice of Eastern meditation and the worldviews that support it. From a Christian perspective, Eastern religions are idolatrous and pantheistic, stressing the worship of many pagan gods. In the Bible we are warned that real spiritual power is associated with idolatry and pagan worship and that this power is demonic. In Deuteronomy 32:16-17, Moses says that when Israel turned to idols and sacrificed to them, "they made him [God] jealous with their foreign gods and angered him with their detestable idols. They sacrificed to demons, which are not God." Psalm 106:34-37 makes the same point:

> They [the Israelites] did not destroy the peoples
>   as the LORD had commanded them,
> but they mingled with the nations
>   and adopted their customs.
> They worshiped their idols,
>   which became a snare to them.
> They sacrificed their sons
>   and their daughters to demons.
>   (Also see 1 Corinthians 10:20.)

Persons who are deeply committed to idolatrous beliefs and practices may well be opening their lives to serious demonic involvement. Unusual effects, like automatically assuming difficult yoga postures, the inability to control or stop the kundalini process, speaking in unlearned languages, temporary manifestations of clairvoyant abilities and the like, certainly suggest that something supernatural is afoot. There are parallels between kundalini symptoms and symptoms that are currently associated with demonized states, including deranged thinking (see Lk 8:35), emotional extremes (deep melancholy, ecstasy), trancelike states or periods of unconsciousness, apparent seizure activity (Lk 9:39), and unusual pain unrelated to illness and injury.[46]

Exercising Discernment

Two related questions that contemporary Christians often raise in relationship to Eastern traditions are whether there are things that we might be able to learn from them and whether it would be appropriate to adapt some of their practices to enrich our own times of prayer and worship. In brief, my answer to the first question is yes, while to the second I say no.

What can we learn from the Eastern traditions? Some very general practices they endorse could definitely be of benefit. For example, most of us could surely benefit by learning to exercise greater control over our attention, especially during personal devotions. We could also benefit from longer, more disciplined and more consistent times of prayer. (I wonder how it might change our lives if we regularly spent one to two hours per day in prayer and Bible study.) It would probably enrich our lives if we were to develop a deeper appreciation for the experiential aspects of prayer and worship and learn to spend more time in quietness, listening and waiting on God, rather than just rushing through habitual prayer lists.

The Eastern system also has a lot to teach us about potential pitfalls in our own religious practices. One of these is the danger of basing one's faith and religious beliefs solely on unusual mystical experiences, particularly if they are precipitated by human efforts and achieved by methods that alter consciousness. This chapter's survey of the effects of Eastern meditation clearly demonstrates that human feelings and experiences, even when incredibly convincing and realistic, can be completely wrong and deceptive. It also highlights the importance of basing one's faith on an objective standard, like the Bible (which is a historical record of God's interactions with human beings since their creation), rather than just personal experiences. Our experiences with God's leading and guiding are vital to our faith and growth, but it is always prudent to check unusual experiences against biblical standards and in prayer, to make sure they are really from God.

An overemphasis on experiences can lead to other dangers too. Believers with this orientation may start depending on their experiences to validate their faith and to assure themselves that they are right with God. This can lead to a continual search for new experiences, in effect turning the believer's affections more toward the experiences than toward God. Believers with these priorities may come to believe that by leading a holy life and engaging in disciplined meditative exercises they can coerce God into giving them the ecstatic experiences they want.

It is certainly legitimate to want to draw near to God and receive all he has to give us. But the biblical record also indicates that *unusual* supernatural contacts between God, or his angels, and humans (such as Moses and the burning bush, the supernatural events accompanying the exodus from Egypt, the visions of the prophets, angelic visits preceding the birth of Christ) were *initiated by God* for his own sovereign purposes. Such encounters come by his choice, not ours. In any case, a heavy reliance on meditative techniques that are similar to those in Eastern traditions or that significantly alter consciousness is dangerous. As we have seen, there is no guarantee that the ecstatic experiences that accompany such practices are from God.

Why do I say it is not appropriate to adapt Eastern meditative practices for Christian use? The purposes of Eastern meditation are very different from the purposes of meditation described in the Bible. One way to appreciate this is to study the way the word *meditate* is used in Scripture.

Virtually all the occurrences of *meditate* in its various forms are in the Old Testament, many in Psalms. In Joshua 1:8 God instructs Joshua, "Do not let this Book of the Law depart from your mouth; meditate on it day and night, so that you may be careful to do everything written in it. Then you will be prosperous and successful." In Psalm 119 the writer uses the word *meditate* in the following ways:

I meditate on your precepts
    and consider your ways. (v. 15)
Then I will meditate on your wonders. (v. 27)
I lift up my hands to your commands, which I love,
    and I meditate on your decrees. (v. 48)
I have more insight than all my teachers,
    for I meditate on your statutes. (v. 99)
My eyes stay open through the watches of the night,
    that I may meditate on your promises. (v. 148)

In this context, to meditate means to *think* deeply and gratefully about God, what he has done, his laws, and his promises and plans for us. Its purpose is to lift our hearts in worship and adoration, to help us comprehend God's sovereign will and to bring our own lives into line with it. It is meant to engage all of our faculties: mind, soul and spirit.

By way of contrast, the goal of Eastern meditation is to shut off all the operations of the mind, to cut out all emotions and sensory impressions and to enter an altered state in which "truth" is revealed by rapturous and paradoxical experiences, not by way of reason or other natural modes of comprehension. In fact, it is noteworthy that many of the significant "truths" conveyed by Eastern meditation ("all is one," "the self is an illusion") contradict the truths conveyed by the meditator's own mind and senses. Biblical meditation of the type described in Psalm 119 does not create such fundamental contradictions.

In addition, the Bible makes it clear that at least one Eastern technique, mantra meditation, is not a method Christians should use. Jesus warns, "When you are praying, do not heap up empty phrases as the Gentiles do; for they think that they will be heard because of their many words. Do not be like them; for your Father knows what you need before you ask him" (Mt 6:7-8 NRSV). Immediately following this admonition, and in response to his disciples' request that he teach them to pray, Jesus gives his disciples the Lord's Prayer, a model of the rationally based communication we should use when seeking to converse with God.

A final reason for avoiding Eastern meditative techniques is that there are definite hazards associated with them. They were devised to support a worldview that is totally antagonistic to Christianity. Furthermore, they seek to replace reason as a means of knowing truth with nonrational insights and intuitions born of highly questionable experiences. The deep and passive altered states created by these techniques, along with the extraordinary experiences they can bring about, open the mind to all sorts of false beliefs about God and reality. Such states can make people very vulnerable to deception, whether from their own imaginations, from the false teachings of other human beings or from demons.

Mystical writers from Maharishi Mahesh Yogi to Christian mystics like

St. John of the Cross[47] and the author of *The Cloud of Unknowing*[48] all warn about the dangers of madness, demonic deception or possession for those who venture out on the mystical path. Their warnings are important, and we need to pay heed to them.

7

Are Human Beings Developing New Powers of Mind?

The idea that human beings might have latent paranormal or spiritual powers, such as ESP or the ability to foretell the future, to heal or to influence people or events with the mind, has been a central tenet of New Age thinking from its inception. In fact, from the New Age perspective the apparent ability to exercise such powers is considered a sure sign of advanced spiritual standing. If such beliefs were confined to New Age circles, they wouldn't be an important cause for concern, because this group is relatively small. But the same beliefs are also becoming increasingly common in popular thinking, both in the United States and in Western Europe. This is evident from the press and media coverage currently devoted to such topics and from recent opinion polls.

According to polls, sizable numbers of Americans now believe in paranormal powers, while many more are uncertain whether they exist but are not willing to rule them out. In a 1990 Gallup Poll 49 percent of the respondents said they believed in ESP (with 22 percent uncertain), and 26 percent (23 percent uncertain) believed in clairvoyance, defined as the ability to "see" events at remote locations or to know information that is not directly available to the senses. Seventeen percent (24 percent uncertain) believed in telekinesis, defined in the survey as "the ability to move or bend objects just using mental energy," and nearly half the sample, 46 percent (with 20 percent uncertain), said they believed in "psychic or spiritual healing or the power of the human mind to heal the body."[1] Recent surveys of U.S. college students have produced very similar percentages.[2] These statistics indicate that *approximately half of the U.S. population either believes that such abilities are real or is open to the possibility that they may be.*

These statistics are rather surprising, particularly in light of the fact that the concept of paranormal powers does not fit very comfortably with Western orthodoxy. Materialists generally reject the idea of paranormal powers because they cannot be explained by known physical principles and seem inextricably intertwined with the spiritual and supernatural. Christians who take the Bible seriously are aware that people can have experiences that might seem paranormal, but would probably hesitate to attribute these to human powers. They would be more likely to attribute them to natural causes (coincidence, one's knowledge of what is likely to happen, self-deception, misinterpretation of events and so on) or to supernatural intervention, either by God or by demons (see Acts 16:16-19).

Significantly, the belief that human beings have unusual hidden powers fits in exceptionally well with New Age or more general mystical perspectives. These systems attribute such abilities to a higher spiritual nature or the "subconscious mind" and assume that they are simply waiting to be developed. Within such systems, any manifestations of these abilities are welcomed and affirmed.

Our present cultural ambivalence on the issue of paranormal powers is important because it creates a situation in which it would be fairly easy for large numbers of people (in particular those who are only moderately committed to a traditional worldview) to adopt a more mystical system of beliefs. Social psychologists have demonstrated that people are not comfortable with dissonance or inconsistency in their beliefs. Once they become aware of important inconsistencies, they either modify the beliefs that don't fit or drop beliefs that seem less important.

In our situation, simultaneously believing in paranormal powers and either materialism or Christianity is bound to create some dissonance. As long as this dissonance is mild—that is, as long as neither set of beliefs is held very strongly—incongruent beliefs can continue to coexist peacefully. But if the balance shifts and one set of beliefs suddenly becomes more salient than the other, the stage is set for change.

Consider what might happen if a nominal Christian, Jew or materialist who also believes in paranormal powers suddenly had a dramatic, realistic mystical experience that was incongruent with his or her worldview. She would be quite likely to assume that her experiences are valid, and so would either modify her worldviews to accommodate the experience or adopt a mystical perspective that places the experience in a positive light.

I discovered a striking example of this principle in action while investigating a "psychic fair" in Barrington, Illinois, with a couple of interested students. Though this fair was rather small, it offered a variety of things to do. One of its features was an extensive collection of rocks and crystals that were ostensibly endowed with beneficial properties—powers to ensure safe travel, to attract money and power, to provide healing for various diseases and ailments, to find one a mate, to block evil, to aid psychic development and so on. "Marlena the Rock Lady" presided over this collection, dispensing comments and helpful advice to prospective customers.

The fair also offered the services of a dozen psychics who specialized in palmistry, psychometry (the art of obtaining information about a person's life or future by concentrating on some personal item) and tarot cards. Marlena gave talks on the virtues of various stones and crystals, while Irene Hughes, a well-known psychic, offered predictions and demonstrated her abilities to people in attendance. There was also a New Age minister, "Reverend James," who conducted a "Personal Predictions and Healing Service."

As my students and I probed for information, we discovered that this psychic fair was a family enterprise. Marlena and the Reverend James were husband and wife; two of their daughters, Melody Joy and Gwen Pippin, were tarot consultants; and a son-in-law helped with the finances. To our great surprise, the Reverend James told us that he had attended Bob Jones University and a conservative Baptist seminary, and that his daughters had both attended Christian secondary schools and Wheaton College. The family was very musical, and according to the Reverend James, they had been involved in an evangelistic singing ministry.

How, we wondered, could a family with this type of background possibly get involved in the psychic-fair business? According to what Marlena and the Reverend James told us, two events were pivotal. Marlena took a class in meditation, and during this time she started having unusual "psychic" experiences. One day while she was driving, a clear voice in her head told her that she would be given special powers to help people. When she objected and said she wouldn't even know where to begin, the voice told her to go home and start with her son's rock collection. The Reverend James had apparently modified his own beliefs after a nontraditional healer cured a back condition that had troubled him for years.

When we asked the Reverend James how he reconciled the obvious biblical warnings against divination with running a psychic fair, his answers were evasive. On the one hand he insisted that the fairs were only for entertainment, implying that he, his psychic readers and their customers didn't really believe in what they were doing and that nothing supernatural was involved. In an unguarded moment, however, he also intimated that he had discovered a way of truth that was broader and more encompassing than Christianity.

This family's "psychic" activities are very sobering, whatever their reasons for engaging in them. Even if they did not believe in what they were doing, their customers evidently did. It is doubtful that the patrons would have paid twenty dollars or more per consultation for the privilege of being fooled. At the very least the family was engaging in deception for pay, giving people meaningless advice and reinforcing their beliefs in psychic powers. On the other hand, if family members had become convinced that their powers were genuine, this could only mean that they had modified their former Christian beliefs considerably.

Examples like this make it clear that this is yet another area in which

Christians need to exercise serious discernment. Fortunately, as with previous topics, there is a considerable body of evidence we can draw on to help us understand "paranormal" phenomena. In this case some evidence comes from the work of parapsychologists and some from magicians who have made it their business to investigate the claims of psychics.

Parapsychologists and Their Search for Answers

Historically parapsychologists have been interested in events that might provide evidence for life after death or for a separate realm of spirits. In their search for such evidence they have investigated many unusual phenomena, including telepathy, clairvoyance and precognition (all classified as types of ESP), psychokinesis, psychic healing, mediumship phenomena (apparent contacts with departed spirits) and manifestations of apparitions or ghosts.

Parapsychology had its beginnings in 1882, when a group of respected leaders and academics at Cambridge University founded the Society for Psychical Research (SPR). The members of SPR were primarily interested in the numerous spirit mediums who were operating throughout North America, Britain and Western Europe at that time. Mediumship had become popular through the influence of an earlier, quasi-religious movement known as spiritualism. According to the tenets of spiritualism (which clearly contradict the Bible; see Deut 18:9-12), people should try to establish regular contact with spirits (departed human beings and others) for advice, knowledge and spiritual guidance. The spiritualists believed that such contacts could be made most easily through individuals who were willing and able to serve as mediums.[3]

Spiritualism had its origins in America in the late 1840s, in the household of a blacksmith named John Fox in Hydesville, New York. In March 1848 the Fox family began hearing strange popping, rapping, banging and scraping noises in their house. The noises grew louder and more insistent, and in time fourteen-year-old Kate discovered that if she snapped her fingers in a particular pattern, whatever was producing the noises would mimic her pattern.

After this discovery Mrs. Fox attempted to use the sounds as a mode of communication. She asked aloud that if the noises were being made by a spirit, it should make two raps. Two raps sounded in an immediate response. The family then worked out a system of communication in which the spirit would rap when they called out a correct letter. Through this means the spirit informed them that he was a thirty-one-year-old man who had been murdered and that his body had been buried in the cellar of the Fox home. Subsequent efforts to search the cellar were hampered by the fact that the ground under the house was waterlogged. No body was ever found, so the murder was never verified. But the strange manifestations continued, eventually drawing crowds of curious onlookers from miles around.

Maggie and Kate Fox, who appeared especially adept at communicating with the spirit, eventually started going on tours around the country, giving lectures and demonstrating various spirit manifestations in séances. In these sessions, which were always held in darkened rooms, attenders reportedly felt touched by invisible hands, saw objects move about or materialize out of thin air, watched musical instruments that seemed to play by themselves and heard the famous rapping noises.

The Fox sisters caught the attention of the American public, and their message proved irresistible. Self-styled mediums sprang up in various places, and do-it-yourself séances became all the rage. Later in their lives, confronted with many charges of fraud, both sisters confessed that the special effects in their séances were produced by fraudulent means. One of the sisters said she had made the rapping noises by cracking her toes. Curiously, shortly after giving these confessions Maggie and Kate Fox retracted them and asserted that the phenomena were real and that they had been coerced into making false confessions. As far as the Fox sisters were concerned, that was where the matter rested.[4]

By the time the SPR was founded in 1882, mediums and spiritualistic practices had spread widely. Spiritualism grew rapidly, partly because it appealed so strongly to curiosity and partly because people were somewhat restive with prevailing worldviews. At the time Christianity was under siege by Darwinism, and the militant, agnostic materialism of that era didn't appeal to many people either. Spiritualism offered an intriguing alternative, complete with "scientific proofs" (mediumship phenomena) to support its basic doctrines.

Most scientists of that era refused to take spiritualism seriously. But members of SPR contended that alleged contacts with spirits should be investigated scientifically. They argued that if the incidents were fraudulent they should be exposed, but if they were genuine they should be examined with care because of what they might reveal about life after death.[5]

As SPR members began investigating different mediums, they discovered that the overwhelming majority were frauds who were using tricks and sleight of hand to convince people that they had genuine powers. A few mediums were never caught cheating, but it was not possible to show beyond reasonable doubt that they had genuine powers either. As a result, SPR investigators eventually lost interest in mediums and turned to the study of thought reading (later known as telepathy), apparitions, haunt-ings, hypnosis and clairvoyance. The next generation of researchers, who were the first to be called parapsychologists, became even more selective. Many concentrated on the various forms of ESP or psychokinesis (PK), which could be studied in normal people under controlled laboratory con-ditions.[6]

The Rhines' Experiments

Parapsychologists continued their research up through the 1920s without much recognition from other scientists, but their cause was strengthened the 1930s and 1940s when J. B. Rhine and his wife Louisa Rhine started publishing significant studies of ESP from Duke University. J. B. Rhine's primary objective was to establish the reality of ESP and PK once and for all, using controlled experiments that could be analyzed with statistics. In order to test for clairvoyance he developed a special set of cards, each bearing one of five symbols—a star, a circle, three parallel wavy lines, a square, a plus sign. Equal numbers of each type of card were mixed thor-oughly, and an experimenter randomly drew twenty-five cards for a test without looking to see what they were. The subject's task was to guess the order of the cards in each stack of twenty-five. Since there were five different kinds of cards, the chance of guessing any one card correctly was one in five, and subjects could be expected to get five out of twenty-five correct by chance alone. By structuring the tests this way Rhine could check the number of cards his subjects guessed correctly, over many runs of twenty-five, to see whether they were exceeding the number they should get by chance.[7]

Rhine did achieve statistically significant results in some of his experiments, although his subjects' average hit rates were usually only slightly better than chance (between five and six on runs of twenty-five). One of Rhine's most successful subjects was a young divinity student named Hubert Pearce. Pearce averaged about eight hits per run, rather than the expected five, over 690 runs (17,250 individual trials). Curiously, however, after this long set of successful runs Pearce could not duplicate his performance. At the conclusion of the successful series he announced that he was under some emotional strain and did not expect to do well in further tests. Thereafter he could not exceed a chance level of performance.[8] This sudden turnabout seemed odd and led some critics to speculate that Pearce had somehow cheated on the first runs but then either couldn't or wouldn't do so on later tests. In fairness to Pearce, however, it should be said that other experimenters have also observed ESP performance drop-offs in this type of task over time.

In order to test PK (the ability to influence physical objects with the mind), Rhine developed a machine that mixed and threw dice in a completely random manner. The subject's task was to try to make the die land with a particular face up at a rate greater than that expected by chance. Rhine's experiments with PK produced a few significant results, but the effects were even smaller than those obtained for ESP.[9] Since his original experiments many new variations and tighter controls have been added to both ESP and PK experiments.

Louisa Rhine took a different approach to the study of ESP. She was interested in the frequency and phenomenology of spontaneous ESP experiences and reasoned that study of many different accounts might yield some important clues. From her extensive collection of cases she discovered that spontaneous ESP experiences came in four basic forms: intuitive impressions (which accounted for 26 percent of the cases), hallucinations (9 percent), realistic dreams (44 percent) and unrealistic dreams (21 percent). She found that spontaneous episodes usually involved a close friend or relative and that the majority of episodes dealt with deaths or personal crises (illness, accidents, births, marriages). Interestingly, those who had had such experiences usually believed that the person in crisis had tried to contact them. Rhine discovered, however, that the people in crisis were usually *not* thinking about the other person at the time. Thus such episodes were evidently not due to conscious attempts to "call" or make contact with the other person.

Rhine did not try to use these case studies to prove the existence of ESP, because she was well aware of their limitations. None of them were independently verified, and many had occurred years before they were written down and sent in. Such reports can easily be compromised by memory distortions, misperceptions and even outright fabrication. Yet taken as a whole, they did provide some interesting phenomenological data.[10]

J. B. Rhine's studies generated a storm of protest among psychologists and other scientists who did not believe in ESP or PK. They insisted that his results were not valid and argued that they were due to methodological weaknesses or outright cheating. Despite all this furor and many legitimate criticisms (which Rhine strove to address in subsequent experiments), the Rhines' work still made an impact. It established the idea that paranormal powers might actually exist, and it provided the impetus for better and more extensive research in this area.

J. B. Rhine also made two strategic moves that helped make the concept of paranormal powers, or "Psi," much more believable, especially to skeptics with a scientific mindset. He (and others) gave Psi phenomena new "scientific" names, and by attributing them to the human mind, he effectively severed their connections with their occult, spiritualistic roots. When Rhine began his work, abilities to see into another's mind, view remote events, prophesy or influence physical objects without touching them were commonly thought of as manifestations of *supernatural* power (usually a spirit working through a human). After Rhine, these same phenomena became known as mental telepathy, clairvoyance, precognition and psycho- or telekinesis, and were conceptualized as *natural,* though undeveloped, powers of the human mind. These changes opened the door for a very gradual (but still tentative) acceptance of parapsychology as a field of inquiry.

Is There Compelling Evidence for Paranormal Powers?

Parapsychologists consider both qualitative and quantitative evidence in their attempts to document paranormal powers. Quantitative evidence comes from controlled studies similar to those pioneered by Rhine, while qualitative evidence is drawn from spontaneous incidents and investigations of individuals who claim to have psychic powers. Parapsychologists check such cases as rigorously as possible, but investigations of this latter type are never considered definitive.

At least a couple of magicians have investigated psychics as well. In general magicians are more skeptical than parapsychologists, and also more adept at spotting clever tricks.

The Evidence for Telepathy

In the early 1970s Russell Targ and Harold Puthoff, physicists at the Stanford Research Institute, published two articles on telepathy and "remote viewing" in respectable scientific journals (*Nature*[11] and *Journal of the Institute of Electrical and Electronic Engineers*[12]). In these studies the person being tested for telepathic powers (the "receiver") remained in a room at the institute with one experimenter while the other members of the research team visited a randomly selected geographic site in the area. Once there, team members got out and walked about, concentrating on the area's distinctive features.

After allowing thirty minutes for the team to reach its destination, the experimenter instructed the receiver to describe and/or draw his or her impressions of the target site. The descriptions and conversations between the experimenter and the participant were taped and transcribed, and this same process was repeated for other sites on succeeding days. After nine sessions of this type, the subject's transcribed comments for each day were given to an independent judge, who then visited the sites and ranked each of the descriptions according to how well they matched the target sites. When a description received a ranking of 1 against its target site, it was counted as a "hit." The total number of hits achieved by participants in nine trials was then compared to the number of hits that would be expected by chance (which Targ and Puthoff assumed to be one in nine).

In Targ and Puthoff's first experiment, conducted on a former police commissioner named Pat Price, seven of Price's nine descriptions were direct hits. In the second, with photographer Hella Hammid, five of her descriptions were direct hits and the other four were near misses (all of these had a rank of 2). According to the experimenters' statistics, the probability of obtaining this many hits by chance was phenomenally small. The portions of Price's and Hammid's descriptions that Targ and Puthoff chose to publish seemed strikingly accurate.[13] Later studies of this type have sometimes succeeded and sometimes failed to demonstrate remote-viewing effects.[14]

Even though Targ and Puthoff's results seemed impressive, as it turned out, their research had two serious flaws. For one, they apparently used the wrong statistics. This was discovered by a blue-ribbon panel of experts from the National Academy of Sciences, commissioned by the Army Research Institute to investigate the authenticity and possible applications of ESP and PK. When they applied the correct statistics to the data, most of the results were no longer statistically significant.[15]

The second problem was uncovered by two psychologists, Dick Kammann and David Marks, who had tried unsuccessfully to replicate Targ and Puthoff's findings in thirty-five successive studies. Thinking they must be doing something wrong, they asked if they might examine Targ and Puthoff's original transcripts and lists, but were refused access. They did succeed, however, in getting copies of the original materials from a judge. They discovered that these lists and transcripts contained clues (most from incidental statements made by the experimenter who stayed with the subject) that could help an astute judge match the transcripts with the appropriate locations.

To check this, they first gave the original lists and transcripts to independent judges. They too were able to match the locations and the descriptions with great accuracy. Then Kammann and Marks edited out the obvious clues and gave the revised transcripts to a second set of judges. These judges could no longer match the locations and descriptions.[16] Thus it was evidently the clues that made the difference.

Some of the most damaging criticisms of Targ and Puthoff's work come from James Randi, a magician who has spent nearly four decades debunking psychics. He became interested in Targ and Puthoff because Uri Geller, a well-known Israeli psychic, had been the star performer in Targ and Puthoff's *Nature* article. Randi had been investigating Geller, and when other researchers at the Stanford Institute found out, they called him covertly to express their deep concern about the quality and objectivity of Targ and Puthoff's research. Their information revealed other very serious problems. It appears that Targ and Puthoff (who, according to Randi, were both members of the Church of Scientology) were so eager to prove that telepathy was real that they disregarded proper experimental procedures and safeguards. In addition, it appears that they may have inflated their success rate by omitting many unsuccessful tests that were never reported.[17]

Another influential set of studies in parapsychology, known collectively as Ganzfield experiments, tested the proposition that telepathy might be enhanced in altered states of consciousness (in this case induced by perceptual deprivation). In these experiments participants were asked to recline, look toward a bright light through a pair of translucent goggles and listen to staticlike white noise through a pair of headphones. This treatment ostensibly induces a mild altered state in about fifteen minutes.

In these studies one experimenter helped participants enter the Ganzfield state while a second randomly selected four different pictures from a large collection and then randomly chose one of the four to be the "target." This was given to a third person, who was to act as the "sender." The sender entered a separate room and concentrated intently on the picture, trying to send it telepathically to the participant in the altered state. After a fixed period the participant removed the goggles and earphones and then ranked the four pictures in terms of how well each matched his or her impressions during the Ganzfield state. Picking the picture that was "sent" constituted a hit. Since hits should occur 25 percent of the time by chance, experimenters checked for sustained hit rates that were significantly higher than 25 percent.[18]

Ganzfield experiments became very popular because they appeared to be relatively successful. According to a 1978 survey by Charles Honorton, twenty-three out of forty-two Ganzfield experiments had obtained statistically significant results, with an overall hit rate of 55 percent (compared to the 25 percent expected by chance). Successful studies had been conducted in nine different laboratories.[19]

But psychologist Ray Hyman disagreed with Honorton's conclusions. After reviewing the same studies, he pointed out serious flaws in all twenty-three successful studies (such as inadequate randomization of the pictures, extraneous cues that could give hints to subjects, errors in statistics and the like).[20] To their credit, the two researchers came together amicably to settle their dispute and eventually published a joint statement in the December 1986 issue of the *Journal of Parapsychology* to the effect that there were still too many confounding factors in the Ganzfield research to attribute the results to Psi or, conversely, to prove that the results were due to artifacts. They agreed that the only way to resolve the issue would be through new, more tightly controlled experiments.[21]

The Evidence for Clairvoyance

Recent investigations of clairvoyant abilities have used the basic card-guessing techniques developed by J. B. Rhine. Like Rhine, subsequent experimenters have found that unselected groups of participants have an overall hit rate of about 5.2, where a rate of 5 would be expected by chance. This small difference is statistically significant because it is based on very large numbers of trials. But it is questionable whether this result is significant in any practical sense, because it indicates that participants are exceeding chance by just two hits in every one hundred tries. Moreover, many investigators suspect that the small differences that have been attributed to Psi may actually be due to subtle confounding variables in the experiments.

The Evidence for Precognition

Precognition, or the ability to foretell the future, is a topic of great popular interest, primarily because there are so many psychics who claim to have this power. Research in this area is difficult, and there aren't many controlled studies to draw on for evidence. Parapsychologists have attempted a few systematic studies, but these have not been very enlightening.

Two enterprising investigators did check to see whether spontaneous precognitive events, or premonitions, had any validity. At "premonition bureaus" in London and New York, people were invited to register their premonitions before the anticipated event was supposed to take place. But in this investigation very few premonitions proved to be accurate.[22]

Some of the more informative evidence on psychic predictions has been published by two magicians, James Randi (a materialist) and Dan Korem (a Christian). Both men have spent years investigating psychics because they believe that psychics are exploiting the unwary with magicians' stage tricks while claiming to have unusual powers. Both cite cases in which unscrupulous psychics have gained incredible control over people's lives and pocketbooks.

In his informative book *Powers: Testing the Psychic and the Supernatural*, Korem describes the techniques often used by psychics. When possible, before interacting with those they intend to dupe, they use covert means to obtain personal information about them. If they succeed, they toss out this information in some offhand way early in their conversation. This throws the prospective client off balance: how would the psychic know such things if he or she didn't have special powers? Thus the psychic gains instant credibility.

If psychics do not have definite information about a person, they begin by making very broad statements that apply to just about everybody and that are subtly complimentary. For example, "At times you are extroverted, affable and sociable, while at others you are introverted, wary and reserved." Or, "You pride yourself on being an independent thinker and do not accept others' opinions without satisfactory proof." While making such statements and eliciting responses from the prospective client, psychics watch for slight changes in facial expression and other clues in the person's bearing, dress, presence or absence of wedding or engagement rings and so forth. Adept psychics can use this information to establish a rough personality profile from which they can make even more specific guesses.

According to Korem, psychics make very clever use of language. They can lead people into giving them critical information without realizing they have done so, and they state their conclusions in such a way that they can retreat from wrong guesses without the person even noticing that they were wrong.[23] Once they have convinced someone that they have genuine powers, they can start offering their services to that person for a fee.

Psychics may eavesdrop, snoop or employ confederates to obtain the specific personal information that can help them look credible. A former assistant to Uri Geller, Yasha Katz, told Randi how he systematically gleaned information for Geller by watching closely as people who were going to be in the audience opened their purses or wallets to pay for tickets.[24] Korem also describes the clandestine way he obtained specific information for many shows he did while in college. He would sit in one of the stalls in the men's restroom prior to a performance until he heard a couple of men discussing something he could use during the show. Noting the color of the shoes the speaker was wearing, he would then exit the stall so he could match the shoes with a face. During the show he would call this man forward, have him concentrate on a card and then make some offhand comment related to the information he had obtained in the restroom. The man, not understanding how Korem could know something so personal and specific, would always be dumbfounded.[25]

Korem and Randi say that all the psychics they have investigated have engaged in trickery of some type to create the illusion that they have special powers. They all rely on a few standard operating techniques, astute observation, snooping and quickness of wit to make themselves look credible. Interestingly, some psychics apparently become so adept that they actually begin to believe they have unusual powers. As far as Randi and Korem are concerned, though, none of the modern psychics have any real paranormal powers.[26]

The Evidence for Psychokinesis

Psychokinesis (PK) is defined as the ability to influence objects or events with the mind alone. Originally this concept was devised to help explain the strange behavior of objects during some séances or poltergeist activity. *Poltergeist* is a German word that literally means "noisy ghost," and poltergeist activity is frequently accompanied by rapping or percussive noises and odd, often destructive movements of objects. Small objects may move through the air as if carried by some invisible hand, while larger objects (sideboards, tables, linen chests) may scrape along the floor in sideways or zigzag movements.[27]

Psychologist Carl Jung reported witnessing one such incident with his mother. One day they heard loud cracking noises coming from a sideboard. When he opened the drawer the sounds appeared to be coming from, he discovered that the blade of their bread knife had been mysteriously broken into four pieces.[28]

In the beginning most researchers believed such incidents either were being faked or were due to the activities of discarnate spirits. Yet they discovered that both mediumship and poltergeist effects seemed to require the presence of particular people, and this suggested that the effects were due to a spirit somehow working through a particular person or were emanating from the human psyche itself. As time wore on and spirits became less fashionable, explanations leaned toward the latter rather than the former. By the time J. B. Rhine conducted his PK experiments in 1943, the idea that PK was a paranormal power was well entrenched.

Rhine and other early experimenters obtained some statistically significant results in their PK experiments, but the effects were even smaller and less reliable than those obtained for ESP. But these early experiments also had methodological flaws that might account for the results that were obtained.[29] Some more recent work on PK utilizes a sophisticated device known as a random event generator (REG), developed by physicist Helmut Schmidt. This apparatus has a display screen on which a light moves rapidly in a circle. The light keeps moving from one discrete point on the circle to the next at a constant speed until it is stopped by an electrical signal produced by the emission of a particle from a radioactive source. After a brief interval the light begins moving again and keeps moving until it is stopped by the next particle. Since the rate of particle emission is essentially random, the location at which the light stops from trial to trial is also random. (However, REGs do need to be checked from time to time to ensure that they are actually operating randomly.) Participants in REG experiments are asked to make the light stop in a designated location, just by willing it to happen.[30]

In general, the presumed PK effects in REG experiments are tiny. Robert Jahn and his colleagues at Princeton have collected a database with millions of REG trials, in very tightly controlled experiments, with the help of many students and a computer. For all his efforts, Jahn found a hit rate of just 50.02 percent, which means that the students were only producing one extra hit in every twenty-five hundred trials. Believe it or not, this tiny effect was statistically significant, but only because Jahn was able to calculate his statistic based on millions of trials. Whether an effect this small has any practical significance is debatable.[31]

In the minds of those who believe in PK, the most convincing evidence for the phenomenon comes not from experiments but from personal experiences or individual cases that appear to defy logical explanation. Yet James Randi and Dan Korem insist that they have not yet found a single person who can demonstrate genuine PK. They say they can explain or duplicate every demonstration of "PK" they have seen with the use of magic tricks.

Some "psychics" can pull off some pretty amazing stunts that look like

PK. James Hydrick, a popular psychic investigated by Korem, was able to make pencils move and telephone pages turn without touching them. He could even rotate a partially folded dollar bill, balanced on the head of a pin, while the bill, the pin and the block of wood supporting them were all placed under an inverted glass fish tank.

Korem discovered that Hydrick's secret was his ability to exhale brief, energetic puffs of air, to direct them precisely and to do this completely surreptitiously. He used a special fish tank for the last trick. One side wasn't quite even along the top, so there was a tiny space between the edge of the tank and the table when the tank was inverted. Hydrick would direct a puff of air toward the tabletop by the crack, and three or four seconds later, when the air current had moved through the slit and reached the bill, the bill would start to turn. In the meantime Hydrick could move away from that side of the tank, making gestures that suggested that he was applying a little "body English" to make the bill move.[32]

What Do We Make of Paranormal Claims?

Having surveyed some of the evidence, we are now in a position to ask whether human beings actually have paranormal powers. In my opinion the evidence for such powers is not convincing. Virtually every self-proclaimed psychic, past or present, who has been carefully investigated either has been exposed as a fraud or simply cannot demonstrate any real powers. Controlled investigations of ESP and PK have produced some statistically significant effects, but these are so small they have no practical significance. And even these small effects are not necessarily due to Psi. They may be due to very subtle but more mundane factors that the experimenter failed to recognize, such as a slightly biased REG generator.

Beyond all this, the single factor that makes the existence of Psi most doubtful is its lack of reliability. It has been consistently difficult for investigators to replicate their own successful outcomes or those of other experimenters. And when replications do succeed, the effects are often marginal. If Psi is real, it should produce some tangible effects that can be obtained in test after test.

Ruling out the possibility that human beings have paranormal powers does not necessarily mean that they do not have experiences which can look like Psi. In fact, from a Christian perspective such experiences are quite possible because there are supernaturally mediated incidents in the Bible that resemble every category of Psi. For instance, Jesus had powers that look like telepathy. He knew what the Pharisees and Sadducees were thinking when they tried to trap him with clever questions (Mt 12:25). Peter demonstrated similar knowledge in his encounter with Ananias and Sapphira. By the power of the Holy Spirit he immediately knew they were being dishonest about the money they were giving, and he correctly predicted that their punishment would be swift and irreversible (Acts 5:1-10).

Jesus also had the ability to see remote events and to know all about people he hadn't met—an ability that resembles clairvoyance. When he met Nathanael for the first time, Jesus described his character and told him that he had seen him under a fig tree before Philip greeted him and asked him to come meet Jesus (Jn 1:45-49). Nathanael was truly astounded by these revelations. Jesus also amazed the Samaritan women he met at a well by giving her an accurate summary of her marital history (Jn 4:16-19). Precognition has its parallel in prophecy, and Jesus, as well as many other individuals in the Old and New Testament record, was supernaturally empowered to predict the future.

In addition to parallels with ESP, there are many biblical events that modern parapsychologists would probably attribute to PK. Jesus turned water into wine (Jn 2:1-10), multiplied loaves and fishes (Mk 6:37-44), withered a fig tree with a word (Mk 11:12-14, 20-21), walked on water (Mt 14:25) and commanded storms to cease (Mt 8:23-27). There are also supernatural events of this type in the Old Testament. Before and during the exodus from Egypt, God brought about many miraculous signs through Moses to establish his sovereignty (Ex 7—12). Years later God enabled the prophet Elisha to increase a small amount of oil to fill many pots so a prophet's widow could pay her debts (2 Kings 4:1-7). Elisha was also enabled to make an iron axhead float so it could be retrieved from a river (2 Kings 6:4-8).

Healing has been classified as a type of PK, and there are numerous examples of this in Scripture as well. Jesus, his disciples, the apostle Paul and Old Testament figures like Elijah and Elisha all accomplished miraculous healings, even raising people from the dead.

All the preceding events were obviously empowered by God. But Scripture also indicates that Satanic or demonic power may manifest itself in events that look paranormal. In Acts 16:16-20, the writer describes a slave girl who was able to tell fortunes (prophesy) because of an indwelling demon. She kept following Paul and those with him, proclaiming that they were "servants of the Most High God" (clairvoyance). When Paul cast the spirit out, she lost these abilities and her owners were infuriated.

People who were demon possessed appeared clairvoyant, at least momentarily, because the demons in them recognized Jesus when he commanded them to leave, and they shouted this aloud in their surprise and dismay (see Mt 8:28-29; Mk 1:23-26, 32-33). Demons may provide the impetus or inspiration for some cases of false prophecy, although the Bible makes it clear that false prophecies can also originate in the prophet's own imagination. Jeremiah warned the Israelites,

Do not listen to what the prophets are prophesying to you;

they fill you with false hopes.

They speak visions *from their own minds,*

not from the mouth of the LORD. (Jer 23:16)

Ezekiel's comments in 13:1-6 are similar.

Revelation 16:13-14 suggests that false prophecies can come from demons: "I saw three evil spirits that looked like frogs; they came out of the mouth of the dragon, out of the mouth of the beast and out of the mouth of the false prophet. They are spirits of demons performing miraculous signs." John implies the same thing when he warns, "Dear friends, do not believe every spirit, but test the spirits to see whether they are from God, because many false prophets have gone out into the world" (1 Jn 4:1; also see 1 Sam 18:10).

The ability of the magicians in Pharaoh's court to duplicate Moses' first three miracles (which might be compared to PK) may also have been a display of Satanic power. If it was, this incident indicates that Satan and his agents can affect physical objects. This ability is also apparent in the story of Job 1:16, 19, where Satan caused fire to fall from the sky which burned up Job's sheep and servants, then sent a "mighty wind" that blew down the house where Job's children were feasting. Thus it is possible that some poltergeist activity and perhaps even a few of the events associated with mediums are due to demonic activity.

All of this suggests that some of the current events that look paranormal may in fact be energized by demonic power. But I think it would probably be a serious mistake to attribute all or even most of this to demons. As Dan Korem points out, most of the biblical accounts of such incidents give no indication that pagan magicians, conjurers or sorcerers could wield unusual power. In fact, when their powers were put to the test—such as when Elijah challenged the priests of Baal to call down fire from heaven and consume the sacrifice (1 Kings 18:16-38), or when only Daniel, but not the Babylonian magicians, enchanters, sorcerers or astrologers, could describe Nebuchadnezzar's dream and interpret it (Dan 2)—they usually failed miserably. Korem concludes that their demonstrations of "power" were created by the same deceitful tricks and illusions that are being used so effectively today.[33]

Demons may be encouraging modern-day psychics in their activities and even deceiving some of them into thinking they actually have real power, but why should they bother to produce supernatural effects when they can achieve the same ends through persons who are willing to trick and deceive, and when other persons are willing to take such demonstrations at face value?

Considering the information at hand, what conclusions can we now draw about paranormal-type experiences? First, they are apparently not due to latent human powers, because confirming evidence is lacking. Second, while some of these experiences may be due to supernatural intervention, most probably are not. Many of the situations that suggest the operation of ESP (aside from those that may represent insight or promptings from the Holy Spirit) are probably due to coincidence or other natural causes. In addition, it now appears that most (if not all) of the contemporary displays of PK, especially those put on by psychics, are feats of trickery.

These conclusions leave still leave us with one unanswered question. If the evidence for paranormal powers is so weak, why do so many people still believe that they are real? Some people probably believe because they want to believe, so it doesn't take much "evidence" to convince them. In other cases the deciding factor appears to have been an unusual personal experience.

The investigative committee commissioned by the army, mentioned earlier in this chapter, came across a striking example of this while interviewing a respected parapsychologist. He told the committee openly that his colleagues were making a serious mistake by trying to get the scientific community to take their research seriously, because *the effects of Psi were not reliable enough to meet scientific standards.* When asked how he could still believe in Psi in the face of such contrary evidence, he answered, "When I was sixteen I had some personal experiences of a psychic nature that were so compelling that I have no doubt that they were real."[34] Because of his experiences, this man had persevered in a very frustrating and unrewarding field, hoping to validate Psi scientifically so he could convince others of what he knew to be true by experience. A few well-placed experiences of this type can apparently make a dramatic impact on a person's beliefs.

8

Healings

Why do I include a chapter devoted to "healings" in this book on New Mysticism? Although it may not be immediately obvious, nontraditional medicine and the healings claimed for it have been very instrumental in drawing people away from traditional worldviews and toward more mystical systems of belief. This happens in several ways. First, since most of the current nontraditional medical treatments are based on beliefs that are inconsistent with traditional Western orthodoxy, every time someone appears to be healed by one of these methods, the worldviews supporting them become more credible. This is especially true in cases where previous medical treatment did not help. In the second place, since New Agers have been the most visible promoters of nontraditional methods, the widespread use of those methods has helped to popularize and legitimize New Age/New Consciousness thought. Third, numerous nontraditional healers have reportedly induced unusual, mystically tinged experiences in their patients while attempting to heal them. Such experiences are bound to make the healer's worldview seem more credible to patients.

The variety of nontraditional healing techniques that are currently available is truly remarkable. For techniques like herbal remedies, acupuncture, acupressure, chiropractic and possibly some message therapies, it is possible to explain apparent benefits at least partially in physiological terms, although the practitioners commonly explain their effects in terms of balancing spiritual energy. At the other end of the spectrum are more esoteric treatments that cannot be directly explained in terms of our current knowledge of physiology. These include aromatherapy (in which a person is exposed to certain aromas to aid healing), ayurveda (an ancient system from India that uses deep meditation, diet, massage, altered sleep patterns and yoga to stimulate the body's healing response[1]), color healing (shining colored lights onto the body to alter its spiritual vibrations), crystal healing (using crystals and other minerals to impart "healing energy"), bioenergetics (which involves the exchange of healing energy between patient and therapist[2]), psychic healing and various forms of shamanism.[3]

According to current surveys, Americans and other Westerners are quite interested in these alternate treatments, and many are already using them. According to a 1991 survey for *Time* magazine, 62 percent of those polled said they would definitely consider seeking help from alternative practitioners if standard medical practices did not work, and 33 percent of the sample had already utilized the services of a nontraditional healer of one type or the other.[4] In a survey published in *The New England Journal of Medicine*, researchers found that one-third of their sample had used at least one type of unconventional therapy in the year preceding the survey. They estimated that Americans made some 425 million visits to providers of nonconventional therapy during that year, at an out-of-pocket cost of approximately 13.7 billion dollars. This exceeded the 388 million visits to regular physicians that year and a comparable 12.8 billion dollars out-of-pocket for traditional medical expenses.[5] These numbers surprised everyone.

Interest in nontraditional medicine has become so great that it has even stirred the U.S. Congress into action. Prompted by the Senate Appropriations Committee, Congress approved a two-million-dollar appropriation for studying the efficacy of nontraditional medical treatments. In line with this mandate from Congress, the normally conservative National Institutes for Health organized a new office for the "study of unconventional medical practices," which started its investigations in 1993.[6]

What are we to make of all these changes in attitudes toward medical treatment? Do they bode well or ill? In my view, some of what is happening is positive and some is definitely negative.

The Holistic Health Movement

The positive aspects of the situation are actually rooted in two developments that began in the mid to late 1970s: a widespread and growing dissatisfaction with traditional medicine alongside the influence of the holistic health movement, a loose confederation of health professionals with an alternate, New Age approach to health and medical treatment. This group gathered strength through the late 1970s by forcefully denouncing many of the objectionable practices of traditional medicine and arguing for a totally different approach to healing.

Even though this group's specific underlying beliefs about illness and healing were at odds with traditional worldviews, many of their criticisms of modern medicine and their *general* suggestions for change were both excellent and timely. Holistic advocates deplored the impersonal, business-as-usual way traditional doctors often treated their patients. They denounced the insensitivity of doctors who concentrated only on patients' physical problems while disregarding their fears and anxieties. They reproached traditional physicians for focusing very narrowly on treating illnesses while largely ignoring prevention. Finally, they criticized the medical establishment for relying heavily on treatments that are themselves very destructive—surgery, powerful drugs, radiation therapy.

The critics argued for a *holistic* approach to medicine, treatment geared toward meeting the needs of the whole person—body, mind and spirit—rather than just physical needs, prevention and wellness rather than just finding cures for illness, and more natural, less harmful cures. They maintained that patients should be empowered and treated as active partners rather than passive bystanders in the healing process.

These were ideas whose time had come, and they fell upon very receptive ears. They were not unique to the holistic health movement—similar criticisms and suggestions for change were being voiced in many different quarters. But the proponents of holistic medicine received most of the credit for these ideas because they promoted them most visibly and forcefully. Their successful advocacy added a great deal of credibility to the holistic health movement, and to New Age/New Consciousness thought along with it.

The criticisms and suggestions for change that were promoted by the holistic health movement have helped bring some positive changes in medicine and our present attitudes toward health. Medical schools are now training doctors to be sensitive to the psychological and emotional needs of their patients and to interact with them respectfully and with care. Medical professionals are focusing more on prevention, particularly by educating people about the dangers of obesity, smoking, drinking and drug use and the benefits of good nutrition and regular exercise. Media and public interest in physical and emotional fitness, or wellness, are probably at an all-time high. Physicians are also more appreciative of the idea that health is related to one's state of mind (this change in perception, however, has probably been driven more by current research on stress-related illness and placebo effects than by the holistic health movement).

Changes of this type have been good, but there are some very negative aspects of our present situation too. Amid the growing acceptance of alternative techniques, people are encouraged to experiment with esoteric practices, many of which are forbidden in Scripture and can draw people away from Christian faith. And many of the alternative treatments whose benefits are still unproven hold out false hopes to people at a time when they are extremely vulnerable and desperate.

Treatments based on New Age thinking can seem tremendously hopeful and empowering, because they suggest that people can heal themselves if they apply enough effort and go about it in the right way. In their desperate search for cures, people with serious illnesses may spend precious money and time on alternative therapies, only to discover later that they have actually reduced their chances of being cured by traditional medicine. Those who become convinced that they can heal themselves but fail to get better are likely to end up carrying a burden of grief and guilt in addition to their illness.

The current openness toward alternative healing methods also creates a climate that is ripe for fraud. And unfortunately, there is plenty of evidence that unscrupulous operators have been quick to take advantage of this situation. False healers have been appearing in many settings, including the arena of Christian faith healing.

Amid all this confusion, I believe three types of information can greatly aid our discernment. One is a basic knowledge of the beliefs and practices involved in holistic medicine; this can help us identify alternative treatments that are incompatible with Scripture. The second is a better understanding of the various psychological and physical factors that can affect physical healing, while the third is a clear set of biblical guidelines that can help us differentiate between natural and supernatural healings.

The Central Tenets of Holistic Medicine

Since holistic medicine is a branch of the New Age movement, its basic assumptions about human nature are consistent with New Age thinking. Here is a summary of some of its basic tenets.

1. Illness is fundamentally a problem of energy disturbances. In the holistic framework, humans are primarily spiritual or "energy" beings who can exercise considerable control over their physical bodies with their minds. The universal "life energy" of which we are composed flows in, out and through us. When this flow is normal, the body is healthy, but when it is restricted or disturbed for some reason, the body develops symptoms of disease. According to this model, then, illness is fundamentally a problem of energy disturbances, and healing is the process of restoring disturbed energy patterns to normal. Presumably this restoration can be accomplished by the person who is afflicted, or by some other person who has learned how to manipulate and restore the energy properly.

I should point out that although these ideas may seem quite new and different to Westerners, the "energy model" is not unique to the holistic health movement. It is actually very old and has cropped up in many diverse cultures over the centuries. It is an integral part of Hinduism, Chinese Taoism, and shamanic lore among the Polynesians and American Indians. Modern Chinese still believe that they manipulate this energy with acupuncture needles, and classic chiropractic theory was based on the idea that one's energy fields could be balanced and restored by manipulation of the spine.

Holistic advocates use the energy model to explain how tribal shamans and psychic or holistic healers of all types are able to assist healing. Their talents are attributed to their ability to manipulate or channel the "life energy" with their minds.[7] "Therapeutic touch," developed by Dolores Krieger, is considered a type of energy manipulation. In crystal healing, various types of crystals are thought to attract or amplify beneficial life energy, so treatment consists of having the patient lie down, relaxing or meditating, with a number of crystals arranged appropriately on the body.

2. *People have the inherent ability to control, or at least influence, their own health and illness.* If human beings can control or influence physical reality with their minds, they should certainly be able to control or influence their own bodies. A corollary to this belief (which is accepted in varying degrees by different people in the movement) is that if people are ill, it is because at some level they *want* to be ill. This proposition implies that people should be able to heal themselves, or at least improve their health, with effort and the appropriate techniques.

3. *The way to health and healing is through the Higher Self.* As you may recall, the Higher Self is thought to operate on a subconscious level, presumably because of opposition from the conscious mind. Thus holistic advocates favor techniques like visualization, meditation and evoking imaginary inner guides as aids to healing. A cancer patient may be encouraged to visualize her white blood cells as ferocious sharks that are attacking and devouring a shrinking tumor. She is to will this attack with all her might while visualizing the attack scene as vividly as possible. Some patients are hypnotized in an effort to make their visualization efforts more effective.

A few investigators have actually checked the activity of white blood cells (which are vital components of the immune system) before and after visualization exercises to see whether the exercises alter the cells' effectiveness. So far the results have been inconclusive or negative.[8]

Radiologist Carl Simonton and his wife, psychologist Stephanie Simonton, used visualization therapy on 159 cancer patients as an adjunct therapy along with their usual chemotherapy and radiation treatments. In their popular book *Getting Well Again*, they reported that these treatments were very beneficial.[9] Unfortunately, however, the Simontons' conclusions were based primarily on anecdotal accounts and simple summary statistics rather than accepted experimental procedures. Since they did not employ control groups, it was not possible to determine whether their patients were healthier than they would have been without visualization or to determine what was responsible for the apparent benefits of treatment. The Simontons gave their patients attention, social support and a renewed sense of hope, and the visualization training provided them with an opportunity to try to do something for themselves. Research indicates that all four of these variables can reduce stress, and stress reduction allows the immune system to operate much more effectively. If the Simontons' patients did show real physical improvement, it may well have been due to stress reduction rather than visualization per se.

4. *Medical treatments should be holistic.* This proposition stems from the belief that illness involves body, mind and spirit and that the spiritual/psychological dimension is probably more important in illness than physical factors.

5. *Medical treatment should be a partnership between the healer and the client and should be focused on wellness and prevention.* These principles are consistent with the belief that it is the patient who is primarily responsible for healing. The role of the healer is to assist the healing process, treating patients with love and respect, giving them hope, helping them to see their illness in the greater scheme of things (showing them that death is not the end of life and that they can learn from their illnesses) and teaching them to take an active role in their own health and recovery.

6. *"Natural" methods of healing are to be preferred over traditional techniques like surgery, radiation and drugs.* This proposition appeals to just about everyone until the word *natural* is defined more specifically. In holistic parlance, "natural" methods are those that fit with the energy model of disease and wellness. Thus favored methods of healing include nutritional therapies (especially the use of herbs or roots) and treatments meant to manipulate spiritual energy. Holistic advocates are particularly interested in shamanic healing techniques, especially among the American Indians, because shamanism has presumably been minimally influenced by Western thinking and is therefore more in tune with effective methods of spiritual healing.

Holistic Medicine and Traditional Medicine

As discussed above, some of holistic medicine's general criticisms and suggestions for change have made an impact on traditional medicine, and doctors are increasingly aware of the mind-health relationship. Other holistic beliefs—for example, that illnesses are due to disturbances in energy fields, that people get ill because in some part of their being they want to or that they can heal themselves with inner spiritual power—have been firmly rejected.

Yet even though traditional physicians do not accept the more eccentric elements of the holistic approach, their new appreciation for the mind-illness connection has encouraged some of them to try treatments that were considered highly unconventional, at least in medicine, just a few years ago. These include biofeedback or autogenic training (a mild type of self-hypnosis) for migraine headaches,[10] progressive relaxation, biofeedback and yoga or other types of Eastern meditation for high blood pressure,[11] group therapy for cancer patients (which may be able to prolong life in some cases[12]), guided imagery as an adjunct technique for fighting cancer, and meditation, acupuncture and hypnosis as treatments for pain. As mentioned previously, treatments of this type have become popular enough to prompt the NIH to create a special office to investigate their efficacy.

The only branch of traditional medicine that has been significantly affected by more esoteric holistic beliefs is nursing. Nursing has had enthusiastic holistic proponents from the very beginning. One of these was Dolores Krieger, who was on faculty at New York University. Krieger developed a diagnostic/healing technique known as "therapeutic touch" which became very popular and is now taught in many mainline nursing schools.[13] The explanations offered for this practice vary, but in a popular nursing text, Barbara Blattner, formerly a teacher at San Francisco State University, describes this laying on of hands as a form of psychic healing, a channeling of "the superconscious energy that is the source and intelligent center of all life."[14]

According to a report by Sharon Fish, the holistic influence in nursing is significant and still gaining momentum. A number of professors of nursing at key positions in prestigious nursing schools—including the University of New York, Catholic University of America, University of Colorado and the University of Minnesota—promote holistic principles in their classrooms and in texts they have written. These texts overtly support such practices as the laying on of hands, Eastern meditation, achieving unity with the Universal Mind, returning to nursing's true roots (shamanism), getting in touch with inner guides, experimenting with the paranormal, journeying out of the body, and more. Unfortunately, students are inclined to take these suggestions seriously because they come from respected authorities.[15]

Why the Apparent Success of Holistic Medicine?

The current, widespread involvement with nontraditional healing raises the obvious question whether such techniques actually work. Unfortunately, it is not yet possible to answer this with objective data because of a lack of adequate research. Plenty of books and articles claim favorable results for holistic techniques, but they are not based on careful studies with appropriate control groups. At this point the only thing we know for sure is that large numbers of people are experimenting with alternate healing techniques, and based on the amount of time and money they are investing in them, many are evidently convinced that they work.

From this perspective the techniques appear to be helping, but how are they doing so? Are they benefiting people by realigning spiritual energy, as the advocates of holistic medicine would have us believe, or are there other, more prosaic reasons for their success?

Based on Scripture and current medical knowledge of healing, I believe there are a number of plausible alternative explanations for the apparent successes and popularity of holistic techniques. These fall into two major categories, natural (that is, physical and/or psychological) and supernatural.

Natural Explanations

1. Some alternative techniques may work by conferring direct physical benefits that are not yet recognized by scientists. According to this explanation, the beneficial effects of certain holistic treatments are due not to energy realignments but to their physical effects in the body. Certain herbal treatments may produce real physical benefits that scientists have yet to study or explain. Acupuncture and acupressure, when used as methods of pain relief, may also fit into this category. Research suggests that they may relieve pain by stimulating the body to release endorphins, our natural painkillers. Chiropractic manipulations may decrease certain types of back or leg pain by relieving pressure on nerves that are compressed or by relaxing the muscles that are producing the pain.

2. Some alternative therapies may bring about real physical improvements indirectly, through the reduction of stress. It is now well established that excessive, prolonged stress can impair health and, conversely, that reductions in chronic stress can improve it. Prolonged stress can provoke or aggravate high blood pressure, diabetes and cancer. Sustained stress can hinder the immune system, impairing its ability to search out and destroy incipient tumors, or invading fungi, viruses and bacteria. Such impairments greatly increase the risk of infectious diseases and cancer.

The anxiety, anger and frustration that frequently accompany very stressful situations can also cause harm by chronically overactivating the sympathetic nervous system. One of the important functions of this system is to help us respond to emergencies with increased alertness, agility and strength. However, it was also designed to operate for *short periods of time*. Continually pushing it into overdrive over weeks or months generates higher-than-normal levels of certain neurotransmitters and hormones that can cause lasting damage, particularly in the cardiovascular system.

That is the bad news about stress, but there is also good news. Just being in very stressful circumstances is not usually sufficient, in and of itself, to produce significant physical damage. The way our bodies respond in such circumstances is quite dependent on psychological variables such as our assessment of the situation and our perceptions of how well we can cope with it. In fact, research indicates that people who react to stress in a positive way, keeping a hopeful outlook and entering an active, problem-solving mode as opposed to slipping into apathy or hopelessness, can minimize or even avoid substantial health risks. Having some sense of control in the situation is another important factor. Even in situations in which external factors are completely out of our control, we can still control *our reactions* to the situation. Keeping even this minimal sense of control can make a big difference. Evidence suggests that our immune systems can consistently function well, even in difficult circumstances, if we can take this positive, active approach.

The psychological component in stress-related illness is very relevant to our present discussion, because it suggests an alternative explanation for the apparent success of holistic therapies. Some of the most obvious benefits of these treatments are psychological. They frequently impart hope, a renewed sense of self-worth and purpose, and a *sense of control*. All of these can reduce distress, and reducing distress can help the body return to a healthier state.

Interestingly, some better-known healers within the holistic tradition are coming up with similar reasons for the apparent successes of their treatments. Noting that all their varied methods of healing are bringing about very similar results, many are now concluding that the particular methods of healing are not as important as the hope, love and sense of meaning and empowerment they are giving their patients. As the healers see it, these new perspectives liberate their patients from negative emotions and despair so they can mobilize their own "inner powers" and heal themselves.[16]

Of course there is one major difference between the healers' position and the stress-reduction hypothesis. The healers favor the view that the "inner powers" in question are spiritual and work by realigning energy, whereas according to the stress-reduction hypothesis the inner powers are simply the physical healing capabilities of the body.

3. Sometimes people may be attributing physical improvements to nontraditional treatments when they are actually due to the body's own ability to heal itself. Healing is a mysterious and complex process in which great numbers and varieties of living cells cooperate, as with a single purpose, to repair other cells or structures that have become dysfunctional. Researchers are beginning to understand how these cells accomplish some of the things that they do, but they do not yet understand the forces that initiate, direct and orchestrate the healing process. The process of healing per se is apparently something that only the body (or God) can do. When doctors intervene—whether by setting and splinting a broken bone, correcting structural problems with surgery or administering antibiotics—technically speaking, they are not healing the body but assisting it so it can more readily or effectively heal itself.

The healing capabilities of our bodies are tremendous. In fact, doctors have estimated that at least 80 percent of the ailments they treat in their offices would resolve themselves successfully in time with no treatment whatsoever. This has two interesting implications. The first is that we are probably visiting doctors' offices more often than we need to, and the second is that medical interventions are probably getting more credit for curing people than they actually deserve. If we go to the doctor, take the medicine prescribed and get better, most of us naturally assume that the medicine was responsible whether it was or not.

These facts have great relevance for our present discussion. If healers can achieve an apparent cure rate that approaches 80 percent no matter what therapy they apply (as long as their treatments aren't harmful), many of their clients are going to improve shortly after the treatment and conclude that it was the treatment that made the difference. This principle alone could explain many of the apparent successes in holistic healing.

4. *Some of the physical benefits attributed to holistic treatments may actually be due to placebo effects or other natural causes.* The medical community has known about placebo effects for years. Research indicates that inert substances, such as sugar pills, can bring about relief of pain in about 35 percent of a wide variety of pain patients, if those patients believe that the substance will help them. These effects actually have a physiological basis. Expecting a substance to relieve pain can actually stimulate the body to release endorphins, which then reduce the pain. Researchers know this happens because it is possible to eliminate the placebo effect with a substance called Naloxone, which blocks the pain-killing activity of endorphins. If people are given Naloxone along with the sugar pills, the placebo effect disappears.

It has also been reported that placebo effects can aid healing, but the physiological reasons for this are not yet known. Possibly the healing effect is actually due to stress reduction. Believing that a treatment is helping may reduce worry and distress and allow the immune system to operate more effectively. In any case, placebo effects may account for some of the apparent successes of nontraditional healers.

Other natural circumstances can also conspire to convince people that healing is occurring when it actually isn't. In some common ailments such as multiple sclerosis, arthritis and back pain, symptoms typically fluctuate from better to worse and back again over time. People with such ailments are likely to seek help when their symptoms are worse; then, in the course of time, they get better. If they happen to get better shortly after receiving treatment, they are likely to attribute their improvement to whatever treatment they just received.[17]

5. *Alternative healing procedures can confer significant psychological benefits.* Many holistic healers make a deliberate effort to communicate love and respect for their clients, listen sympathetically to their problems, encourage them to take charge of their own lives, and help them see that their illness

may have a greater meaning. If clients gain renewed courage, hope and a sense of meaning from their healer, they are very likely to conclude that the treatments were worthwhile even if they didn't help physically. They may even decide that their healing was "spiritual" rather than physical.

6. *Some apparent healings are fraudulent, perpetrated by temporarily convincing a patient that he or she is healed or by more deliberate tricks.* Fraudulent "healings" have been documented among nontraditional healers of various types and among faith healers who claim to be Christians. The so-called psychic surgeons who were based primarily in Brazil and the Philippines are a case in point. These healers required their patients to go through extensive preparations before "surgery"—fasting, praying, saying incantations, getting anointed with oil and so on—apparently to build up their expectations. During the operations (which were accompanied with impressive oozings and spurtings of blood), the surgeons appeared to open their patient's abdomens with their bare hands, reach in and yank out disgusting-looking growths and tumors. Then, with a final flourish, they would use their psychic powers to heal the wound instantaneously, leaving no trace of scarring.

Knowledgeable investigators were able to show that these "miracles of healing" were pure trickery. The surgeons would "operate" only on people whose abdomens were fat enough to be kneaded and creased to look as if they had been opened. The blood and "tumors" that appeared to come from within the patient were actually the blood and body parts of cows and chickens, and the bloody special effects were accomplished with the aid of accomplices and magic tricks.[18] Unfortunately, many innocent people (including many Westerners) were duped by these tricks and wasted precious time and money pursuing them.

A trick "healing miracle" that has been used for effect in Christian circles is causing a "shortened" leg to grow. Magician James Randi explains this and other maneuvers (like appearing to give sight to the blind and causing the lame to walk) in his important book *The Faith Healers*.[19] Faith healer W. V. Grant began with a moment of ecstatic insight, then announced that someone was present who had a shortened leg that needed to be adjusted.

He would then call out the name of a likely prospect, based on information he had gleaned before the meeting. (Preferably this was a person who had had a leg injury as a child, had a slight limp and was wearing loose-fitting shoes or boots.) Grant would bring the person on stage and seat him or her on a chair facing across the stage but turned slightly toward the audience. Then Grant lifted both legs parallel to the floor with one hand. When he did so, the leg that was farther away from the audience appeared about two inches longer than the closer leg. After Grant prayed vigorously for healing, the shorter leg appeared to lengthen before everyone's eyes.

Grant apparently accomplished this illusion with two simple maneuvers. To show the audience how uneven the legs were to begin with, he would lift both legs with one hand while swinging both of them slightly away from the audience. Simultaneously he twisted his hand, pulling out the heel of the shoe on the foot that was farther from the audience. By the time the two legs were lifted into place, from the audience's perspective the farther leg looked about two inches longer than the closer leg, according to the positions of the heels. Next, while praying mightily (and thereby distracting the audience's attention), Grant slowly swung both legs back toward the audience and twisted his hand in the opposite direction, gradually pushing the heel of the shoe back against the foot and bringing the heels into line. These moves, plus the expectations of his audience, created the strong illusion that the nearer leg was lengthening.[20]

Randi also exposed a faith healer named Peter Popoff who was able to call out names and addresses, tell people what was wrong with them and then proceed with "healings" that astounded his audiences. Randi discovered that this faith healer had gone high-tech. Before the show his wife and assistants would interview people in the audience, getting their names, addresses and specific ailments on prayer cards. Then Popoff's wife would exit the hall and enter a trailer where she could watch the proceedings through closed-circuit TV and feed Popoff information about selected candidates over a radio transmitter. Popoff wore a tiny receiver, which looked like a hearing aid, in his ear. Randi succeeded in exposing Popoff as a fraud by recording the short-wave transmissions from Popoff's wife during an entire healing service.

Popoff also used other tricks to make it look as if he was healing people. During preliminary interviews Popoff's wife and assistants would pick out a few people who had real disabilities, but were able to walk fairly well, and instruct them to sit in rented wheelchairs, presumably so they could be assisted to the front of the hall. During the service, with his wife's directions, Popoff could call out these individuals, act as if he had healed them, and get them to get out of their chairs and walk around to prove it. Sometimes he would even plop into the wheelchair himself and have the "healed" person push it around the auditorium, all to thunderous applause and adulation.[21]

People who have been manipulated in services like these respond in different ways. Some realize that they have been duped and get very angry, but many others continue to insist that something miraculous happened, even after they realize their physical condition has not changed and are confronted with direct evidence of fraud, like Randi's tapes. In these individuals the desire to believe in the healer and in miraculous healings apparently overtakes objectivity and common sense.[22]

Randi's insights and discoveries are valuable. They serve as a timely reminder that there are still wolves masquerading as sheep, and that one of their favorite pastimes is fleecing (and confusing) the flock.

But *are* some nontraditional healings being assisted supernaturally? This question is easier to answer if taken in three parts. (1) What are the distinguishing characteristics of supernatural healing? (2) Are there nontraditional healings that exhibit these characteristics? (3) If there are, how are we to interpret them?

The Marks of Supernatural Healing

One could argue that all healing is supernatural, since God designed the healing capabilities of our bodies and apparently assists natural healing in response to the prayers of his people (see Ps 103:2-3; Jas 5:13-16). For our purposes, however, I am defining supernatural healing as a miraculous event, *one that clearly transcends natural healing processes.*

Natural healing has several important characteristics. One is the fact that it is not always easy to confirm. Doctors distinguish between *pathological disorders* like cancer, cataracts, skin eruptions, arthritic conditions, paralysis, infected toenails and so on, whose symptoms are obvious to any outside observer, and *functional disorders* like recurrent headaches, chronic fatigue or back pain, whose symptoms are apparent only to the person experiencing them. When a pathological disorder is healed, it is obvious to everyone. But when a functional disorder is healed, the only evidence is the patient's word (and this can be influenced by many factors).

Another important aspect of natural healing is the fact that it is *gradual*. Healing may be faster or slower depending on one's general state of health and state of mind (stress) or the presence or absence of medical intervention, but it still takes time. The medical literature does document healings described as "spontaneous remissions"—for instance, a cancerous tumor (or a group of them) that unexpectedly reverses course and disappears in a matter of weeks or months.[23] Even though they are uncommon, spontaneous remissions are still considered natural, because they can be explained physiologically and do not actually occur within seconds. Our immune systems do have the ability to search out and destroy tumors and remove the debris, though it is very unusual for this to happen after tumors have grown large and spread. Spontaneous remissions are rare, and they are improbable in light of medical experience, but they can still be explained naturally.

Supernatural healings, as described in the Bible, contrast sharply with natural healings. All the supernatural healings in the Bible apparently occurred instantaneously (except for the case of King Hezekiah, in 2 Kings 20:1-7, who was healed within a three-day span that God had announced in advance and then validated by making a shadow on the stairs move backwards). They also occurred on command, right when the person who was instrumental in the healing attempted them. In addition, all the people supernaturally healed in scriptural accounts had observable pathological conditions, In Jesus' personal ministry there were no failed attempts or cases in which symptoms returned after a short time. *Everyone* was healed

(Lk 6:19). Finally, many of the healings in the Bible involved physical events that do not take place in the normal process of healing—such as the restoration of neurons in the central nervous system. In light of current medical knowledge, the healings in the Bible are truly amazing.

According to the Gospels, Jesus healed many paralytics and cripples. Luke 6:6-11 tells how Jesus healed a hand that was "shriveled" and had the man prove it was healed by stretching it out in front of everyone in the synagogue. The hand had apparently been deformed and paralyzed, which implies that there had been neural damage either in the motor-control areas of the brain or somewhere along the neural route from the brain to the hand. The muscles of the hand were atrophied, tight and unresponsive, and the injury was apparently an old one, which indicates that this man's natural powers of healing had failed to undo the damage.

From a physiological standpoint the immediate healing of this man's hand is amazing. In order to make the hand appear normal and function again, Jesus probably had to add many more cells to the existing muscle and skin tissue to restore the movement and elasticity in the joints and connective tissue which were stiff and tight for lack of use, and repair any nerve or brain damage that had been done. This latter feat is especially significant, for adults do not generate new neurons in the brain or spinal cord, and damaged neurons do not function normally. In fact, when neurons in the brain and spinal cord are damaged, they usually die. Existing neurons can sometimes compensate for those that are lost, by sending out branches to the affected muscles, but if this is going to occur it usually comes within a few months of the injury. By his act of healing Jesus must have created new neurons, "rewired" existing neurons so they could take over lost functions or repaired neurons that were still alive but damaged. And he did this instantaneously. None of this can be explained in terms of natural processes.

The healing of the man who was crippled from birth, recorded in Acts 3:1-10, is even more astounding. In his case, muscles in his feet and legs that were weak from disuse had to be restored and strengthened, and any bone or neural abnormalities had to be repaired. All of this *instantaneous* replacing and repairing is incredible enough, but if, as the passage suggests, this man had never walked, the miracle is amazing for another reason.

Walking upright is a very complicated process, and it takes young children a long time and a good many bumps to learn how to do it. While children are learning to walk, neuronal circuits are apparently formed in motor areas of their brains which can later automatically command the complicated, highly orchestrated muscle movements that are necessary for walking. To enable this man to walk, the Holy Spirit not only had to repair his feet and legs but also had to activate (or create) neurons in the motor areas of the brain and then lay down all the complicated neuronal circuits that are normally established gradually through long hours of practice. Yet when this man rose to his feet, not only did he know how to walk, but he could run and jump as well.

In light of our present knowledge Jesus' healing of the man born blind, recorded in John 9:1-8, is another incredible accomplishment. Scientists now know that when neurons in the visual area of the brain are not used during the first months of life, they deteriorate and lose their ability to function normally. This has been established by experiments with animals and in cases where surgeons have corrected congenital cataracts in adults who had never been able to see. Simply removing the clouded lenses and correcting for their loss with glasses does not enable these individuals to see correctly. They have permanent alterations in the neurons in the visual areas of the brain. So in order for Jesus to give this man normal vision, he would have had to repair any structural problems in the eyes and then replace lost neurons, establishing all the intricate connections between them which support normal vision. This act is clearly supernatural.

By way of summary, then, what are the characteristics of healings that are unquestionably supernatural? I would include the following. The healings are instantaneous, are carried out on command, and correct pathological disorders that are clearly visible to everyone. They defy natural explanation and are frequently *creative* in the sense that they require the creation of new tissue (muscle, skin, bone or neurons). They may also involve the immediate and obvious reshaping of bone and other structural elements or the repair or replacement of neurons in the brain (which does not happen naturally).

Holistic Healings and the Supernatural

Do any holistic healings meet the criteria for supernatural healing? This question is difficult to answer because the evidence is sketchy. There are numerous anecdotal accounts of apparent physical healings, but most of these are not corroborated by independent medical evidence.

The work of Olga Worrall, who worked out of Mt. Washington's United Methodist Church in Baltimore, is one exception. She has apparently carried out healings that have been verified by physicians. After her attempts to heal, cancerous tumors of the brain, throat and abdomen have gradually regressed and disappeared over a period of weeks or months, a swollen lymph node on a woman's face shrank and returned to normal within a few minutes, and a child's uncontrolled eye movements gradually disappeared over a period of three months.[24] These are healings of pathological disorders, but they were not instantaneous or creative.

Worrall did encourage people to continue with conventional medical treatment while she was attempting to heal them, so it is possible that the tumor regressions were partly due to radiation or chemotherapy and partly due to the fact her clients had received new hope. Yet there were indications that some other power might have been at work. Some who received her touch described powerful sensations of heat infusing their bodies, and if reports are to be believed, she sometimes induced the same sensations in people she happened to be praying for who were many miles away.[25]

Superficially at least, Worrall could have passed for a Christian healer. Many of her healings were conducted in church, with the pastor's blessing and with prayer. In this setting she did give God the credit for her healings. But Worrall was also a committed psychic who described "visits" from discarnate spirits and deliberate journeys out of the body. She was a very popular speaker on the holistic health circuit.

On the whole, the holistic healings that are being reported do include some healings of pathological disorders, and some of these may have been immediate, although this is far from certain. Some of the healings that were purportedly immediate (for example, spirit-assisted surgeries performed by a Brazilian healer called Arigo) may well have been fraudulent.[26]

In any case, reports of holistic healing never include acts of *creative* healing. None of the reported healings have accomplished anything as profound as the biblical examples cited above.[27] And the reported healings of pathological disorders generally involve the disappearance of cancers or tumors. If supernatural assistance is present in some of these healings, it is clearly not of the same order as the power of God in the miraculous healings in the Bible.

The Bible doesn't tell us whether Satan has been granted healing powers. The story of Job (Job 1—2) tells us that Satan does have the power to inflict illness (Job's boils) or even death (Job's sons and daughters) if God allows it. Since he has the power to inflict physical damage on our bodies, he may also have the power to destroy tumors and other diseased tissue if he chooses to do so. One way Satan might make it seem that he has dramatic healing power is to work through indwelling or oppressing demons. Some New Testament accounts indicate that demons can inflict various types of physical disorders—muteness (Mt 9:32-33), apparent epilepsy (Mk 9:17-27), crippling (Lk 13:10-13) and blindness (Mt 12:22). All Satan would have to do to pull off a dramatic "healing" would be to order the demon who is causing a problem to cease and desist, right after the ministrations of some healer.

The Bible does tell us that Satan will be able to produce some amazing signs and wonders in the end times (Mt 24:24; 2 Thess 2:9), but it doesn't say whether any of these will be healings. Even if they are, they will evidently not be based on real creative power, because these passages also say that such wonders will be "deceptive" and "counterfeit." Satan may have the power to deceive and destroy, but the awesome ability to create or restore living cells on command belongs to God alone.

9

Communication
with Spirits

Among the various types of mystical experiences that are heralded today, some of the most persuasive are those that appear to be direct contacts with spirits (human or otherwise). Some of these occur spontaneously, while others are deliberately sought. In the spontaneous encounters, people suddenly and quite unexpectedly sense that they are in the presence of a spirit, whom they usually identify as a close friend or relative who has died. Many merely "sense" this presence briefly, but others say they have actually heard, seen or felt the touch of the spirit.[1]

Those who deliberately seek contact with spirits use channelers, mediums, their own channeling efforts or, most recently, "psychomanteums." (A psychomanteum is a darkened chamber equipped with a mirror that ostensibly facilitates contacts with the dead.) Raymond Moody, who popularized near-death experiences in his book *Life After Life*, is currently promoting the psychomanteum as a way to contact departed relatives and friends and alleviate grief. In a more recent book, *Reunions*, Moody documents the extraordinary experiences that many of his clients have had in the psychomanteum.[2]

Contemporary contact experiences are reportedly very persuasive, very realistic and according to some surveys, remarkably common. In a 1984 survey Andrew Greeley asked his respondents, "Have you ever felt as though you really were in touch with someone who had died?" A surprising 42 percent of the sample said yes (up from the 27 percent who said yes to the same question in 1973).[3] Among the widows in Greeley's study, 64 percent reported having such experiences at least once or twice, and 35 percent of this group reported such experiences "several times" or "often."[4] In a study of fifteen Western European nations conducted by Gallup International, the percentage of people who reported contact with the dead, using the same question Greeley used, ranged from 9 percent in Norway and Denmark to 41 percent in Iceland. The weighted average for all these countries was 23 percent. Twenty-seven percent of U.S. citizens answered yes in the same survey.[5]

An indicator of our collective belief in spirit contacts is the continuing popularity of channeling. By conservative estimates, tens of thousands of Americans have sought out channeled advice, whether in private sessions, in workshops or through books and tapes, and the proceeds from the sale of channeled material are substantial.[6] Millions of Americans have been given favorable introductions to channeling through motion pictures (such as the popular *Ghost*) and television. Prominent channelers and their "entities" have even made guest appearances on popular network TV programs like the *Oprah Winfrey Show*. (Raymond Moody and some of his successful psychomanteum clients were also featured on her show in December 1993.)

In light of the biblical warnings against such pursuits, the growing interest in spirit contacts and the proliferation of contact experiences creates a very unwholesome climate, to say the least. These experiences are providing dramatic support for mystical belief systems, and the widespread promotion and endorsement of techniques for making such contacts is no doubt encouraging further spiritual experimentation.

The psychomanteum is likely to prove particularly seductive, especially for those who are struggling with grief. To hear that a well-known psychiatrist recommends this technique as a form of grief therapy could provide a very strong incentive to try it, even among people who should know better.

A Closer Look at Channeling

According to channelers, channeling is a process whereby human beings allow a spiritual entity to temporarily enter and use their bodies so the spirit can interact with other humans. When these spirits are taking over, the channelers appear to enter a trancelike state, and a short time later a being with a different personality appears to emerge. This entity may differ from the channeler in gender, tone of voice, style of speech, mannerisms and accent. Most channelers say they are not aware of anything that happens while this spirit is in charge.

Channeling is very similar to the older practice of trance mediumship, although there are some notable differences. Mediums usually limited their contacts to human spirits, their messages were often personal (and thereby potentially verifiable), and they tried to prove the authenticity of their contacts with physical manifestations (rapping sounds, table lifting, apparent materializations of hands or apparitions). In contrast, channelers claim to contact many types of spirits (humans, angels, ascended masters, UFO-nauts, dolphins and others). They usually relay very general, feel-good-about-yourself messages and do not attempt any supernatural displays of power. In fact, the only observable signs that separate entities may be in control are the apparent changes in personality, the nature of the messages and the channelers' claims that the entities are real. This lack of tangible evidence makes it virtually impossible to determine objectively whether the entities are real and may partly explain why researchers are avoiding this entire area.

From a historical perspective, channeling is just the latest variation in a long line of methods for making contact with the spirit world. Shamanism is probably the oldest and most widespread method. It has been documented in geographic areas as diverse as Siberia, North and South America, Africa, Tibet, Finland, the West Indies and Korea. Throughout recorded history, shamans—also known as "healers," "medicine men" or "witch doctors"—have entered trance states to intercede with the spirits on behalf of their peers. According to the Old Testament, mediumship, spiritualism, and related practices like divination, fortunetelling and soothsaying also flourished among the cultures that surrounded Israel (see Lev 19:26, 31; 20:6, 27; Deut 18:9-13).

In Western countries public interest in mediumship has waxed and waned over the years. It was fairly strong from the 1850s through the early 1900s, paralleling the rise and decline of spiritualism. But as more and more mediums were caught engaging in fraudulent behavior (primarily in their efforts to prove, with physical evidence, that spirits were present), public interest waned. In the present generation, which is largely uninformed about mediumship's past embarrassments, public interest in mediumship in the form of channeling has revived and is again fairly strong.[7]

It's hard to estimate how many people are actually engaged in channeling, but the numbers may be in the tens of thousands in the United States. In 1987, Jon Klimo estimated that there were probably at least one thousand channelers operating in the Los Angeles area alone.[8] Prospective channelers have certainly been getting plenty of incentives to try this activity for themselves in recent years. In New Age circles, channeling is encouraged because it is thought to enhance spiritual growth. Numerous self-help books and weekend workshops are available to help aspiring channelers get started. In addition to the channelers, there are probably hundreds of mediums who are still operating among the scattered groups of spiritualists in the United States and Canada.

Channelers and Their Entities

While most channelers work within a relatively small circle of people, a few have accumulated impressive followings. One of these was the late Jane Roberts, who channeled an entity named "Seth." Roberts, an aspiring writer and poet, was apparently enticed into channeling through a series of bizarre "mystical" experiences. As she tells the story, one evening, while writing poetry, she was startled as her mind suddenly filled with an "avalanche of radical new ideas" that burst forth with terrific power and that she felt compelled to record on paper. Writing furiously, she turned out a one-hundred-page manuscript entitled "The Physical Universe as Idea Construction." Roberts was intrigued because she was sure she was in contact with some higher power, but she was disturbed because the ideas put forth in the manuscript completely contradicted her own view of reality.

Shaken and uncertain what to do next, Roberts and her husband, Robert Butts, began experimenting with a Ouija board. They soon started receiving messages from a spirit that identified itself as Frank Withers. After a few sessions, however, Withers retreated, explaining that he was simply a fragment of a larger personality named Seth who now wanted to communicate through Roberts. Seth identified himself as an "energy essence personality" who had evolved beyond physical incarnations.

After a few more sessions with the Ouija board, Roberts began to receive Seth in trance and take dictation from him. In ensuing encounters, which Roberts said she didn't remember, Seth dictated five separate books, which she dutifully took down in automatic writing. (Roberts also channeled three books for other entities, one of whom claimed to be the spirit of the well-known psychologist William James.)

Seth's books promoted many of the themes that are now central in New Age/New Consciousness thought: human beings are extensions of God and are therefore "gods"; they have unlimited potential that needs to be developed; human beings do not die, they simply reincarnate; and reality is a creation of the mind. The "Seth books" became exceedingly popular.[9] In fact, these works helped to launch the current channeling movement.

Helen Schucman was another early channeler whose work became very influential. She was a trained psychologist in the psychiatry department of Columbia University's College of Physicians and Surgeons when she first began hearing a persistent inner voice in 1965. This voice kept telling her, "This is a course in miracles. Please take notes." Schucman, whose background was Jewish and who claimed to be an atheist, was reportedly unnerved by the voice. She became even more upset when the voice identified itself as Jesus Christ. She was afraid that she was losing her mind. With encouragement from her immediate supervisor and her husband, however, she finally gave in and started taking dictation.

Unlike Roberts, Schucman remained aware of what she was writing while the messages were coming in. Her source dictated messages off and on over the next eight years (1965-1973), and the final result was a massive, twelve-hundred-page, three-volume work entitled *A Course in Miracles*.[10] The set consisted of a text, a workbook filled with "spiritual" exercises and an instructor's manual. First published in 1975, the set has by now sold hundreds of thousands of copies, its reputation boosted by word of mouth and by endorsements in popular self-help books like *Love Is Letting Go of Fear* by psychiatrist (and convert) Gerald Jampolsky.[11]

The *Course in Miracles*, which was ostensibly dictated by Jesus, maintains a semblance of Christianity by using Christian terminology. In the process, however, it twists and redefines critical doctrines. According to the *Course* God is an impersonal, undifferentiated mind, and Jesus is just one of his "sons" like the rest of humanity. Jesus is holy, but so is everyone, since everyone is an extension of God. The *Course* posits that humans do not need salvation and that there was no need for Jesus to atone for our sins by death on the cross, because we are already "sons" and thereby eternally secure. This treatise assures its readers that God has no intention of punishing anyone, "sins" are merely mistakes that can be corrected, and death is only an illusion. The "miracles" the *Course* refers to are not instances of divine intervention as recorded in the Bible, but rather times when people recognize their own divinity and grasp the "true" spiritual nature of reality.[12]

A Course in Miracles has spawned several books that purport to explain and interpret it. One of the most successful is Marianne Williamson's *A Return to Love: Reflections on the Principles of "A Course in Miracles,"* published in 1992 by HarperCollins. After Williamson appeared on the *Oprah Winfrey Show* that same year, and Winfrey announced she was so impressed that she was giving away one thousand copies to friends, Williamson's book quickly jumped to the bestseller list in New York City.[13]

Unfortunately, both the original *Course* and *Return to Love* are apparently attracting many converts, including many nominal Christians who are not sufficiently trained in Scripture or doctrine to recognize that these works are completely incompatible with the Bible.

On the contemporary channeling scene, there are at least a dozen popular channeler-entity teams. One of the more successful is an attractive former housewife named J. Z. Knight, who channels Ramtha. Ramtha modestly identifies himself as a thirty-five-thousand-year-old "Ascended Master" who was once a barbarian warrior/king, then a Hindu god, and who has now progressed beyond deity itself. Knight appears to drop into a deep cataleptic trance when Ramtha enters, and Ramtha, a powerful male presence, strides about with great vigor and speaks to his attentive followers in a stylized, archaic manner.

In recent years, the Knight-Ramtha team has lost some of its appeal because Ramtha's personality appears to have soured (his messages became sermons of doom and gloom rather than love and peace) and Knight has been accused of fakery. (One staff member heard her practicing Ramtha's voice in an unguarded moment.) Whatever Ramtha's actual identity, his appearances have been profitable for Knight: he has made her a millionaire several times over.[14] According to channel watchers, however, Penny Torres Rubin, who channels Mafu (described in chapter two), has now surpassed Knight in popularity.[15]

Kevin Ryerson and Jach Pursel both discovered their ability to channel while experimenting with Eastern meditation. Ryerson channels several entities, including John, who claims to have been a member of the Hebrew Essene sect at the time of Christ; Tom McPherson, a rustic Irishman who speaks with a brogue; and Obadiah, a Haitian who speaks in a West Indian dialect. Critics have watched Ryerson closely to see whether these characters ever get confused (which would indicate that he is creating them), but apparently this hasn't happened. They remain consistent with their cultural background. Jach Pursel, a former regional insurance supervisor in Florida, channels Lazaris, who claims to be a "group entity" from another dimension. In order to meet heavy demands for private readings, public talks and weekend workshops, Pursel has reportedly spent as long as forty hours a week unconscious, with Lazaris in control.[16]

Another important group of entities I should mention are the extraterrestrials or "Space Brothers," who claim to have come from other parts of the universe or from an "etheric realm" close to earth. These entities have manifested through various channelers and have sent messages through people who claim to have made contact with UFOs. Messages from the Space Brothers have been coming in for the last forty years or so and now fill several volumes.[17] In recent years some of these sources are even identifying themselves as Jesus (or "Sananda") and are describing the way UFOs are going to be assisting at his Second Coming.[18]

The Variety of Channeled Entities
The variety of beings that have reportedly been channeled by various individuals in recent years is enough to strain credulity. The list includes the channeler's own "Higher Self," God, various gods, "the Universal Mind," group entities like Seth and Lazaris, Jesus, angels, ascended masters, extraterrestrials, human spirits, demons, fairies, dolphins and even plants.[19]

Though channeling enthusiasts apparently take this list in stride, it is very difficult for a nonenthusiast to do so. In fact, from an outsider's perspective the list looks like the work of some practical joker who is trying to see just how much foolery devotees will accept without becoming suspicious. The list is also curious, because it doesn't seem likely that the channelers themselves would deliberately create such outlandish entities, especially if their goal was to establish a loyal following. It is possible that some, like P. T. Barnum, enjoy probing the outer limits of people's credulity. If a joke is being perpetrated, however, it may well be aimed at both the channelers and their followers.

The Messages Brought by Channelers
The general messages coming forth from various entities are fairly consistent, and they echo familiar themes: God is an impersonal force, reality is a creation of the mind, and all beings, human and otherwise, are divine

extensions of God who are evolving and growing, through a series of embodied and disembodied lives, toward an eventual reunion with God. Significantly, many entities are emphasizing the "Higher Self," encouraging followers to make contact with this part of their being and to follow its counsel trustingly even though it may at times seem strange or alien to them. Another channeled message that has been consistent (and that has also been imparted to a number of near-death experiencers) is that a time of great upheaval, change and catastrophe is soon to come upon the earth. In many scenarios this time is to be followed by a millennium or "New Age" in which human beings will be making unprecedented spiritual advances.[20]

Messages of this latter type are especially common from the Space Brothers. In some versions of this message, people are told that the Brothers will be standing by with their UFOs to collect and evacuate the "more spiritually advanced" (those who subscribe to New Age thought or similar mystical systems) to safer places until the upheaval settles down. In a few cases the Brothers have even referred to this process of collection as "the Harvest,"[21] a chilling echo of the words Jesus used to describe the final separation of the righteous and the wicked which will take place at "the end of the age" (see Mt 13:24-30, 36-39). But note that Jesus says the harvesters will be *his* angels, not Space Brothers in UFOs.

More About Psychomanteums

Psychomanteum is actually another name for the ancient Greek oracles of the dead. These were places designed for the express purpose of facilitating contact with spirits. Those who visited an oracle for this purpose were required to live in very dimly lit underground rooms and passageways for up to a month (probably a very effective way of inducing sensory deprivation). At the end of this time they were led by priests into a large "hall of visions" that was illuminated with torches. There they gazed into a huge, highly polished metal caldron (perhaps through water) until apparitions appeared in its mirrored surfaces.[22]

This use of the caldron is closely related to the divinatory practices of mirror, crystal and water gazing, which have long been associated with fraud and deception (think of the fortuneteller with her crystal ball and other unscrupulous diviners). These practices have cropped up time and again across the centuries, but they have also always been disparaged, dismissed as superstitious nonsense and banned by religious authorities.

So why would Moody become interested in a technique that, by his own admission, has such a shabby reputation? Moody says that he was partly prepared for this through his work with near-death experiencers. He had observed that the reunions between experiencers and their departed loved ones had a tremendous therapeutic effect. After such encounters experiencers not only were reassured about their loved ones but also lost their fear of death. Moody reasoned that anyone who was bereaved could benefit if he or she could somehow have such reunions, but he couldn't think of any reasonable way to make this happen.

By his account, the idea of using mirror gazing for this purpose virtually fell into his lap. One day when he was walking through a used-book shop, a book inexplicably fell off the shelf and dropped at his feet. The book was an intriguing, persuasive account of mirror gazing, and as he read, he began to see the possibilities.[23]

Moody's psychomanteum is quiet, far from distractions like clocks and telephones, dark except for a very dim light source, and comfortable. It contains a large mirror and a low, comfortable chair that is set at an angle with the mirror so viewers cannot see their own reflection. Moody uses a day-long procedure to prepare his clients for the use of this chamber. He and the client start with a leisurely walk in the woods, enjoying the scenery and discussing the person the client hopes to see. This is followed by a light lunch and a continued discussion of the deceased, augmented by photos and mementos which are meant to evoke strong memories of the person. Sometimes clients spend time in a special bed listening to tapes that help induce a profound state of relaxation. Finally, after dusk, the client is ready to enter the psychomanteum. (Apparitions are apparently more likely at night.)

The purpose of all this preparation is to fill clients' minds with vivid memories and to help them achieve a mild altered state of consciousness which Moody likens to hypnogogia (the state between sleeping and waking). Once inside the psychomanteum, clients are instructed to relax deeply, think about the person they want to contact and watch in the mirror. Most of these sessions last an hour or so.

According to Moody, the experiences these procedures produced totally surprised him. As a pilot study he had invited several mature, well-educated, emotionally stable people to participate. Of the ten who tried his procedure, five had visionary encounters with dead relatives on their first try.

An accountant in his mid-forties attempted to contact his mother who had died a year earlier and whom he missed very much.

> There is no doubt that the person I saw in the mirror was my mother! I don't know where she came from but I am convinced that what I saw was the real person. She was looking out at me from the mirror. . . . I could tell she was in her late 70s, about the same age as . . . when she died. However, she looked happier and healthier than she had at the end of her life. Her lips didn't move, but she spoke to me and I clearly heard what she had to say. She said, "I'm fine," and smiled happily.
>
> I stayed as relaxed as I could and just looked at her. . . . Then I decided to talk to her. I said, "It's good to see you again." "It's good to see you too," she replied. That was it. She simply disappeared.[24]

A physician, who had prepared to see his aunt, unexpectedly encountered his nephew instead.

> I suddenly had a very strong sense of the presence of my nephew, who had committed suicide. I was close to this nephew. . . . There was a very strong sense of his presence and I heard his voice very clearly. He greeted me and brought me a very simple message. He said, "Let my mother know that I am fine and that I love her very much." This experience was profound. I know he was there with me. I didn't see anything but I had a very strong sense of him and of his presence.[25]

In another case a woman who came to see her late grandfather first saw him in the mirror.

I was so happy to see him that I began to cry. Through the tears I could still see him in the mirror. Then he seemed to get closer and he must have come out of the mirror because the next thing I knew, he was holding me and hugging me. It felt like he said something like, "It's okay, don't cry." Before I knew it, he was gone. . . . It was great to see him again. . . . Even though I miss him, it nice to know that he's happy where he is.[26]

Moody was so intrigued by these initial results that he decided to try the psychomanteum himself. He prepared to see his maternal grandmother, whom he had loved dearly, but after about an hour in the psychomanteum without any success, he came out. Later, while sitting in an adjoining room, he was surprised when a young woman walked into the room and came up to him. For about a minute Moody did not recognize her, but he then realized that she was his *paternal* grandmother, who had died some years earlier. She was much younger than he remembered her and looked somewhat different. But she did have an intimate knowledge of their family, and Moody recognized her "presence." His memories of her were mixed, for their relationship had not been that happy.

Moody states that his grandmother looked like any other person, although she seemed to be surrounded by some type of light or an indentation in space that set her apart from the physical surroundings. He spoke to her and heard her speak, but for some reason she would not let him touch her. In a conversation that probably lasted at least an hour, they discussed their relationship and other family issues. They said goodby, noting that they would meet again, Moody left the room, and when he returned she was gone.[27]

Since 1990 Moody has observed and interviewed three hundred people who have used the psychomanteum, and he has found that at least 50 percent have significant apparitional visions on their first attempt. Many of those who don't succeed on the first try do succeed in subsequent attempts.[28] Moody has also discovered that about 25 percent of those who do succeed are visited by a deceased person they did not prepare for, and another 25 percent do not have the visit until after they leave the psychomanteum. (However, these visits usually do occur within twenty-four hours of the session.) In about 10 percent of the cases the apparitions appear to come out of the mirror, and in another 10 percent of cases clients seem to journey into the mirror to meet their intended party. Moody indicates that everyone who has had a reunion like this invariably says it was *real* and profoundly affecting.[29]

Reviewing the surprising success rate of mirror gazing, Moody suggests several applications for this technique. He believes it should definitely be used in grief therapy and suggests that it might also provide a breakthrough in attempts to study spirit contacts scientifically, since its success rate is so high. He himself began giving demonstrations of mirror gazing in his classes to get his students more involved in the study of psychology.

Possible Explanations for "Spirit Contacts"

From a Christian perspective, the beginning point for explaining the current rash of spirit contacts is to consult the Bible to find out what types of spiritual contacts are possible. It is clear from Scripture that contacts between humans and supernatural beings—whether God, the Holy Spirit, angels, demons or Satan—are definitely possible. But the Bible does not tell us whether it is possible for living humans to see or interact with spirits of the dead, apart from God's permission and intervention.

Aside from Jesus' own appearances after his death, which constitute a special case, only twice in the Bible are such interactions recorded. One was the transfiguration, when Peter, James and John were allowed to watch and listen as Jesus conversed with Moses and Elijah, who had lived on earth centuries earlier (Mt 17:2-4). (Elijah didn't die because he was taken up to heaven in a whirlwind [2 Kings 2:11-12], but Moses did [Deut 34:5].) God evidently used this powerful supernatural event to authenticate Jesus' divinity.

In the other case King Saul sought to communicate with the dead prophet Samuel through a medium at Endor (1 Sam 28:7-19). The medium succeeded in contacting Samuel but was evidently shocked and terrified at what transpired. She recognized Saul, which contributed to her fear, because the king had previously expelled all the spiritists and mediums from the land on threat of death.

Saul paid a heavy price for this and other acts of disobedience. Samuel told him that God had become his enemy and prophesied with deadly accuracy that Saul and his sons would be killed by the Philistines the next day. In this case it would seem that God allowed Samuel to appear to make Saul's disobedience an object lesson for the Jews—and for later believers who would read about the incident.

Even though the Bible does not tell us whether unsanctioned contacts between the living and the dead are possible, it does tell us very clearly that we are not to seek such contacts or to consort with evil spirits. In Leviticus God warns the Israelites not to engage in divination (seeking to know the future or hidden information through spirit contacts) or sorcery (seeking to harm others by manipulating supernatural power; Lev 19:26). He says, "Do not turn to mediums or seek out spiritists, for you will be defiled by them. I am the LORD your God" (19:31). "I will set my face against the person who turns to mediums and spiritists to prostitute himself by following them, and I will cut him off from his people" (20:6). "A man or woman who is a medium or spiritist among you must be put to death. You are to stone them; their blood will be on their own heads" (20:27).

In the same vein, God warns the Israelites,

When you enter the land the LORD your God is giving you, do not learn to imitate the detestable ways of the nations there. Let no one be found among you who sacrifices his son or daughter in the fire, who practices divination or sorcery, interprets omens, engages in witchcraft, or casts spells, or who is a medium or spiritist or who consults the dead. Anyone who does these things is detestable to the LORD, and because of these detestable practices the LORD your God will drive out those nations before you. (Deut 18:9-12)

Two Old Testament passages help explain why such practices are detestable to God. According to Deuteronomy 32:15-17,

He [Israel] abandoned the God who made him
and rejected the Rock his Savior.

They made him jealous with their foreign gods
    and angered him with their detestable idols.
They sacrificed to demons, which are not God.

As I pointed out in chapter six, Psalm 106:34-37 similarly rebukes the Israelites for turning to idols and demonic powers. These passages and others indicate that in the worst case, idol worship amounts to spiritual prostitution, substituting the worship of demons for the worship of Almighty God. They also suggest that practices like divination, witchcraft, mediumship, spiritism and consulting the dead, which were an integral part of the pagan religious systems of the Canaanites, are likely to involve or invite demonic activity.

Using scriptural guidelines, we cannot rule out the possibility that some spontaneous contacts with spirits of the dead are genuine. We do not fully understand the way the Holy Spirit works, and it is at least conceivable that some contacts may be gifts from a loving God to reassure those who are grieving. Yet this does not seem consistent with God's strong prohibitions against seeking such contacts. Would he allow people to have spontaneous experiences of this type which might encourage them to seek further contacts or to discount his warnings about dabbling in this area? This doesn't seem very likely.

Although we cannot be sure, there is probably one conclusion we *can* draw. Based on God's sovereignty over human life, it is probably safe to say that human beings cannot actually contact the dead except by God's provision and according to his will. If this is so, though, it must mean that many of the apparent contacts between the living and the dead that are being reported today are not genuine, and we need to search elsewhere to find suitable explanations for them.

Possible Natural Explanations

The most obvious natural explanation for the apparent spirit contacts that are occurring is that they are imaginary—the joint effect of strong desires, misinterpretations of natural events and being in an altered state of consciousness. Altered states seem particularly relevant here, because channelers and mediums appear to work in trance states, people using psycho-manteums do so in deep states of relaxation, and many of the spontaneous contacts with spirits apparently occur at night, when people are more relaxed or prone to sleep.

Yet it is apparent from Moody's work that people do not need to be in an altered state to have very profound experiences. In 25 percent of the cases he collected, the contacts occurred *after* the person had left the psychomanteum and had ostensibly reentered a normal conscious state.

In the case of channelers, evidence suggests that some entities (or at least some of their messages) are being created in the channeler's own mind. Many messages contain material that is mundane, meaningless or inaccurate—hardly the type of performance that one would expect from a spiritual entity with a superior intellect.[30] In *The Aquarian Gospel of Jesus Christ,* channeled by Levi Dowling, the source wrongly names Herod Antipas instead of Herod the Great as the ruler of Jerusalem when Jesus was born, states that Jesus once visited the city of Lahore in Pakistan—even though Lahore didn't exist until six hundred years after Christ—and asserts that Jesus visited the magicians in Persepolis, although that city was destroyed by Alexander the Great in 330 B.C. and was never rebuilt. In spite of such mistakes, many readers accept Dowling's book as "proof" of Jesus' occult past.[31]

In many cases channeled materials are limited by the intellectual capacities and grammatical competence of the channeler.[32] If a channeler makes certain grammatical errors in normal speech, the same mistakes are likely to appear when he or she is channeling. It is also of interest that channelers themselves are often unsure how much of their message is coming from their own mind and how much from some other source. Because of this confusion, some channelers speculate that their primary source might actually be the Higher Self. But to them this is still acceptable, since the Higher Self is thought to be a reliable source of spiritual information.[33]

In cases where the channeled entities are not real, channelers are apparently either fooling themselves or engaged in deliberate fraud. In the latter case they could be faking to gain fame and fortune, or perhaps to promote a particular worldview. In our current climate, mysticism is in, skepticism is on the decline, and channeling can be very lucrative. The fraud explanation is also consistent with what we know about the mediums of the recent past. Almost all were caught using trickery to make their performances more convincing. History may simply be repeating itself.

One self-deception hypothesis that has been offered suggests that channelers are deceiving themselves by slipping into a self-induced hypnotic trance. This explanation is intriguing, because all the elements of channeling can sometimes be seen in hypnosis. If a hypnotist suggests the presence of a fictitious character, highly susceptible subjects will interact with the character as if it were real. Some very susceptible subjects can be hypnotically regressed to a "former life" and start acting like different people, complete with new mannerisms and accents and unique life histories. Proponents of the hypnotic explanation argue that if hypnotic regression can stimulate the imagination to create another person, the hypnotic state should also be capable of conjuring up a convincing entity during a channeling session.[34] For this to work, however, channelers would have to be very susceptible to hypnosis and able to enter and exit deep trance states without the aid of a hypnotist. This does not seem very likely.

A second version of the self-deception hypothesis suggests that channelers are afflicted with multiple personality disorder (MPD) and their channeled entities are simply misidentified alternate personalities. Unfortunately, this hypothesis still doesn't explain very much, because clinicians do not yet have a good understanding of MPD. To muddy the waters still further, some clinicians who have worked with MPD patients suggest that at least some the alternate personalities in MPD are due to possession, either by discarnate human spirits or by demons.[35]

Spirit Contacts and Demons

Several lines of evidence suggest demons may be involved in channeling. In the first place, biblical warnings would lead us to believe that channeling, like mediumship, very likely invites demonic activity and deception. In the second place, channeling resembles demon possession. According to the channelers, they are allowing powerful spirit beings to enter and control their bodies while they are "set aside" and are not aware of what is going on. They appear to manifest other personalities when these beings are in charge.

A third argument for demonic involvement in channeling comes from the messages the channelers receive. These echo New Age themes and even some haunting refrains from the Garden of Eden: "Trust in your Higher Self, which is God within you. It will never mislead you. Partake generously of the fruit God has forbidden (interactions with the spirit realm), because this will make you wise and powerful like a god. Don't be afraid of death or God's punishment; both are only illusions." Even channeled messages about the Higher Self are suspect. Why should the Higher Self seem alien or be so difficult to contact if it is really an integral part of the self? And why do channeled entities so often admonish their followers to follow its dictates without question? Might this not be a coverup for demonic activity in a person's life?

Those who are experimenting with the psychomanteum are also walking on dangerous ground. Even though this practice may seem innocent enough to some people (like a fascinating and effective way to alleviate grief), the use of the psychomanteum to contact dead loved ones is a form of divination. It is an attempt to learn hidden things about the spirit world and death through contacts with spirits. So this too is an open door for deception.

The messages coming through departed loved ones in psychomanteum-induced encounters are suspect, because they are too reassuring and bland. "All is well." "We are fine." "We are waiting for you." There is no urgency. People are not being admonished to accept Jesus Christ, to hold fast to their faith in a darkening world or to tell others that they need to accept Jesus as Lord or be lost forever. The messages that are coming forth are very similar to those being reported by near-death experiencers. Both promote an easy form of universalism. In essence they are telling people to relax and enjoy their lives, because everyone gets to heaven in due time.

Conclusions

All these observations imply that demons may well be involved in a number of contemporary spirit-contact experiences, especially those that are deliberately sought out. But lest we attribute too much to demons, we need to remind ourselves that the nature and extent of their involvement probably vary greatly from one situation to the next. At one end of the spectrum, it is likely that a number of seeming contacts with spirits have natural causes. For example, one may have a strong sense of another's presence simply because of a sudden vivid memory. Memories of this type can be triggered by smells or sights that are particularly associated with the person. Such memories can evoke strong emotions.

There are probably other cases in which demonic influence is indirect—for instance, encouraging an erstwhile medium or channeler to lie, cheat and defraud other people. Some psychomanteum experiences may simply be hallucinations, brought on by entering a very relaxed (hypnotic?) state with strong expectations and memories. Other psychomanteum episodes may involve deceptive visions and/or the actual manifestation of a masquerading demon. It is very interesting in this regard that Moody actually describes psychomanteum-induced contacts as "*visionary* apparitions." Finally, it is quite possible that some channelers are indwelt by demons who are posing as wise and helpful entities.

10

UFO Experiences

I f you have recently picked up a popular book on UFOs or perused any of the sensational headlines about UFOs on supermarket tabloids, you are probably wondering whether this topic is actually serious enough to write about. It is, because UFO experiences and messages from beings who claim to be from outer space are becoming increasingly influential in New Age circles, and well beyond.[1] At the behest of these strange voices, some people have made drastic changes in their lives, leaving responsible positions with good salaries, moving from urban to rural areas, adopting simple lifestyles, and then waiting trustingly for further orders.[2]

In addition to this small core of people who take UFOs very seriously, there is a much larger group of Westerners who at least believe UFOs are plausible. According to a 1990 Gallup Poll, 47 percent of Americans questioned said they believed UFOs are real, and 14 percent claimed they had actually seen them.[3] In another survey taken the same year, 54 percent agreed with the statement "Some unidentified flying objects are really space vehicles from other civilizations."[4] According to William Alnor, a Christian who is actively researching this field, beliefs in UFOs are at an all-time high around the world. In recent years major UFO conferences have been held in Europe, Russia and Japan, as well as the United States, and UFO cults are spreading rapidly, even in Two-Thirds World countries.[5]

The field of UFOlogy is currently a divided house. There are a few well-trained, careful researchers with good scientific credentials whose work is both believable and important, but there are also scores of self-styled "experts" who are not trained as scientists and who seem more interested in proving their theories or providing sensational copy than in careful investigation. This latter group is turning out popular books and articles with such outlandish claims that they are making the entire field look farcical. In fact, the atmosphere that now exists has apparently driven many responsible investigators from the field.

Tales of Abduction

Much of the sensationalizing and speculation centers on UFO abduction stories. In these accounts, aliens impose a trancelike state on human beings, forcefully remove them to waiting UFOs and then subject them to traumatic medical exams with heavy sexual overtones. A major problem with these abduction stories is the fact that they are almost always obtained under hypnosis, often with heavy-handed questioning—circumstances likely to produce a great deal of confabulation.

Unfortunately, the people who are collecting these stories often have only minimal training in psychology or hypnosis, and they tend to ignore the problems because their direct manner of questioning produces the results they expect. In their own thinking, the fact that witnesses usually do not recall abductions or medical exams unless they are hypnotized proves that the aliens tried to erase these memories, and the fact that they obtain very similar testimonies from many different witnesses validates their beliefs that the abductions are real. Because they trust their methods, they believe what the witnesses tell them. But the data they have obtained in this manner has led them into the wildest kinds of speculation.[6]

Other factors, like deliberate deception and hoaxing on the part of individuals and sects who want to perpetuate saucer myths, have added to the current confusion.[7] In fact, the testimony of one of the most widely known abduction witnesses, Whitley Strieber, is now suspect. Strieber wrote two long, shocking accounts of his abductions which became best-sellers, and one of these, *Communion*, was even made into a movie.[8] Recently, however, Strieber has completely reversed his position on UFO abductions. Along with the last edition of *Communion Letter*, a regular newsletter that he published for subscribers, he sent a letter to his readers that stated, "[The UFOlogists'] interpretation of the visitor experience is rubbish from beginning to end. The abduction reports that they generate are not real. They are artifacts of hypnosis and cultural conditioning. What is really behind our experience? We are."[9]

Strieber does not come out and say in this letter that his own abduction accounts are not to be believed, but this is implied. He may or may not be implying that his own experiences were confabulated under hypnosis or were fiction from the start. Strieber is a fiction writer, and judging by his prior publications, *The Wolfen* and *The Hunger* (which his editors described on a flyleaf in *Communion* as "a novel of terror beyond your imagining" and "the ultimate novel of erotic hunger"), he would certainly have been capable of creating *Communion* from his own imagination. Strieber reassures his readers in *Communion* (p. 4) that most of what he is relating in the book existed in clear, normal memory *before he was hypnotized* to help him remember the details. All in all, it is difficult to tell whether Strieber is a victim or an opportunist who took advantage of a lucrative market and a convenient way out.

At any rate, sensational abduction testimonies plus deliberate deceptions and hoaxes have all contributed to wild rumors that the U.S. government is secretly cooperating with the aliens, that they have joint, top-secret bases under the desert in Nevada and New Mexico, that the aliens are doing genetic experiments in an effort to interbreed with the human race and so on. Responsible investigators protest that rumors like these are proliferating without a shred of substantial evidence.[10]

On the saner side of UFOlogy, one of the most respected and careful UFO researchers is Jacques Vallee, who has training in astrophysics and computer science. His interest in UFOs was piqued early in his career when he observed two unexplainable objects with a small telescope. Checking around, he found that other colleagues and professional astronomers had seen the same objects, but as was their custom, they had systematically destroyed the pertinent data because they couldn't account for it by known physical principles. This attitude angered Vallee and launched him into his own thirty-year attempt to study the phenomenon as thoroughly and objectively as possible.

Vallee is one of the most vocal critics and debunkers of much of the popular UFO hysteria, yet he also believes there is a genuine, worldwide UFO phenomenon that is supported by the testimony of thousands of reliable witnesses.[11] In support of this thesis he points out that the number of remote sightings of UFOs is now enormous, and he estimates that there have been at least five thousand documented cases of "close encounters" in which witnesses have watched UFOs at close range, often seeing or even interacting indirectly with their occupants.[12] In a sizable number of cases, multiple witnesses have observed the same event, and in some instances there have apparently been physical signs of landing—patterned indentations in the ground, burnt patches of grass, higher-than-normal levels of radiation and lower-than-normal levels of microorganisms in the soil surrounding the landing site.[13] Vallee argues that this data shouldn't simply be ignored.

Historical and Cultural Perspectives on UFOs

One of Vallee's major contributions has been to show that UFO phenomena are not just a recent development. He found that very similar events have been recorded for centuries. Mysterious flying objects, lights and signs in the sky were apparently common at times over Japan and Western Europe during the Middle Ages.[14] Certain religious miracles, like the appearances of "Mary" at Fatima (in Portugal in 1917), at Lourdes (in France in 1858) and near Mexico City in 1531 ("Mary of Guadalupe"), are strikingly similar to UFO encounters. In both situations, witnesses see strange globes of light of varying intensity, luminous entities that appear close to or within the light, miraculous healings, and other unusual events. Vallee argues, fairly persuasively, that both types of event are probably being staged by the same agents.[15]

Closer to our own time, there was a wave of sightings of a mysterious "flying machine" over many parts of the United States in the late 1890s. It started in 1896, when startled residents of San Francisco spotted a large, elongated dark object in the sky that carried brilliant searchlights and was capable of flying against the wind. Later, beginning in April 1897, this object made an astonishing number of appearances in the Midwest, often traveling slowly and majestically over large urban areas like Omaha, Milwaukee and Chicago, where large crowds gathered to watch the spectacle.

Witnesses described the craft as having turbines, wheels, wings, powerful lights and a glass cockpit through which the occupants were clearly visible. Some people said the occupants looked strange, but most thought they looked like normal humans. At times the airship abandoned its stately pace and darted about like a modern UFO, changing course and altitude abruptly, swooping at impossible speeds, circling, landing, taking off or sweeping the countryside with powerful beams of light. It also made mechanical noises, like the clunking and rumbling of engines or the whooshes made by compressed air.

On occasion farmers in the Midwest were startled to see the contraption sitting on the ground right on their own land, apparently being "fixed" by one of its occupants. By and large these occupants looked and acted like the farmers—they were taciturn, bearded and dressed in clothes of the period. They usually asked the farmers for some simple thing, like a flask of water from the well or some other common object. But when the farmers became curious and wanted to see the "airship" at closer range, the pilots let it be known in no uncertain terms that they were not at liberty to let them in.[16]

Starting in 1946, right after World War II, Americans and people in other parts of the world started spotting UFOs that looked like "flying saucers" or alien spacecraft. These also had elongated shapes, carried bright lights and maneuvered at impossible speeds and angles. However, these models were more advanced than the airships seen fifty years earlier. They were not equipped with obvious mechanical devices, nor did they make throbbing engine sounds. They would hover silently or whir and hum, making noises like those that come from powerful electrical equipment.

These vessels were sleek and sophisticated and appeared to be powered by an advanced propulsion system. And the occupants of the saucers looked different from the pilots of the airships. Most still looked like humans, although they were dressed quite differently, but others looked like aliens. These were humanoid in the sense that they had heads, eyes, bodies, arms and legs, but they were also markedly different from humans. The UFOnauts sported evidences of advanced technology, such as weapons that could stun or paralyze people with rays of light.

In recent years the predominant shape of UFOs has changed again. People are still seeing saucers, but more frequently they are reporting craft with a triangular shape.[17] One recent rash of sightings of this type occurred over Belgium. According to a report in the October 10, 1990, edition of *The Wall Street Journal*, there were more than twenty-six hundred sightings in that country in the course of that year.

UFO sightings since 1946 have usually occurred in waves. Typically there are a number of sightings in the same area over a period of weeks or months, and then the activity stops, reappearing somewhere else after a time. These waves now seem to be occurring at shorter intervals, and the number of sightings and close encounters being reported worldwide appears to be increasing.

One wave of sightings occurred in northern Israel, near Mt. Carmel. From December 1990 through 1992 there were at least two hundred sightings in this region. Reports of landings (many close to Elijah's cave) and "strange fire" also became increasingly common during that period. These events, plus the fact that Mt. Carmel is only twenty miles from the Valley of Armageddon, apparently set off speculations in the region that these events are important signs and portents of things to come.[18]

The Appearance of the UFOnauts

From eyewitness accounts, UFOnauts appear to come in great variety.

There are reports of humanoids of giant stature, humans like ourselves, winged creatures, dwarfs that are dark and hairy with bright eyes and deep voices, dwarfs with smooth, pale, gray complexions, oversized heads and silvery voices. Curiously, the latter two types are similar to the "gnomes" and "sylphs" described in medieval literature.[19]

Another very interesting characteristic UFOnauts display is an ability to change their appearance, chameleonlike, depending on the culture they are visiting. In the United States they sometimes look like science-fiction monsters, in South America they appear sanguine and quick to fight, in France they behave like rational, peace-loving tourists, and as we have already seen, in the Midwest of the 1890s they looked like rugged individualists, much like the American farmers of the time.[20]

The Psychological and Spiritual Impact of UFO Encounters

The psychological impact of UFO sightings varies a great deal, depending on the perceived strangeness and closeness of the contact. Many of the brief sightings that occur at a distance probably do not have much of an impact on people's beliefs. Witnesses simply do not know what to make of these incidents, and feeling no urgency to assimilate them, they simply file them away in a compartment of memory.

In the 1890s, when the American populace was confronted by the "airship" and its occupants, most apparently greeted the spectacle with amazement, curiosity and a sense that there was definitely something strange going on. Yet these sightings apparently did not produce a great deal of fear or foreboding, because the pilots looked human and the airship resembled what the people imagined an elaborate flying machine might look like. (According to current expert opinion, however, a physical craft like this would not have been able to fly on its own due to its poor aerodynamic design!) The fact that most witnesses saw the airship only from a distance and for a brief time also minimized its impact.

More recent "close encounters," which involve watching a UFO close at hand, seeing it land and perhaps getting a glimpse of its occupants, have been harder for witnesses to assimilate. Such experiences are full of contradictions. UFOs seem to violate the laws of physics. They may swoop, rise straight up at impossible speeds or simply vanish in midair, and their occupants often look like something out of a science-fiction movie. The very thought that such things actually exist strongly contradicts both consensual reality and everyday experience. Yet these encounters seem real, not imaginary. Such inherent contradictions impel witnesses to search for plausible explanations. They are often forced to reevaluate some of their basic religious beliefs in the process.

Another characteristic of the UFO encounter that encourages such reevaluation is its spiritual impact. Curiously, even though the UFO phenomenon seems to offer a rational explanation for itself (that is, the UFOnauts must be beings that evolved, or were created, on another planet), witnesses usually interpret these events as more than accidental encounters with other physical beings. To witnesses the experiences seem to carry important *spiritual* implications. Witnesses often get the impression that they have been selected for contact and that the event has some revelatory purpose.[21]

Starting in the early 1970s a mystical element was added to the UFO encounters. At this point contactees began reporting unusual psychic events in connection with their experiences. These included dreaming of a sighting before it occurred, hearing distinct messages within one's head before and after the contact, precognition of future events, and episodes of apparent telepathic communication. Some contactees were reportedly healed of chronic ailments, and a few even had out-of-body or levitation experiences. Since the 1970s these "paranormal" side effects have apparently become the rule rather than the exception.

The aftereffects of UFO contacts of this type can be profound. They can precipitate significant changes in lifestyle, alter religious beliefs and leave contactees with "paranormal" talents that are difficult for them to cope with. Based on his research, Vallee believes that major encounters of this type are much more frequent than anyone realizes. He has found that only a small percentage of those who have had such experiences will come forward on their own initiative and share them with researchers. This means that the frequency of such encounters is probably being greatly underestimated.[22]

Two Popular Explanations for UFOs

UFOs are commonly accounted for in one of two ways, either by the "natural phenomenon" explanation or by the "extraterrestrial" hypothesis. According to the former, all the apparent UFO incidents can be explained in terms of ordinary physical principles. Remote sightings of UFOs are usually explained as misperceptions of airplanes, man-made satellites, stars, planets (especially Venus), luminous swamp gas or earthquake lights (electrical discharges set off by earthquakes). Close encounters with UFOs are attributed to hoaxes, deliberate storytelling, overactive imaginations, self-deception, false memories created under hypnosis and the like. According to Vallee, the strict naturalistic explanation is generally favored by skeptics and scientists who are unfamiliar with some of the reliable observational data that is available.[23]

In actuality, natural explanations of this sort evidently do account for many apparent UFO incidents. Yet they do not do a good job of explaining certain features of other experiences, like UFOs' ability to move in ways that appear to violate the laws of physics, or times that many reliable witnesses, interviewed separately, report seeing the same aerial maneuverings or the same UFOnauts emerging from a spacecraft.[24]

According to the extraterrestrial hypothesis, UFOs are physical space vehicles controlled by intelligent beings from some other part of the universe who are probably visiting Earth as part of a scientific survey. Vallee argues that this explanation fails on several counts. For one, it seems unlikely that the UFOs and their occupants are physical unless they have learned to manipulate space and time in ways we can scarcely imagine. The craft and their pilots have the ability to appear and disappear instantaneously, to alter their shapes and appearance continuously and even to merge with other objects.

In addition, the sheer number of sightings and close encounters now on record argues against an extraterrestrial hypothesis. Vallee estimates that there are at least five thousand close encounters on record. Research indicates that most of these occur late at night, either around 12:00 midnight or at 3:00 a.m., when most people are sleeping and frequency of incidental sightings would therefore be low. If these "landings" were deliberately being scheduled to minimize the possibility of detection, the actual number of landings would probably be at least ten times greater than the number of sightings that have been reported. However, fifty thousand landings are far more than would be needed to collect enough plant, animal and mineral specimens for a scientific survey![25]

A third argument Vallee raises against the extraterrestrial hypothesis is the observation that UFO sightings are not a recent phenomenon. They have apparently been occurring throughout recorded history, and certainly for the last six hundred years or so. UFOs and their occupants apparently change their appearance to adjust to the cultural expectations of the people who see them. In fact, they consistently stay about one jump ahead of human technology and ideas. (Some of the features of UFO encounters are actually anticipated in works of fiction several years before they are reported.) Vallee argues that *physical* extraterrestrials from some remote location in the heavens who were engaged in a scientific survey wouldn't stay near Earth so long and wouldn't or couldn't change their appearance as readily as the agents humans have been observing.[26]

Vallee derives a fourth argument against the extraterrestrial hypothesis from the peculiarities of the medical exams that are ostensibly carried out during abductions. So far there have been at least six hundred reported cases of medical exams that involve the removal of bodily fluids and tissues. Almost invariably abductees say these exams are traumatic, and many ostensibly leave visible scars. These facts are puzzling in light of current medical capabilities.

If UFOnauts were really interested in secret, large-scale collections of human blood, sperm or ova, they could get such materials faster and with less possibility of detection by raiding blood and sperm banks or collections of embryos at major research hospitals. It is not necessary to inflict pain or leave scars to collect fluid and tissue samples; human doctors routinely take such samples for lab tests. Even the UFOnauts' apparent (but unsuccessful) attempts to erase memories are suspect, because medical doctors now routinely administer drugs that *completely* erase memory during surgery. If we were dealing with advanced aliens, they should be able to carry out all these procedures at least as effectively as human doctors.

On the basis of these arguments and observations, Vallee concludes that the purpose of the apparent abductions and exams must not be the collection of biological samples, but rather the creation of a particular kind of experience. In short, he thinks these experiences are being staged, deliberately, *as a way to manipulate human beliefs.*[27]

Vallee's Conclusions About UFOs

Vallee rejects both the natural phenomenon and the extraterrestrial explanations for UFOs and draws some striking conclusions of his own. He believes that the UFOnauts are real, conscious beings, but he doubts that they are physical, because of their ability to transcend time and space. He concludes that they are probably based on or near Earth rather than somewhere in outer space, because they have apparently been making regular contacts with humans throughout the centuries. He observes, "If there is a form of life and consciousness that operates on properties of space time that we have not discovered, then it doesn't have to be extraterrestrial. It could come from any place, and any time, even from our own environment. . . . *It could also coexist with us and remain undetected*"[28] (italics added).

As a third point, Vallee warns his readers that the UFOnauts may not be as benign or as interested in human welfare as they would like us to believe. He bases this conclusion on the observation that their contacts with humans have been consistently deceptive or manipulative, and in all known cases of verbal communication their assertions have been systematically misleading.[29] Finally, Vallee wrestles with the question of what these agents are trying to accomplish through their contacts. He concludes that all of their actions, now and through the ages, seem to have been directed toward one major purpose: *to manipulate and control our religious beliefs.*

Vallee suspects that the UFO mythology that is presently shaping up may be preparing us for a new form of religion (and a "New Age" of irrationality and mysticism). Through his extensive travels and contacts he has found that there are now UFO/New Age subcultures in every country which subscribe to the belief that humans have a higher destiny, that we are now poised on the brink of incredible spiritual growth and that the Space Brothers are here to help us make that transition at the appropriate time. Other elements in this new belief system include an increased acceptance of "paranormal" powers, growing faith in helpful spirit beings, and a new hope that these beings will "save" enlightened human beings from the destruction and upheaval that is predicted to come upon the earth.[30]

This latter message came through very pointedly while Vallee was participating in a panel discussion with Andrija Puharich and others at a New Age conference in San Francisco. Describing his latest experiences with Uri Geller, Puharich explained to the audience that he was regularly receiving messages from some mysterious cosmic source on his tape recorder, but the tapes kept vanishing and there was nothing he could do to prevent it. Puharich told the audience that experiences like these had convinced him that both he and Geller are being guided by a very high source of wisdom. He then commented that the only course for humankind was to place its destiny firmly in the hands of these helpful spirits.

Vallee was greatly disturbed by this. He asked, "Shouldn't we know something more about the helpful stranger before we jump on board? . . . When we are asked to suspend all our rational thoughts, to forget our obsolete critical faculties, to throw control overboard, then the time has come to take all the data and go away with it to a quiet place to think."[31]

Christian Perspectives on the UFO Phenomenon

The time has also come for us to take all this data and try to make sense of it. Considering the three explanations for UFOs that have been discussed, I believe we can immediately rule out the extraterrestrial hypothesis on the basis of Vallee's expert opinion that it doesn't fit the data. But the proposition that some apparent UFO sightings might be due to natural causes, whether physical or psychological, does have merit. This hypothesis seems especially plausible in cases where a person simply sees a distant moving light that *could* be a UFO. Any ambiguous physical event like this, plus a little imagination, could easily create the impression of a UFO sighting. However, the naturalistic hypothesis does not adequately explain sightings in which one or several credible witnesses see a UFO maneuvering and landing at close range.

Human factors may also be at work in apparent abduction episodes. For instance, episodes that are "remembered" under hypnotic examination may be unintentionally confabulated. This seems especially likely in the case of witnesses who come to an abduction specialist of their own accord, already familiar with other abduction accounts and convinced that they too have had such an experience. In such a case it probably wouldn't take much prompting for a hypnotized witness to come up with a compelling story. Other abduction accounts may be deliberately faked.

Still, assuming that some abduction witnesses are truthfully describing what they do remember, there are two aspects of these experiences that are not so easy to explain. Before they are hypnotized, many witnesses say they remember seeing a UFO, watching it at close range and being conscious after the episode; yet there seems to be a gap in time and memory between these last two events. It is difficult to explain what they saw before this lapse or why they apparently lost memory of it.

From a Christian perspective, Vallee's explanation of UFOs is the most striking because of its parallels with demonic activity. UFO investigators have noticed these similarities. Vallee himself, drawing from extrabiblical literature on demonic activities, establishes a number of parallels between the UFOnauts and demons. But he carefully avoids saying that the two are one and the same.[32] Pierre Guerin, a UFO researcher and a scientist associated with the French National Council for Scientific Research, is not so cautious: "The modern UFOnauts and the demons of past days are probably identical."[33] Veteran researcher John Keel, who wrote *UFOs: Operation Trojan Horse* and other books on this subject, comes to the same conclusion: "The UFO manifestations seem to be, by and large, merely minor variations of the age-old demonological phenomenon."[34]

To appreciate these parallels, take a moment to review Vallee's main conclusions. UFOnauts are real, but not physical, and they can transcend space and time as we know it. They are based on or near the earth, and in fact may be coexisting with us. They are consistently deceptive and manipulative, and their major purpose is to shape and control our religious beliefs.

Now consider Ephesians 6:10-12, where Paul warns Christians, "Finally, be strong in the Lord and in his mighty power. Put on the full armor of God so that you can take your stand against the devil's schemes. For our struggle is not against flesh and blood, but against the rulers, against the authorities, against the powers of this dark world and against the spiritual forces of evil in the heavenly realms." This one passage tells us that unseen, intelligent aliens (nonhumans) dwell among us and "in the heavenly realms," probably close to the earth. They are spiritual beings, so they do transcend space and time. (This means it would probably not be difficult for them to move in ways that physical objects cannot, or to change their appearance at will.) This passage also tells us that demons are powerful, organized opponents who scheme to deceive us.

In John 8:44-45 Jesus describes Satan this way: "He was a murderer from the beginning, not holding to the truth, for there is no truth in him. When he lies, he speaks his native language, for he is a liar and the father of lies." This and other passages indicate that Satan and his legions are exceptionally adept at deception and cunning manipulation. And it probably goes without saying that one of Satan's primary aims is to control and manipulate religious beliefs, in an effort to keep people from seeing the truth and turning to Jesus Christ.

The parallels between Vallee's description of UFOnauts and the biblical portrayal of demons is just too striking to ignore. The question is apparently not *whether* demons are involved in UFO incidents but *how* and to what extent.

Considering what we know about the usual activities of demons, there are several possibilities. They may be encouraging some of the deception and hoaxes that are being carried out (although humans are perfectly capable of doing these things on their own). This is highly speculative, but demons may be shaping abduction episodes in witnesses' minds through visions while the witnesses are in an altered state. This might happen while they are hypnotized or during the "lost time" that follows some UFO encounters. In partial support of this idea, UFO researcher Jenny Randles has discovered that witnesses do seem to enter an altered state during the abduction experience. They describe going through a "breakpoint" in time, after which they leave ordinary space-time behind and appear to be moving through a lucid dream until they return to normal consciousness.[35]

In the close encounters in which credible witnesses see globes of light, spacecraft and/or alien beings, demons may again be inducing visions or possibly making themselves visible. (Angels are able to make themselves visible, and demons are described as fallen angels in the Bible.[36])

In the final analysis, of course, we can only speculate about the degree of demonic involvement and their mode of intervention in UFO incidents. The one thing that is clear about these incidents is that they are working to Satan's advantage. UFO experiences, like other mystical experiences that are now in evidence, can shake up witnesses' religious beliefs and draw them away from the truth.

11

The Larger
Picture

*T*hus far I have examined "New Mysticism," a loose collection of beliefs and mystical perspectives that could potentially coalesce into a new religious system in the United States and other Western countries. I have identified the beliefs that are incorporated in this system, tracing their origins to Eastern and New Age thought, contemporary psychology, spiritualism, paganism and Christianity. I have also scrutinized some of the experiences that appear to be validating these beliefs and giving them impetus: near-death and out-of-body experiences (NDEs and OBEs), "paranormal" incidents, unusual healings, kundalini arousal, channeling, spontaneous and psychomanteum-induced contacts with spirits, and UFO encounters. In addition, we have explored the characteristics of altered states of consciousness and noted how closely they are associated with extraordinary experiences. It is now time to step back from this peculiar montage and examine the larger picture.

From this perspective, two arresting features come sharply into focus: the diverse mystical experiences have some striking commonalities, and these experiences are shaping beliefs, both in individuals and in Western culture as a whole.

Common Elements in Current Mystical Experiences

The common features of these varied experiences are particularly informative.

1. *All the experiences appear to convey a spiritual message.* From the point of view of experiencers, these events afford a glimpse into another reality, strengthening their belief in the existence of higher spiritual powers and reassuring them that there is more to human life than mere physical existence.

2. *Virtually all the experiences seem very real and very meaningful.* When experiencers describe these events, they stress their reality and meaningfulness in very emphatic terms. They use words and phrases like "astounding," "eye-opening," "life-changing," "of ultimate importance in my life." Experiencers seem utterly sincere and insistent on this point.

3. *The experiences are timely.* They are occurring at a time when our culture seems increasingly ready to accept them and many people are actively pursuing them.

4. *Most of these experiences are associated with altered states of consciousness.* This appears to be a very consistent and important feature of the mystical experiences we have considered. To review briefly: hypnotic, sensory-deprivation, drug and Eastern meditative states have all served as prior conditions for ecstatic visions, visits to otherworldly places and encounters with various spirit beings. OBEs most frequently occur during deep relaxation or in a twilight state of sleep, but can also occur in other altered states. NDEs occur when the NDEr is close to, or in, an unconscious state. Channelers appear to operate in trance states. Deep relaxation apparently facilitates visionary apparitions in the psychomanteum. Many spontaneous spirit contacts and UFO sightings occur at night, when people are relaxed and sleepy or have just awakened from sleep. Some UFO episodes apparently have a dreamy, surrealistic quality. And some UFO abductees report "missing time" and "remember" abduction and examination scenes

through hypnosis or deep relaxation.

All of this strongly suggests that there is a relationship between altered states and mystical experiences, yet this relationship is apparently neither direct (cause-and-effect) nor simple. On the one hand, even though mystical experiences frequently occur in altered states, being in an altered state is not sufficient to produce a mystical experience. In fact, among all the unusual effects that altered states typically produce, true mystical experiences are relatively uncommon. (Mystical encounters do seem to occur more frequently, however, as altered states are deepened, or when certain drugs, like LSD or phencyclidine ["angel dust"], are used.)

On the other hand, it is apparently not necessary to be in an altered state for profound mystical experiences to occur. For instance, among psychomanteum users, 25 percent of those who report apparent contacts with the dead have them sometime after leaving the cubicle, evidently while fully awake and alert. And many close encounters with UFOs appear to occur while witnesses are in full control of their faculties. These two observations suggest that we cannot simply attribute all current unusual experiences to altered states. Something more must be involved.

One thing that is apparent from the data is that altered states are likely to magnify the impact of mystical experiences. As described in chapter four, altered states can evoke vivid imagery, set off unconstrained imaginative processes, intensify emotions and make people very suggestible. They impair judgment and critical thinking and can impart a profound sense of reality, meaning or spiritual significance to just about anything, whether the event has any basis in reality or not.

Demonic invovement may help explain some of the connections between altered states and mystical experiences, especially in cases where experiencers are engaging in practices that are forbidden in the Bible. Demons probably have very limited access to human minds under normal circumstances, especially among Christians. But their influence is probably greater in persons who deliberately turn from God and engage in pagan or spiritualistic practices. Being in an altered state could magnify the impact of any such influence.

Demons may be staging some of these experiences (perhaps in the form of visions) and timing them to occur while experiencers are in altered states to increase their effectiveness. This could explain why the mystical experiences occur frequently in altered states even though altered states are neither necessary nor sufficient to explain all of them. This hypothesis would help account for the occult, antibiblical nature of so many of the experiences. It also leaves open the possibility that some of the unusual experiences have their origins elsewhere—for instance, in the mind/brain system itself.

5. All the experiences that involve apparent spirit contacts convey similar messages. Channeled messages from sources as different as "Seth," Helen Schucman's "Jesus," "Mafu" and the "Space Brothers" are very similar, and they all bear a striking resemblance to New Age thought—which isn't surprising, since New Agers have incorporated channeled information into their belief system from the start. The messages that are coming forth by now have a familiar ring:

☐ "The Higher Self is God within you."

☐ "Physical reality and death are illusions."

☐ "You will not face hell or judgment."

☐ "You have inner spiritual powers that are waiting to be developed."

☐ "Trust us, we are here to help you."

A significant number of channeled messages include implicit or direct attacks on Christians, claiming that we have botched things or misinterpreted and distorted Jesus' teachings. There are also many attacks on the truthfulness of the Bible.

The implied messages from NDE and psychomanteum experiences reinforce these ideas and add some others, suggesting that death is just a transition, that everyone goes to "heaven" and that God accepts everyone so there is no hell or judgment. Both types of experience also convey the idea that it is fine to converse with spirits of the dead or the spirit guides who assist with NDEs. Virtually all of these encounters convey the impression that the spirits involved are good and they have our best interests at heart. Surprisingly, this is true even for many of the UFO witnesses who say they were abducted, terrorized and subjected to traumatic examinations. These witnesses often conclude that they must have needed this type of experience in order to shake up their beliefs and start them on the correct spiritual path.[1]

The similarities in the messages are obvious, but what do they mean? In cases where the "spirit contacts" are imaginary or faked, the similarities undoubtedly reflect the fact that the channelers, NDErs, psychomanteum clients and other advocates share certain beliefs that are manifested in their experiences (or performances). In cases where the spirit contacts are real, the similarities in the messages probably imply that the messages are coming from a common supernatural source—Satan.

6. *Experiences that involve apparent spirit contacts are apparently followed by similar "paranormal" aftereffects.* Kenneth Ring and Christopher Rosing found that 50 percent of the NDErs they studied reported strange aftereffects including peculiar energy flows, ecstatic visions, mysterious trembling and shaking, and episodes of "mind expansion."[2] (As you may recall, Ring interpreted these symptoms as manifestations of kundalini arousal.) Ring, Rosing and other researchers have also found that sizable numbers of NDErs encounter poltergeist activity and report meetings with beings of light, spirits of the dead or UFO contacts. Some say they have acquired unusual powers like ESP or the ability to heal or channel following their experiences.[3] More recently Ring found the same pattern of aftereffects in a set of NDErs and a group of UFO contactees.[4] Strange aftereffects like these can occur in other situations too. The "kundalini" symptoms that Ring identified in NDErs are more typically found in long-term practitioners of Eastern meditation and other religious practices. (See chapter seven.) The poltergeist and spirit-contact phenomena are also commonly associated with occult or spiritualistic practices.

From a Christian perspective, this list of aftereffects looks like just one more indication of demonic involvement. But insiders like Kenneth Ring, who are documenting these effects, give them quite a different spin. When Ring compared NDErs and UFO witnesses, he found some intriguing commonalities between them in addition to the aftereffects. Compared to controls, significant numbers in both groups reported "psychic" episodes or spirit contacts that predated their NDE or UFO experiences and often extended back into childhood.[5]

Based on these and other findings, Ring suggests that the NDEs and UFO episodes are just a part of a larger pattern of spiritual events in the lives of these experiencers. He believes that these multiple experiences are being engineered by spiritual forces and that their ultimate purpose is to transform the experiencers into the "Omega Prototype," the ultimate, enlightened spiritual human being. This forced program of spiritual development, he says, is just beginning and is apparent among NDErs, UFO witnesses and others because they just happen to be more spiritually sensitive than most people. Ring is convinced that these experiencers are simply on the forefront of a wave of change that will soon engulf and transform us all.[6]

The Impact on Belief

One of the most pronounced effects of the mystical experiences considered in this book is their ability to alter beliefs, both in individuals and in society as a whole. Investigators with very different worldviews agree on this point. NDE researchers Kenneth Ring and Bruce Greyson have both concluded that this is one of the most significant effects of the NDE experience.[7] Stanislav and Christina Grof (also of New Age persuasion) argue that belief change is the primary effect of many "spiritual" experiences, including shamanic crises (painful, involuntary visionary episodes involving attacks and tortures by demons, which ostensibly prepare shamans for their calling), meditation-based experiences and kundalini arousal, OBEs, paranormal events, channeling, past-lives regressions, spirit contacts and UFO encounters.[8] Traditional scientist Jacques Vallee[9] and a number of Christian investigators[10] have reached similar conclusions about the effect of UFO encounters.

Significantly, these authors also agree that these experiences are not occurring randomly but are the result of deliberate, nonhuman efforts to alter human beliefs. From the New Age perspective the experiences are being orchestrated by benevolent spirits, our "collective unconscious" or the Higher Self to hasten our spiritual advancement. Vallee never clearly states what he thinks the UFO agents are, but he obviously doesn't think their intentions are good. Christian writers invariably identify the UFO-nauts as demons who are using the UFO encounters to confuse people and keep them from turning to Jesus Christ.

Today's mystical experiences affect individuals by challenging their worldview. These experiences contradict the basic tenets of materialism, and most are also unacceptable by strict biblical standards. Yet to experiencers the events seem extraordinarily real and meaningful. To reconcile the contradictions this creates, people must either discount their experiences or modify their beliefs. Unfortunately, it appears that many people are modifying their beliefs rather than questioning the validity of their experiences.

As discussed in chapter seven, such mystical experiences are most likely to have an impact on people who are only modestly committed to their present worldview. Given some recent surveys on religious commitment in America, this is particularly alarming. According to some careful research carried out by John Green, Lyman Kellstedt, James Guth and Corwin Smidt, only 19 percent of American adults are "committed" to their religious beliefs.[11] Another 22 percent are described as "modestly religious," 29 percent as "nominally religious" and 30 percent as "secular."[12] If these estimates are accurate, an increase in the frequency or impact of mystical experiences could serve as an effective means of drawing many people further into mysticism.

In addition to their impact on the beliefs of individuals, mystical experiences are affecting some of our collective beliefs. Today's changing climate and the seeming abundance of extraordinary experiences are helping to create the impression that we are entering a unique, portentous era of human history. New Agers and New Mystics believe this because it fits with their view that we are soon to enter an age of unparalleled spiritual development. Christians also take it seriously because it fits with their belief that Jesus' Second Coming may be near. Yet the impression that we are entering portentous times may or may not be true. Mystical experiences of the type we are seeing now are not new in the long sweep of history, and although they appear to be more frequent now than in living memory—that is, in the past eighty years or so—they may not be more frequent now than they have been at other times in the past, such as at the turn of the twentieth century, when spiritualism was in vogue.

It is also possible that estimates of the frequency and import of mystical experiences are somewhat exaggerated. One factor that could contribute to this is the contrast between our present very open and accepting attitudes toward such events and the skeptical, even sarcastic manner in which they would have been treated just a few years ago. This contrast serves to magnify the importance of these events in our minds.

Today's more open climate makes it much easier for people to talk about their experiences in public without fear of ridicule. Thus part of the perceived increase in the frequency of these events may be due to the fact that people didn't share such experiences in the past but are willing to do so now. Media fascination with the new and the strange is undoubtedly another factor. It is very easy to get a distorted sense of the significance of certain events if the information-gatherers in our mass communications system are selective in their reporting.

A third and very important way in which mystical experiences are shaping collective beliefs is through the support they provide for the religious system that is evolving within New Mysticism. To review briefly, this system retains the idea of a personal, loving Creator God but minimizes or ignores his holiness, righteousness and justice. In this system God does not punish sin and accepts everyone unconditionally (universalism). Jesus is also retained as a great spiritual leader, but he is no longer the Redeemer, nor was his death on the cross necessary for salvation. Many New Mystics believe that Jesus is coming to earth a second time to usher in a new spiritual millennium and that there will be some very difficult times on earth before this is accomplished. But they believe that helpful spirits are standing by to assist the faithful so they can get through these times. Such beliefs about God and Jesus can be traced to channeled materials, especially Schucman's *A Course in Miracles*. The new view of Jesus' Second Coming is currently being promoted by the "Space Brothers."[13]

In this new religious system, humans are portrayed as spiritual beings of great worth and goodness, with unlimited potential and growing spiritual powers. They are "gods" in process who do not die but either go to heaven after their sojourn on earth or are reincarnated. Thus far the problems of evil, sin and injustice have been largely ignored. (Sins are basically treated as mistakes that can be corrected.) Interestingly, unlike many other religious systems, this one does not require people to do good works to get to heaven. People get there because it is their nature to be there and they are already good enough. These views of death and human nature are receiving support from NDEs, OBEs, psychomanteum encounters, episodic "paranormal" incidents and channeled messages.

Another important feature of this new religious system is its open and very trusting view of the spirit world. The various types of spirit contacts that are now in evidence (spontaneous, channeled, psychomanteum-related, UFO contacts, NDEs and others) all reinforce the view that it is not only possible but also quite acceptable to contact spirits of the dead and other spiritual beings for advice and assistance. It is generally assumed that the spirits in question have our best interests at heart and that they are contacting us to assist our spiritual advancement.

Very recently it has become popular within this system and among many New Agers to refer to the various nonhuman spirits as "angels." Books and articles on angels have become a hot commodity. Many of these books are sure to create confusion. Their authors range from conservative evangelicals like Billy Graham, who wrote *Angels: God's Secret Agents* in 1975, to New Mystics who are blending Christian terminology and concepts with what are basically New Age beliefs.

The person who apparently sparked this new interest in angels was novelist Sophy Burnham. Her *A Book of Angels*, which was published in 1990, and its sequel, *Angel Letters*, had together sold approximately 800,000 copies as of December 1993. Burnham ostensibly obtained much of her information for these books from her own guardian angel, Ennis, and his friends Kennish, Asendar and Tallithia. Burnham conducts workshops for people who would like to make firsthand contact with angels. She leads them in guided meditation to silence their minds and activate their imaginations, and when they have settled into their own "sacred spaces" they listen for the voices of angels.[14]

What Do All These Changes Mean?

Christians cannot review the common features of today's mystical experiences, or their impact, without questioning their implications for the future or concluding that Satan and his legions are seriously involved. In fact, it would be very easy just to attribute the current mystical scene to a giant Satanic conspiracy, or perhaps even jump to the conclusion that these events are paving the way for Jesus' Second Coming. But we need to weigh the evidence carefully to avoid hasty or inaccurate conclusions.

In the first place, the idea that Satan is responsible for everything that is happening is an obvious oversimplification, because it leaves out both God's sovereignty over history and human culpability. In my opinion, it also attributes too much power to Satan. The mystical experiences that are attracting so many people are not occurring in a vacuum. Satan would not get far with them if they didn't satisfy a yearning in the human heart.

This yearning is created by a void that has not been filled with God. When we accept Jesus Christ as Savior, his Spirit fills that space within us. We begin to sense his presence and guidance and to recognize his mighty miracles all around us—the uniqueness of earth and its ecosystems, our very existence, the fact that we are perfectly equipped to enjoy our world, the mysterious inner workings of our bodies. But if we reject God's plan of salvation, we remain empty and must rummage around through whatever is left over to try to find meaning and purpose in life. It is evidently at this point that Satan enters the picture, offering all kinds of counterfeit experiences and religious beliefs for the unsaved to pick through.

These interrelationships are very well illustrated in 2 Thessalonians 2:8-12, which describes God's sovereignty, human culpability and Satan's role in the powerful mystical experiences that will be associated with the antichrist ("the lawless one") before Jesus' Second Coming.

> And then the lawless one will be revealed, whom the Lord Jesus will overthrow with the breath of his mouth and destroy by the splendor of his coming. The coming of the lawless one will be in accordance with the work of Satan displayed in all kinds of counterfeit miracles, signs and wonders, and in every sort of evil that deceives those who are perishing. *They perish because they refused to love the truth and so be saved.* For this reason God sends them a powerful delusion so that they will believe the lie and so that all will be condemned who have not believed the truth but have delighted in wickedness.

According to this passage, Satan will be producing some very impressive signs and wonders in the last days, but those who are taken in by them and perish will do so because they refused to accept Jesus Christ as Savior, not because Satan has the power to keep them from being saved. God allows them to become ensnared in Satan's deceptions because they have rejected his plan of salvation.

There are pros and cons associated with the idea that today's spiritual events are paving the way for Jesus' Second Coming. In support of this argument, several characteristics of the end times described in Scripture might be related to the current developments within New Mysticism. For instance, people will turn away from God, and there will be a marked increase in wickedness (for example, see Mt 24:10-13; 1 Tim 4:1-2; 2 Tim 3:1-5; 4:3-4). There will be false Christs and false prophets (Mt 24:10-11, 24-25) and the appearance of the antichrist himself (2 Thess 2:1-12; 1 Jn 2:18-23). The powers of these individuals will apparently be authenticated with counterfeit signs and miracles (Mt 24:24; 2 Thess 2:9). In addition, many people will apparently turn to idolatry and the worship of demons (Rev 9:20-21).

In Matthew 24 Jesus warns of persecutions: "Many will turn away from the faith and will betray and hate each other, and many *false prophets* will appear and deceive many people. Because of the *increase of wickedness*, the love of most will grow cold" (vv. 10-12). "False Christs and false prophets will appear and perform *great signs and miracles* to deceive even the elect—if that were possible" (v. 24). Second Thessalonians 2:1-12 describes the coming of the antichrist and specifically links the counterfeit signs and miracles that will take place with the works of Satan. And Revelation 9:20-21 adds this snapshot of life on earth in the midst of the plagues that God will send as part of his final judgment: "The rest of mankind that were not killed by these plagues still did not repent of the work of their hands; *they did not stop worshiping demons, and idols* of gold, silver, bronze, stone and wood. . . . Nor did they repent of their murders, their magic arts, their sexual immorality or their thefts."

There are several ways in which New Mysticism could conceivably prepare the way for such events. It could contribute to increasing apostasy and wickedness in its role as a false religion. If the mystical experiences that are supporting it continue at their present rate and maintain their credibility, New Mysticism could conceivably become a substantial rival to Christianity. It sounds like Christianity (incorporating God, Jesus, angels, heaven and so on) and offers the same rewards (heaven and eternal life), but it leaves out Christianity's exclusivity and "tedious" requirements (the need to submit totally to God's will, to follow *his* plan of salvation, to love and serve others above ourselves). It minimizes sin, eliminating the fear of punishment and hell, and allows followers to live as they please. It also encourages contact with the spirit world and all types of occult and spiritualistic practices. New Mysticism could definitely lead people away from God and into an increasing alliance with evil spirits.

One of the more obvious ways that New Mysticism might prepare the way for future events is through its encouragement of interactions with the spirit world. The mystical experiences that give it strength beckon to humans in very seductive ways, and the belief system it offers not only explains these experiences in very upbeat terms but also encourages seekers to pursue them with promises of more and better things to come. The spiritual beings who are ostensibly behind these experiences are even portrayed as angels, helpful spirits who have started making more extensive contacts with humans in order to help them develop into full-fledged, interacting citizens in the community of spirits. It is conceivable that these deceptions, especially if augmented by signs and miracles, could eventually prepare the way for the worship of evil spirits. This would fit with Paul's warning in 1 Timothy 4:1: "The Spirit clearly says that in later times some will abandon the faith and follow deceiving spirits and things taught by demons."

This is more speculative, but it is also possible that some of the messages coming through from the spirit world will serve to keep the unsaved from realizing what is actually happening when the final events that precede Christ's Second Coming begin to unfold. Mystical experiences might presage and prepare people for the more startling signs and wonders to come. The frequent messages from the Space Brothers, and now from "Jesus" as well, speak of his Second Coming. These might conceivably prepare the way for the coming of the antichrist. And the frequent warnings of disasters and severe trials that are to precede the spiritual millennium may be an attempt to keep the unsaved from realizing that these events are God's judgments.

These arguments support the notion that New Mysticism is preparing the way for Christ's return, but we also need to consider the factors that might argue against it. From a more conservative stance, one could argue that all the changes that are taking place simply reflect a shift in cultural beliefs and interests and that Satan has merely switched his tactics accordingly. For many years materialism has been the major alternative to Christianity in the West, but its appeal is diminishing. It may be that Satan and his legions are encouraging the development of New Mysticism to help create an effective replacement for materialism.

We also need to remember that there have been many other times in history when Christians were sure that Jesus' coming was at hand but it wasn't. Jesus has warned us that "no one knows about that day or hour, not even the angels in heaven" (Mt 24:36). The many channeled messages that say the time is at hand grab our attention because they reinforce our own suspicions. But here we need to consider the source. If the angels in heaven do not know the day or hour, human beings and *fallen* angels will not know the time of Jesus' coming either. Besides, there is no guarantee that these messengers are telling the truth.

So, considering the pros and cons, what are we to make of our current situation? Above all, we need to keep in mind that any conclusions in this area are necessarily speculative and tentative. New Mysticism may or may not be preparing the way for end-times events. But either way, what is clear is that this system of beliefs is developing into a deceptive and appealing alternative to Christianity. This should probably be our most immediate concern. We need to be on our guard so its deceitful practices and false teachings do not invade either our lives or our churches. We may also need to rethink our strategies for evangelism.

How Should We Respond?

First, we need to stay informed about the developments within New Mysticism, especially the new ideas, experiences or practices (such as the use of the psychomanteum) which are continually emerging from it. By staying informed we can reduce the risk of confusion and avoid questionable practices.

In addition, in this age when so many voices are urging us to seek out and place our trust in vague inner urgings and mystical feelings, I believe that it is more important than ever to exercise our God-given ability to use careful discernment. We need to be especially careful when evaluating new "spiritual" practices, amazing testimonies or book-length accounts of stunning spiritual experiences. The market for books of this latter type is very strong, and it is very difficult for anyone to verify their truthfulness. This creates an open door for exploitation, so it is likely that there are a number of books on the market that are either highly exaggerated or fraudulent. This also applies to books aimed at the Christian market. (There are still wolves masquerading as sheep—see Matthew 7:15-23—and sheep can be misled.)

We need to know and depend on the truth of Scripture and strengthen our relationship with the Lord. But we need to do this prudently, in time-honored ways such as submission of our lives to God's will, confession and repentance, prayer, Bible study and fellowship with other Christians. At present there is a large potential for deception and confusion in the area of spiritual development. This is partly due to the fact that many Christians are searching for more meaningful spiritual experiences and partly due to the current blending of New Mysticism and Christianity. Unbiblical techniques are getting mixed in with legitimate spiritual disciplines, and it can be difficult to tell which is which.

How do we sort them out? There are some general guidelines which can help. In the first place, it is probably wise to steer clear of techniques that rely on altered states of consciousness, because these can be highly deceptive. It is also important to question the basic purpose of a technique (and our own motives for trying it). Is its overriding purpose the attainment of a closer, more yielded walk with God, or is it the attainment of experience itself? We need to ask whether the experiences that are promised are the kind that Christians should be seeking. For instance, the Bible does not encourage us to seek transcendent visions or contact with angels. Such experiences are described in Scripture, but these were initiated by God, for his purposes, and not by human efforts.

The Bible does encourage us to seek a close relationship with God. Perhaps, then, the highest experience we should aspire to is to become more aware of God, to attain a clearer sense of his reality and presence, to apprehend more of his holiness and to sense some measure of his love for us. Yet can any technique facilitate such experiences? Wouldn't a genuine experience of this type depend on God's willingness to reveal himself to us rather than our own efforts?[15] We need to be wary of techniques that promise to deliver spiritual experiences by human effort.

Notes

Chapter 1: The Current Shift Toward Mysticism

[1]See Donald G. Bloesch, "Lost in the Mystical Myths," *Christianity Today*, August 19, 1991, pp. 22-24.

[2]George H. Gallup Jr. and Frank Newport, "Belief in Psychic and Paranormal Phenomena Widespread Among Americans," *The Gallup Poll News Service* 55 (August 6, 1990).

[3]Kendrick Frazier, "UFOs as ET Spacecraft? Belief Strong, Steady," *Skeptical Inquirer* 16 (Summer 1992): 346.

[4]I describe placebo effects more extensively in chapter eight, "Healings."

[5]Claudia Wallis, "Why New Age Medicine Is Catching On," *Time*, November 4, 1991, p. 75.

[6]David Eisenberg et al., "Unconventional Medicine in the United States," *The New England Journal of Medicine* 328 (January 28, 1993): 246-52.

[7]See Russell Chandler, *Understanding the New Age* (Dallas: Word, 1988), pp. 71-74.

[8]"New Poll Offers Big Picture of Religion in America," *Christianity Today*, May 27, 1991, p. 50.

[9]So far the evidence that experiencers can disrupt the operation of electrical devices is based only on the frequency with which they report such disturbances as compared to nonexperiencers. To my knowledge these abilities have not been tested objectively.

[10]See, for instance, Kenneth Ring and Christopher Rosing, "The Omega Project: An Empirical Study of the NDE-Prone Personality," *Journal of Near-Death Studies* 8 (Summer 1990): 223-24.

[11]Jeneane Prevatt and Russ Park, "The Spiritual Emergence Network," in *Spiritual Emergency*, ed. Stanislav Grof and Christina Grof (Los Angeles: Jeremy P. Tarcher, 1989), pp. 225-27.

[12]Andrew Greeley, "Mysticism Goes Mainstream," *American Health*, January/February 1987, p. 47.

[13]Data obtained from James Davis and Tom Smith, *General Social Surveys: Cumulative Codebook* (Chicago: National Opinion Research Center, University of Chicago, 1987), p. 140.

[14]Greeley, "Mysticism Goes Mainstream," p. 47.

[15]Andrew Greeley, "Hallucinations Among the Widowed," *Sociology and Social Research* 71 (1987): 258-59.

[16]Gallup and Newport, "Belief in Psychic and Paranormal Phenomena," p. 6.

[17]George Gallup, *Adventures in Immortality* (New York: McGraw Hill, 1982), p. 76.

[18]Glen O. Gabbard and Stuart Twemlow, *With the Eyes of the Mind* (New York: Praeger, 1984), p. 12.

[19]This was the annual conference of the International Association for Near-Death Studies, held on the campus of Washington University, June 25-27, 1993.

[20]There are surveys that have attempted to determine whether Christians differ from non-Christians with respect to beliefs about anomalous events or even whether they occur at different rates in the two groups. However, the criteria used to separate Christians from non-Christians are usually so loose and unreliable (for example, simply asking respondents if they are Christian) that the results do not tell us very much. Many people will say they are Christian when asked, simply because this is still a socially acceptable thing to do.

[21]To clarify, I am using *Christian* to refer to a person who has genuinely accepted Jesus Christ as Savior and Lord and accepts the Bible as God's revealed truth and as a standard for his or her own life. By *nominal Christian* I mean a person who professes to be a Christian but doesn't take the faith very seriously, hasn't genuinely accepted Jesus as Savior or disagrees in significant ways with the Bible or fundamental Christian doctrines.

Chapter 2: New Age Thought & Its Contributions to the New Mysticism

[1]Raymond Moody with Paul Perry, *Reunions* (New York: Villard Books, 1993), pp. 98-100.

[2]Vignette depicted in a videotape of Monroe's work, *Life After Death* (Cos Cob, Conn.: Hartley Films).

[3]Information taken from various pieces of literature published by the Monroe Institute, describing its operations.

[4]See Russell Chandler, *Understanding the New Age* (Dallas: Word, 1988), pp. 80-88.

[5]Jon Klimo, *Channeling* (Los Angeles: Jeremy P. Tarcher, 1987), p. 24.

[6]Douglas Groothuis, *Unmasking the New Age* (Downers Grove, Ill.: InterVarsity Press, 1986), pp. 131-33.

[7]Joel Whitton and Joe Fisher, *Life Between Life* (New York: Warner Books, 1986), pp. 43-51.

[8]Marilyn Ferguson, *The Aquarian Conspiracy* (Los Angeles: Jeremy P. Tarcher, 1980), pp. 68-78, 154.

[9]The conference, entitled "The New Age: A Scientific Evaluation," was held at the Hyatt Regency O'Hare in Chicago on November 4-6, 1988.

[10]Groothuis, *Unmasking the New Age*, pp. 16-18.

[11]Ferguson, *Aquarian Conspiracy*, pp. 23-43.

[12]Ibid., pp. 100-101. Also see Dave Hunt, *Peace, Prosperity and the Coming Holocaust* (Eugene, Ore.: Harvest House, 1983), pp. 56, 109, 123-28.

[13]"New Poll Offers Big Picture of Religion in America," *Christianity Today*, May 27, 1991, pp. 50-51.

Chapter 3: The "Higher Self" & Subconscious Processes

[1]Roger Sperry, "Lateral Specialization in the Surgically Separated Hemispheres," in *The Neu-*

rosciences: Third Study Program, ed. F. O. Schmitt and F. G. Worden (Cambridge, Mass.: MIT Press, 1974).

[2]Joseph Bogen, "The Other Side of the Brain: An Appositional Mind," in *The Nature of Human Consciousness*, ed. Robert E. Ornstein (San Francisco: W. H. Freeman, 1973), p. 119.

[3]Robert Ornstein, *The Psychology of Consciousness* (New York: Harcourt Brace Jovanovich, 1977), pp. 36-39.

[4]For a nontechnical summary, see Sally Springer and Georg Deutsch, *Left Brain, Right Brain*, 4th ed. (New York: W. H. Freeman, 1993), chaps. 1, 6.

[5]Cited in Bogen, "Other Side of the Brain," p. 113.

[6]Ronald Kotulak, "With Half a Brain His IQ Is 126, and Doctors Are Dumbfounded," *Chicago Tribune*, November 7, 1976, sec. 1, p. 6.

[7]Michael S. Gazzaniga, "The Split Brain in Man," *Scientific American* 217 (August 1967): 24-29.

[8]Springer and Deutsch, *Left Brain, Right Brain*, pp. 29-30.

[9]Jerre Levy, "Right Brain, Left Brain: Fact and Fiction," *Psychology Today* 19 (May 1985): 42.

[10]Roger Sperry, "Some Effects of Disconnecting the Cerebral Hemispheres," *Science* 217 (September 24, 1982): 1224-25.

[11]Michael Gazzaniga and Joseph E. JeDoux, *The Integrated Mind* (New York: Plenum, 1978), pp. 147-48.

[12]Ibid., p. 148.

[13]Michael Gazzaniga, *The Social Brain* (New York: BasicBooks, 1985), pp. 72-73.

[14]Gazzaniga and JeDoux, *Integrated Mind*, pp. 149-50.

[15]Jerre Levy, "Psychological Implications of Bilateral Asymmetry," in *Hemisphere Function in the Human Brain*, ed. Stuart J. Dimond and J. Graham Beaumont (New York: Halsted, 1974).

[16]Ornstein, *Psychology of Consciousness*, pp. 34-39.

[17]Ibid., p. 33.

[18]See Ornstein, *Psychology of Consciousness*, and Robert Ornstein, *The Nature of Human Consciousness* (San Francisco: W. H. Freeman, 1973).

[19]See Robert Ornstein, *The Mind Field* (New York: Grossman, 1976).

[20]Gazzaniga, *Social Brain*, pp. 47-48.

[21]Levy, "Right Brain, Left Brain," pp. 38, 42-43.

[22]Michael Gazzaniga, "Right Hemisphere Language Following Brain Bisection," *American Psychologist* 38 (May 1983): 525-29.

[23]Gazzaniga, *Social Brain*, p. 70.

[24]Jay J. Myers, "Right Hemisphere Language: Science or Fiction," *American Psychologist* 39 (March 1984): 315-19.

[25]Gazzaniga, "Right Hemisphere Language," pp. 527-31.

[26]See Joseph B. Hellige, "Hemispheric Asymmetry," *Annual Review of Psychology* 41 (1990): 55-80 for a recent review.

[27]Wendy Heller, "Of One Mind," *The Sciences*, May/June 1990, p. 44.

[28]Hellige, "Hemispheric Asymmetry," p. 58.

[29]Springer and Deutsch, *Left Brain, Right Brain*, pp. 151-53.

[30]Ibid., pp. 102-4.

[31]Sperry has not only abandoned the "two-minds" hypothesis but also dropped his former

materialistic explanation of mind. See Roger Sperry, "The New Mentalist Paradigm and Ultimate Concern," *Perspectives in Biology and Medicine* 3 (Spring 1986): 413-21.

[32]Levy, "Right Brain, Left Brain," p. 44.

[33]Wilder Penfield, *The Mystery of the Mind* (Princeton, N.J.: Princeton University Press, 1975), pp. 38-39.

[34]J. Allan Hobson, "Dreaming," in *States of Brain and Mind,* ed. J. Allan Hobson (Boston: Birhhauser, 1988), p. 31.

[35]See J. Allan Hobson and R. W. McCarley, "The Brain as a Dream State Generator: An Activation-Synthesis Hypothesis of the Dream Process," *American Journal of Psychiatry* 134 (1977): 1335-48.

[36]F. Crick and G. Mitcheson, "REM Sleep and Neural Nets," *Journal of Mind and Behavior* 7 (1986): 229-50.

[37]Jonathan Winson, "The Meaning of Dreams," *Scientific American,* November 1990, pp. 86-96.

Chapter 4: Altered States & Extraordinary Experiences

[1]Woodburn H. Heron, D. K. Doane and T. H. Scott, "Visual Disturbances After Prolonged Perceptual Isolation," *Canadian Journal of Psychology* 10 (1956): 13-18.

[2]Marvin Zuckerman, "Hallucinations, Reported Sensations and Images," in *Sensory Deprivation: Fifteen Years of Research,* ed. John P. Zubek (New York: Appleton-Century-Crofts, 1969), pp. 95-96.

[3]Ibid., pp. 123-25.

[4]A. Michael Rossi, "General Methodological Considerations," in *Sensory Deprivation: Fifteen Years of Research,* ed. John P. Zubek (New York: Appleton-Century-Crofts, 1969), p. 27.

[5]Benjamin Wallace and Leslie E. Fisher, *Consciousness and Behavior,* 3rd ed. (Needham Heights, Mass.: Allyn & Bacon, 1991), pp. 202-3.

[6]John C. Lilly, *The Center of the Cyclone* (New York: Bantam Books, 1972), p. 41.

[7]Lilly had legal permission to experiment with LSD at that time.

[8]Ibid., pp. 43-58.

[9]The conference was held October 16-18, 1981, at the McCormick Inn in Chicago, and offered fourteen hours of continuing-education credit for people in several prominent professional organizations, including the American Psychological Association. It was sponsored by the Institute for the Advancement of Human Behavior in Portola, California.

[10]Ernest R. Hilgard, *Divided Consciousness: Multiple Controls in Human Thought and Action,* expanded ed. (New York: John Wiley & Sons, 1986), p. 163.

[11]Ibid., p. 164.

[12]Ibid., p. 165.

[13]Ernest R. Hilgard and Josephine R. Hilgard, *Hypnosis in the Relief of Pain* (Los Altos, Calif.: William Kaufmann, 1975), pp. 103-63.

[14]Council on Scientific Affairs of the American Medical Association, "Scientific Status of Refreshing Recollection by the Use of Hypnosis," *Journal of the American Medical Association* 253 (April 5, 1985): 30-35.

[15]Wallace and Fisher, *Consciousness and Behavior,* pp. 101-2.

[16]Laura Shapiro, "Rush to Judgment," *Newsweek,* April 19, 1993, pp. 54-60.

[17]Martin Gardner, "The False Memory Syndrome," *Skeptical Inquirer* 17 (Summer 1993): 370.

[18]Evidence supplied in a personal communication from Pamela Freyd, executive director of the False Memory Syndrome Foundation.

[19]Gardner, "False Memory Syndrome," p. 370.

[20]Elizabeth Loftus, "The Reality of Repressed Memories," earlier draft of an article forthcoming in *American Psychologist*.

[21]Gardner, "False Memory Syndrome," pp. 371-72; also from Pamela Freyd, personal communication.

[22]Hilgard, *Divided Consciousness*, pp. 24-39.

[23]Frank Barron, Murray Jarvik and Sterling Bunnell Jr., "The Hallucinogenic Drugs," in *Altered States of Awareness: Readings from "Scientific American,"* ed. Timothy J. Teyler (San Francisco: W. H. Freeman, 1972), p. 102.

[24]Ibid., p. 105.

[25]Wallace and Fisher, *Consciousness and Behavior*, pp. 80-81.

[26]Ibid.

[27]See Arnold M. Ludwig, "Altered States of Consciousness," in *Altered States of Consciousness,* ed. Charles T. Tart (New York: John Wiley & Sons, 1969), pp. 9-22; and G. William Farthing, *The Psychology of Consciousness* (Englewood Cliffs, N.J.: Prentice-Hall, 1992), pp. 207-12.

[28]Ibid., p. 15.

[29]See John P. Zubek, ed., *Sensory Deprivation: Fifteen Years of Research* (New York: Appleton-Century-Crofts, 1969), pp. 255-69, and Herbert Benson, *The Relaxation Response* (New York: Morrow, 1975), p. 64.

[30]Wilder Penfield, "The Interpretive Cortex," *Science* 129 (1959): 1721.

[31]Ibid., 1719-20.

[32]Wilder Penfield, "The Role of the Temporal Cortex in Certain Psychic Phenomena," *Journal of Mental Science* 101 (1955): 451-65.

[33]Vernon M. Neppe, "Near Death Experiences: A New Challenge in Temporal Lobe Phenomenology? Comments on 'A Neurobiological Model for Near-Death Experiences,' " *Journal of Near-Death Studies* 7 (Summer 1989): 247.

[34]Andreas Mavromatis, *Hypnogogia* (London: Routledge & Kegan Paul, 1987), pp. 14-35.

[35]Ronald Siegel, "Hallucinations," *Scientific American* 237 (1977): 132.

[36]See Ronald Siegel, *Fire in the Brain* (New York: Dutton, 1992), for some case studies of individuals who have had very realistic and complex hallucinations that apparently had a definite physiological cause.

[37]Neil R. Carlson, *Foundations of Physiological Psychology*, 2nd ed. (Needham Heights, Mass.: Allyn and Bacon, 1992), p. 129.

[38]William Edmonston Jr., *The Induction of Hypnosis* (New York: John Wiley & Sons, 1986), pp. 6-21.

[39]See Deuteronomy 18:21-22; 13:1-5; and Jeremiah 23:16.

[40]Please see chapter six for a fuller explanation of "biblically based meditation." There is a big difference between the way "meditation" is described in the Bible and the way it is used in Eastern religions and New Age thought.

Chapter 5: Near-Death & Out-of-Body Experiences

[1]Raymond Moody, *The Light Beyond* (Toronto: Bantam Books, 1988), pp. 48-49.

[2]I have changed this woman's name to conceal her identity.

[3]Glen O. Gabbard and Stuart Twemlow, *With the Eyes of the Mind* (New York: Praeger, 1984), p. 12.

[4]George Gallup, *Adventures in Immortality* (New York: McGraw Hill, 1982), p. 76.

[5]Ramond Moody, *Life After Life* (New York: Bantam Books, 1975).

[6]Kenneth Ring, *Life at Death* (New York: Coward, McCann & Geoghegan, 1980).

[7]Michael Sabom, *Recollections of Death* (New York: Harper & Row, 1982).

[8]Ibid., p. 52.

[9]Margot Grey, *Return from Death* (London: Arkana, 1985), pp. 56-72.

[10]D. Scott Rogo, *Leaving the Body* (New York: Prentice-Hall, 1983), pp. 88-106, xi-xii.

[11]Gabbard and Twemlow, *With the Eyes of the Mind*, pp. 5-8.

[12]Michael Sabom is an exception. See note 17.

[13]See Robert A. Morey, *Death and the Afterlife* (Minneapolis: Bethany House, 1984), or John W. Cooper, *Body, Soul and Life Everlasting* (Grand Rapids, Mich.: Eerdmans, 1989), for readable arguments for this position.

[14]Carol Zaleski, *Otherworldly Journeys* (New York: Oxford University Press, 1987), pp. 26-42.

[15]In George Ritchie's *Return from Tomorrow* (Waco, Tex.: Chosen Books, 1978), Ritchie presents himself as a Christian, but Tal Brooke, who was associated with Ritchie prior to his own conversion, indicates that Ritchie's beliefs are suspect. For example, Brooke was present when Ritchie told a sympathetic audience of two hundred that one night in 1958 he had an experience that revealed his true mission on earth. A voice (whom he called "God") told him to go out to a mountain and observe the brilliant lights in the sky. The voice told Ritchie that these lights were massive "mother ships" that were poised for a celestial command to pick up a remnant of true believers before the earth was plunged into darkness and catastrophe. Ritchie was to serve as a modern-day Noah in this scenario. See Tal Brooke, *The Other Side of Death* (Wheaton, Ill.: Tyndale House, 1979), pp. 33-37.

Betty Malz's well-known NDE, described in *My Glimpse of Eternity* (Old Tappan, N.J.: Revell, 1977), has also become controversial. A freelance writer, Lorna Dueck (whose story appeared in *Christian Week* magazine), traveled to Terre Haute, Indiana, where Malz's NDE took place, and interviewed three of Malz's doctors. They all flatly denied that she had died, and her primary physician said that she was never in a coma or anywhere near death. According to hospital personnel, the event is not recorded in hopital records either. Malz's publisher and the editor who checked out the story believe that she is telling the truth and that the doctors and the hospital are covering up what really happened for fear of malpractice suits. See Ken Sidey, "Doctors Dispute Best-Selling Author's Back-to-Life Story," *Christianity Today*, July 22, 1991, pp. 40-43.

[16]*Harper's Bible Dictionary*, ed. Paul J. Achtemeier (San Francisco: Harper & Row, 1985), s.v. "visions."

[17]I met Sabom and asked him about his current views of NDEs at the 1993 International Association for Near-Death Studies (IANDS) conference. He is still uncertain about what they are, but as an evangelical Christian, he is very concerned about the way NDEs are being interpreted.

[18]Sabom, *Recollections of Death,* pp. 81-86.

[19]Ibid., pp. 63-80.

[20]John Palmer and R. Lieberman, "The Influence of Psychological Set on ESP and Out-of-Body Experiences," *Journal of the American Society for Psychical Research* 69 (1975): 257-80.

[21]H. J. Irwin, *An Introduction to Parapsychology* (Jefferson, N.C.: McFarland, 1989), p. 202.

[22]Rogo, *Leaving the Body,* pp. 100-102.

[23]Gabbard and Twemlow, *With the Eyes of the Mind,* p. 207.

[24]Ibid., pp. 222-25.

[25]Rogo, *Leaving the Body,* p. 169.

[26]Gabbard and Twemlow, *With the Eyes of the Mind,* p. 138; and Rogo, *Leaving the Body,* pp. 59, 180-83.

[27]P. M. H. Atwater, *Coming Back to Life* (New York: Ballantine, 1988), pp. 7-8.

[28]Grey, *Return from Death,* p. 76.

[29]Satwant Pasricha and Ian Stevenson, "Near-Death Experiences in India," *The Journal of Nervous and Mental Disease* 174 (1986): 167-68.

[30]Maurice Rawlings, *Beyond Death's Door* (Nashville: Thomas Nelson, 1978), pp. 22, 66.

[31]Ibid., pp. 118-20.

[32]See Juan C. Saavedra-Aguilar and Juan S. Gomez-Jeria, "A Neurobiological Model for Near-Death Experiences," *Journal of Near-Death Studies* 7 (1989): 205-22; Melvin Morse, David Venecia Jr. and Jerrold Milstein, "Near Death Experiences: A Neurophysiologic Explanatory Model," *Journal of Near-Death Studies* 8 (Fall 1989): 45-53.

[33]Saavedra-Aguilar and Gomez-Jeria, "A Neurobiological Model," pp. 207-8.

[34]Michael A. Persinger, "Modern Neuroscience and Near-Death Experiences: Expectancies and Implications—Comments on 'A Neurobiological Model for Near-Death Experiences,' " *Journal of Near-Death Studies* 7 (1989): 234.

[35]Vernon M. Neppe, "Near-Death Experiences: A New Challenge in Temporal Lobe Phenomenology? Comments on 'A Neurobiological Model for Near-Death Experiences,' " *Journal of Near-Death Studies* 7 (1989): 247.

[36]Ernst Rodin, "Comments on 'A Neurobiological Model for Near-Death Experiences,' " *Journal of Near-Death Studies* 7 (Summer 1989): 255-56.

[37]Sabom, *Recollections of Death,* pp. 176-78.

[38]L. J. Meduna, *Carbon Dioxide Therapy* (Springfield, Ill.: Charles C. Thomas, 1950), pp. 23-35.

[39]Morse, Venecia and Milstein, "Near Death Experiences," p. 50.

[40]Gabbard and Twemlow, *With the Eyes of the Mind,* pp. 13-18.

[41]See Stephen LaBerge, "The Psychophysiology of Lucid Dreaming," in *Conscious Mind, Sleeping Brain,* ed. Jayne Gackenbach and Stephen LaBerge (New York: Plenum, 1988), pp. 135-53. Lucid dreaming occurs during REM sleep while virtually all of the voluntary muscles are paralyzed. The muscles that move the eyes are spared, so dreamers can use their eyes to signal an outside observer. They employ distinctive eye movements (for example, four large up-and-down movements in rapid succession) to make the signal clear. Lucid dreamers have been able to produce these movements while physiological recording instruments indicate that they are in REM sleep. Some have even been able to send signals related to the content of their dreams.

[42]Sue Blackmore, "A Theory of Lucid Dreams and OBEs," in *Conscious Mind, Sleeping Brain,*

ed. Jayne Gackenbach and Stephen LaBerge (New York: Plenum, 1988), pp. 373-75.

⁴³Sabom, *Recollections of Death*, pp. 61, 194, and Gabbard and Twemlow, *With the Eyes of the Mind*, pp. 33-36.

⁴⁴Gabbard and Twemlow, *With the Eyes of the Mind*, pp. 30-33.

⁴⁵Bruce Greyson, "Can Science Explain the Near-Death Experience?" *Journal of Near-Death Studies* 8 (1989): 87.

⁴⁶Kenneth Ring and Christopher Rosing, "The Omega Project: An Empirical Study of the NDE-Prone Personality," *Journal of Near-Death Studies* 8 (Summer 1990): 222.

⁴⁷S. Wilson and T. Barber, "The Fantasy-Prone Personality: Implications for the Understanding of Imagery, Hypnosis and Parapsychological Phenomena," in *Imagery: Current Theory and Research Application*, ed. A. A. Sheikh (New York: John Wiley & Sons, 1982).

⁴⁸Ring and Rosing, "Omega Project," pp. 217-21.

⁴⁹Rogo, *Leaving the Body*, pp. 68-79.

⁵⁰Ibid., pp. 63-66.

⁵¹Atwater, *Coming Back to Life*, pp. 27, 45, 95, 146.

⁵²Mark Albrecht and Brooks Alexander, "Thanatology: Death and Dying," *Journal of the Spiritual Counterfeits Project*, April 1977, p. 6.

⁵³Robert Monroe, *Journeys out of the Body* (Garden City, N.Y.: Doubleday, 1970).

⁵⁴Cited in Rogo, *Leaving the Body*, p. 102.

⁵⁵Albrecht and Alexander, "Thanatology," p. 7.

⁵⁶Ibid., pp. 7-8.

⁵⁷Moody, *Light Beyond*, p. 22.

⁵⁸Raymond Moody with Paul Perry, *Reunions* (New York: Villard Books, 1993). Also see chapter ten for a full account.

⁵⁹Kenneth Ring, *Life at Death* (New York: Quill, 1980), p. 140.

⁶⁰Moody, *Light Beyond*, pp. 41-44.

⁶¹Atwater, *Coming Back to Life*, p. 74.

⁶²Ring, *Life at Death*, pp. 185-86.

⁶³Grey, *Return from Death*, pp. 107-10.

⁶⁴Atwater, *Coming Back to Life*, p. 117.

⁶⁵Cherie Sutherland, "Changes in Religious Beliefs, Attitudes and Practices Following Near-Death Experiences: An Australian Study," *Journal of Near-Death Studies* 9 (1990): 21-30.

⁶⁶See Cherie Sutherland, "Psychic Phenomena Following Near-Death Experiences: An Australian Study," *Journal of Near-Death Studies* 8 (Winter 1989): 98-101; and Ring and Rosing, "Omega Project," 223-26. Ring, Grey, Atwater and Sabom have made similar discoveries.

⁶⁷Ring and Rosing, "Omega Project," p. 225.

⁶⁸See Brooks Alexander, "Tantra: The Worship and Occult Power of Sex," *Spiritual Counterfeits Project Newsletter* 11 (Summer 1985): 1-12.

⁶⁹Kenneth Ring, *Heading Toward Omega* (New York: Quill, 1985), pp. 226, 51; Atwater, *Coming Back to Life*, pp. 185-91; Greyson, "Can Science Explain the Near-Death Experience?" p. 86.

⁷⁰Greyson, "Can Science Explain the Near-Death Experience?" p. 87.

Chapter 6: Eastern Meditation & Mystical Experiences

¹Daniel Goleman, *The Meditative Mind* (Los Angeles: Jeremy P. Tarcher, 1988), p. 66.

[2]Maharishi Mahesh Yogi, *Meditations of Maharishi Mahesh Yogi* (New York: Bantam Books, 1968), pp. 17-18.

[3]See the pamphlets "TM: Penetrating the Veil of Deception" and "An English Translation of Transcendental Meditation's Initiatory Puja," both available from the Spiritual Counterfeits Project, P.O. Box 4309, Berkeley, CA 94704.

[4]Alain Danielou, *Yoga: The Method of Re-integration* (New York: University Books, 1955), p. 18.

[5]Goleman, *Meditative Mind*, pp. 104-7.

[6]Ibid., pp. 10-11, 13.

[7]Ibid., pp. 110-13.

[8]Ibid., pp. 10-38.

[9]Ibid., p. 45.

[10]Ibid., pp. 20-33.

[11]Herbert Benson, *The Relaxation Response* (New York: Morrow, 1975), pp. 59-60.

[12]R. Keith Wallace and Herbert Benson, "The Physiology of Meditation," *Scientific American* 226 (1972): 84-90.

[13]R. Keith Wallace, Herbert Benson and A. F. Wilson, "A Wakeful Hypometabolic Physiologic State," *American Journal of Physiology* 221 (1971): 795-99.

[14]See the following three articles from Deane H. Shapiro Jr. and Roger N. Walsh, eds., *Meditation: Classic and Contemporary Perspectives* (New York: Aldine, 1984): Larry C. Walrath and David Hamilton, "Autonomic Correlates of Meditation and Hypnosis," pp. 637-44; Donald R. Morse et al., "A Physiological and Subjective Evaluation of Meditation, Hypnosis and Relaxation," pp. 645-64; and P. B. C. Fenwick et al., "Metabolic and EEG Changes During Transcendental Meditation: An Explanation," pp. 447-530.

[15]David S. Holmes, "The Influence of Meditation Versus Rest on Physiological Arousal: A Second Examination," in *The Psychology of Meditation*, ed. Michael A. West (Oxford: Clarendon, 1987), pp. 81-103.

[16]Ibid., p. 82.

[17]Peter Fenwick, "Meditation and the EEG," in *The Psychology of Meditation*, ed. Michael A. West (Oxford: Clarendon, 1990), p. 105.

[18]Robert R. Pagano et al., "Sleep During Transcendental Meditation," in *Meditation: Classic and Contemporary Perspectives*, ed. Deane H. Shapiro Jr. and Roger N. Walsh (New York: Aldine, 1984), pp. 527-30.

[19]Fenwick et al., "Metabolic and EEG Changes," pp. 461-62.

[20]See Michael M. Delmonte, "Personality and Meditation," in *The Psychology of Meditation*, ed. Michael A. West (Oxford: Clarendon, 1987), for a good review.

[21]Ibid., p. 121.

[22]Leon S. Otis, "Adverse Effects of Transcendental Meditation," in *Meditation: Classic and Contemporary Perspectives*, ed. Deane H. Shapiro Jr. and Roger N. Walsh (New York: Aldine, 1984), pp. 201-2.

[23]Ibid. pp. 203-5.

[24]Ibid., p. 207.

[25]Deane H. Shapiro Jr., "Adverse Effects of Meditation: A Preliminary Investigation of Long-Term Meditators," *International Journal of Psychosomatics* 39 (1992): 62-66.

[26]Frederick J. Heide, "Relaxation: The Storm Before the Calm," *Psychology Today*, April 1985, pp. 18-19.

[27]Jack Kornfield, "Obstacles and Vicissitudes in Spiritual Practice," in *Spiritual Emergency*, ed. Stanislav Grof and Christina Grof (Los Angeles: Jeremy P. Tarcher, 1989), p. 155.

[28]Ibid., pp. 154-56.

[29]Ibid., pp. 156-57. Also see Goleman, *Meditative Mind*, pp. 12-13.

[30]See Lee Sannella, *The Kundalini Experience* (Lower Lake, Calif.: Integral, 1987), pp. 25-30, for a pro-kundalini point of view.

[31]See Brooks Alexander, "Tantra: The Worship and Occult Power of Sex," *Spiritual Counterfeits Newsletter* 11 (Summer 1985): 1-10, for an informative Christian article on tantra.

[32]Ibid., pp. 93-97.

[33]Stanislav Grof and Christina Grof, "Spiritual Emergency: Understanding Evolutionary Crisis," in *Spiritual Emergency*, ed. Stanislav Grof and Christina Grof (Los Angeles: Jeremy P. Tarcher, 1989), p. 15.

[34]Kornfield, "Obstacles and Vicissitudes," pp. 159-61.

[35]Ibid., pp. 98-101.

[36]Lee Sannella, "Kundalini: Classical and Clinical," in *Spiritual Emergency*, ed. Stanislav Grof and Christina Grof (Los Angeles: Jeremy P. Tarcher, 1989), pp. 105-8.

[37]Sannella, *Kundalini Experience*, pp. 101-3.

[38]Ibid., pp. 37-47.

[39]Grof and Grof, "Spiritual Emergency," p. 15.

[40]Bruce Greyson, "Death Experience and Kundalini," address given at the 1993 conference of the International Association of Near Death Studies, in St. Louis, Missouri, June 26.

[41]Grof and Grof, "Spiritual Emergency," pp. 2-26.

[42]Jeneane Prevatt and Russ Park, "The Spiritual Emergence Network (SEN)," in *Spiritual Emergency*, ed. Stanislav Grof and Christina Grof (Los Angeles: Jeremy P. Tarcher, 1989), pp. 225-30.

[43]Arthur J. Deikman, "Experimental Meditation," in *Altered States of Consciousness*, ed. Charles C. Tart (New York: John Wiley & Sons, 1969), pp. 203-9.

[44]Arthur J. Deikman, "Bimodal Consciousness," in *The Nature of Human Consciousness*, ed. Robert Ornstein (San Francisco: W. H. Freeman, 1973), pp. 75-76.

[45]See Peter Fenwick et al., "Psychic Sensitivity, Mystical Experience, Head Injury and Brain Pathology," *British Journal of Medical Psychology* 58 (1985): 35-36; and T. Sensky, "Religiosity, Mystical Experience and Epilepsy," in *Research Progress in Epilepsy*, ed. F. Clifford Rose (London: Pitman Medical, 1983), pp. 214-20.

[46]C. Fred Dickason, *Demon Possession and the Christian* (Chicago: Moody Press, 1987), pp. 41-43.

[47]St. John of the Cross *The Dark Night of the Soul* 46-49, 78-79.

[48]*The Cloud of Unknowing and the Book of Privy Counseling*, ed. William Johnston (Garden City, N.Y.: Doubleday/Image, 1973), pp. 9-10.

Chapter 7: Are Human Beings Developing New Powers of Mind?

[1]*Emerging Trends* (Princeton Religious Research Center) 13 (November 1991): 3.

[2]Wayne S. Messer and Richard A. Griggs, "Student Belief and Involvement in the Paranormal

and Performance in Introductory Psychology," *Teaching of Psychology* 16 (December 1989): 187-91; and David F. Duncan, J. William Donnelly and Thomas Nicholson, "Belief in the Paranormal and Religious Belief Among American College Students," *Psychological Reports* 70 (1992): 15-18.

[3]Harvey J. Irwin, *An Introduction to Parapsychology* (Jefferson, N.C.: McFarland, 1989), pp. 13-15.

[4]Ibid., p. 17.

[5]Ibid., pp. 17-19.

[6]Joseph H. Rush, "Parapsychology: A Historical Perspective," in *Foundations of Parapsychology*, ed. Hoyt L. Edge et al. (Boston: Routledge & Kegan Paul, 1986), pp. 17-18, 20-25.

[7]Irwin, *Introduction to Parapsychology*, pp. 61-66.

[8]Ibid., pp. 66, 72-76.

[9]Ibid., pp. 124-28.

[10]Ibid., pp. 35-55.

[11]Russell Targ and Harold E. Puthoff, "Information Transmission Under Conditions of Sensory Shielding," *Nature* 152 (October 1974): 602-7.

[12]Harold E. Puthoff and Russell Targ, "A Perceptual Channel for Information Transfer over Kilometer Distances: Historical Perspective and Recent Research," *Proceedings of the Institute of Electrical and Electronics Engineers* 64 (March 1976): 329-54.

[13]Russell Targ and Harold E. Puthoff, *Mind Reach Scientists Look at Psychic Ability* (New York: Delacorte, 1977), pp. 46-106.

[14]Committee on Techniques for the Enhancement of Human Performance, "Paranormal Phenomena," in *Enhancing Human Performance*, ed. Daniel Druckman and John A. Swets (Washington, D.C.: National Academy Press, 1988), pp. 176-78.

[15]Ibid., pp. 178-84. Targ and Puthoff assumed that each of the judges' nine rankings within a series would be independent, or *uninfluenced*, by the other rankings. However, this was probably not true since the same judge did all nine rankings. Rankings that are not independent require a different statistical analysis from those that are.

[16]David Marks and Richard Kammann, *The Psychology of the Psychic* (Buffalo, N.Y.: Prometheus Books, 1980), pp. 26-40.

[17]James Randi, *Flim-Flam* (Buffalo, N.Y: Prometheus Books, 1980), pp. 131-50.

[18]Committee on Techniques for Enhancing Human Performance, "Paranormal Phenomena," p. 191.

[19]Charles Honorton, "Psi and Internal Attention States: Information Retrieval in the Ganzfeld," in *Psi and States of Awareness*, ed. B. Shapin and L. Coly (New York: Parapsychology Foundation, 1978), pp. 79-90.

[20]Ray Hyman, "The Ganzfield Psi Experiment: A Critical Appraisal," *Journal of Parapsychology* 49 (1985): 3-49.

[21]Ray Hyman and Charles Honorton, "A Joint Communique: The Psi Ganzfeld Controversy," *Journal of Parapsychology* 50 (1986): 351-64.

[22]Irwin, *Introduction to Parapsychology*, p. 113.

[23]Dan Korem, *Powers: Testing the Psychic and Supernatural* (Downers Grove, Ill.: Intervarsity Press, 1988), pp. 11-29, 37-60.

[24]Randi, *Flim-Flam*, p. 157.

[25]Korem, *Powers*, p. 51.

[26]Ibid., p. 18.

[27]Irwin, *Introduction to Parapsychology*, pp. 170-77.

[28]Ibid., p. 121.

[29]Edge et al., *Foundations of Parapsychology*, pp. 244-45.

[30]Irwin, *Introduction to Parapsychology*, pp. 126-27.

[31]Committee on Techniques for Enhancing Human Performance, "Paranormal Phenomena," p. 186.

[32]Korem, *Powers*, pp. 122-24.

[33]Ibid., pp. 167-91.

[34]Committee on Techniques for Enhancing Human Performance, "Paranormal Phenomena," pp. 201-2.

Chapter 8: Healings

[1]See Craig Lambert, "The Chopra Prescriptions," *Harvard Magazine*, September/October 1989, pp. 23-28.

[2]See Claudia Wallis, "Why New Age Medicine Is Catching On," *Time*, November 4, 1991, pp. 68-71.

[3]See Paul C. Reisser, Teri K. Reisser and John Weldon, *New Age Medicine* (Downers Grove, Ill.: InterVarsity Press, 1987), for an excellent, in-depth discussion of the various alternative treatments from a medical and Christian point of view. Paul Reisser is a Christian physician.

[4]Wallis, "Why New Age Medicine Is Catching On," p. 75.

[5]David Eisenberg et al., "Unconventional Medicine in the United States," *New England Journal of Medicine* 328 (January 28, 1993): 246-52.

[6]Daniel Glick, "New Age Meets Hippocrates," *Newsweek*, July 13, 1992, p. 58; and Richard Stone, ed., "NIH Dabbles in the Unconventional," *Science* 257 (September 18, 1992): 1615.

[7]Reisser, Reisser and Weldon, *New Age Medicine*, pp. 33-49.

[8]See Rob Wechsler, "A New Prescription: Mind over Malady," *Discover*, February 1987, pp. 51-61.

[9]O. Carl Simonton, Stephanie Matthews-Simonton and James Creighton, *Getting Well Again* (Los Angeles: Jeremy P. Tarcher, 1978).

[10]Steven L. Fahrion, "Autogenic Biofeedback Treatment For Migraine," in *Research and Clinical Studies in Headache* 5 (1978): 47-71. Fahrion received a good part of his training at the Mayo Clinic.

[11]For a biofeedback example, see Steven Fahrion et al., "Biobehavioral Treatment of Essential Hypertension: A Group Outcome Study," *Biofeedback and Self Regulation* 11 (1986): 257-75. The authors are all employed at the Menninger Clinic. I heard them describe the benefits of biofeedback, relaxation training, meditation and hypnosis at a conference called "Biobehavioral Treatment for Essential Hypertension," sponsored by the Menninger Clinic, on October 12-13, 1990.

[12]David Spiegel et al., "Effect of Psychosocial Treatment on Survival of Patients with Metastatic Breast Cancer," *The Lancet*, October 14, 1989, pp. 888-91.

[13]Dolores Krieger, *The Therapeutic Touch* (Englewood Cliffs, N.J.: Prentice-Hall, 1979).

[14]Barbara Blattner, *Holistic Nursing* (Englewood Cliffs, N.J.: Prentice-Hall, 1981), pp. 84-85

[15]Sharon Fish, "Nursing's New Age," *Spiritual Counterfeits Project Newsletter* 14, no. 3 (1989)·
4-7.

[16]Richard Carlson and Benjamin Shield, eds., *Healers on Healing* (Los Angeles: Jeremy P.
Tarcher, 1989).

[17]Rex Gardner, *Healing Miracles* (London: Darton, Longman and Todd, 1986), pp. 35-38.

[18]James Randi, *Flim-Flam* (Buffalo, N.Y.: Prometheus Books, 1987), pp. 176-87.

[19]James Randi, *The Faith Healers* (Buffalo, N.Y.: Prometheus Books, 1987).

[20]Ibid., pp. 128-30.

[21]John Tierney, "Fleecing the Flock," *Discover* 50 (November 1987): 50-58.

[22]Ibid., p. 58.

[23]Gardner, *Healing Miracles*, pp. 24-27.

[24]Reisser, Reisser and Weldon, *New Age Medicine*, pp. 101-3.

[25]Editors of Time-Life Books, *Powers of Healing* (Alexandria, Va.: Time-Life Books, 1989), pp.
93-94.

[26]See Reisser, Reisser and Weldon, *New Age Medicine*, pp. 109-12, 127, and Randi, *Flim-Flam*,
173-77, for opposite points of view on Arigo's powers.

[27]Reisser, Reisser and Weldon, *New Age Medicine*, p. 125.

Chapter 9: Communication with Spirits

[1]Erlandur Haraldsson, "Representative National Surveys of Psychic Phenomena: Iceland,
Great Britain, Sweden, USA and Gallup's Multinational Survey," *Journal of the Society for
Psychical Research* 53 (1985): 152.

[2]Raymond Moody with Paul Perry, *Reunions* (New York: Villard Books, 1993), p. 112.

[3]Andrew Greeley, "Mysticism Goes Mainstream," *American Health*, January/February 1987, p.
47.

[4]Andrew Greeley, "Hallucinations Among the Widowed," *Sociology and Social Research* 71
(1987): 258-59.

[5]Haraldsson, "Representative National Surveys," pp. 155-56.

[6]Katherine Lowry, "Channeling," *Omni*, October 1987, p. 50.

[7]Jon Klimo, *Channeling* (Los Angeles: Jeremy P. Tarcher, 1987), pp. 1-3, 61-64.

[8]Ibid., p. 64.

[9]Ibid., pp. 28-34.

[10]Ibid., pp. 38-42.

[11]Martin Gardner, "Marianne Williamson and *A Course in Miracles*," *Skeptical Inquirer* 17 (Fall
1992): 19.

[12]Dean Halverson, "*A Course in Miracles*: Seeing Yourself as Sinless," *Journal of the Spiritual
Counterfeits Project* 7, no. 1 (1987): 18-29.

[13]David Gelmman with Donna Foote, "A Miracle on Your Doorstep," *Newsweek*, March 23,
1992, p. 65.

[14]Editors of Time-Life Books, *Spirit Summonings* (Morristown, N.J.: Time-Life Books, 1989), pp.
137-42.

[15]Ibid., pp. 142-43.

[16]Ibid., pp. 145-46.

[17]Klimo, *Channeling*, pp. 42-56.

[18]William M. Alnor, "The Alien Obsession," *Journal of the Spiritual Counterfeits Project* 17 (1992): 28-37.

[19]Ibid., pp. 168-84.

[20]Alnor, "Alien Obsession," pp. 28-30; Klimo, *Channeling,* p. 160.

[21]Klimo, *Channeling,* pp. 53-55.

[22]Moody and Perry, *Reunions,* pp. 54-62.

[23]Ibid., p. xii.

[24]Ibid., p. 89.

[25]Ibid., p. 91.

[26]Ibid., p. 93.

[27]Ibid., pp. 24-29.

[28]Ibid., pp. 111-12, 180.

[29]Ibid., pp. 112-21.

[30]Ibid., pp. 14, 147-50.

[31]Eric Pement, "Don't Touch That Dial," *Cornerstone* 17, no. 87 (1988): 18.

[32]Klimo, *Channeling,* p. 14.

[33]Ibid., pp. 193, 321.

[34]Ibid., pp. 222-24.

[35]Ibid., pp. 237-38.

Chapter 10: UFO Experiences

[1]William M. Alnor, "The Alien Obsession," *Journal of the Spiritual Counterfeits Project* 17 (1992): 28-37.

[2]Jacques Vallee, *Dimensions* (Chicago: Contemporary Books, 1988), p. 278.

[3]"Belief in Psychic and Paranormal Phenomena Widespread Among Americans," *Gallup Poll News Service* 55 (August 6, 1990): 3.

[4]Cited by Kendrick Frazier, "Who Believes in Astrology and Why?" *Skeptical Inquirer* 16 (Summer 1992): 346.

[5]Alnor, "Alien Obsession," p. 29.

[6]Jacques Vallee, *Revelations* (New York: Ballantine Books, 1991), pp. 170-71.

[7]Ibid. This entire book deals extensively with deliberate deceptions and coverups.

[8]Whitley Strieber, *Communion* (New York: Avon, 1987), and *Transformation* (New York: Avon, 1988).

[9]From Strieber's letter to his readers which accompanied the final issue of *Communion Letter* 3 (Spring 1991). Cited by John Trott, "The Grade Five Syndrome," *Cornerstone* 20, no. 96 (1991): 17-18.

[10]Vallee, *Revelations,* p. 227.

[11]Vallee, *Dimensions,* p. 225.

[12]Vallee, *Revelations,* p. 242.

[13]Ibid., pp. 217-24.

[14]Vallee, *Dimensions,* pp. 9-22.

[15]Ibid., pp. 155-61, 195-218. I can't go into Vallee's data and arguments here, but they are provocative and are certainly worth pondering.

[16]Ibid., pp. 42-49.

17Alnor, "Alien Obsession," p. 31.

18Ibid., p. 28.

19Ibid., p. 166.

20Ibid., p. 160.

21Ibid., p. 195.

22Ibid., pp. 169-80.

23Vallee, *Revelations*, pp. 241-42.

24Ibid., pp. 214-24.

25Ibid., pp. 242-48.

26Ibid., pp. 251-52.

27Ibid., pp. 249-51.

28Ibid., p. 237.

29Vallee, *Dimensions*, pp. 158-61, 280.

30Ibid., pp. 278-81.

31Ibid.

32Ibid., chap. 4.

33Cited in John Ankerberg and John Weldon, "UFO Encounters," *Journal of the Spiritual Counterfeits Project* 17 (1992): 22.

34Ibid.

35Vallee, *Revelations*, p. 254.

36For the identification of demons as fallen angels see Matthew 25:41 and Revelation 12:7; for incidents in which angels have become visible see 2 Kings 6:16-17; Luke 1:11, 28; 2:9, 13.

Chapter 11: The Larger Picture

1Kenneth Ring, *The Omega Project* (New York: Morrow, 1992), pp. 189, 243-46.

2Kenneth Ring and Christopher Rosing, "The Omega Project: An Empirical Study of the NDE-Prone Personality," *Journal of Near-Death Studies* 8 (Summer 1990): 222.

3See Cherie Sutherland, "Psychic Phenomena Following Near-Death Experiences: An Australian Study," *Journal of Near-Death Studies* 8 (Winter 1989): 98-101; Ring and Rosing, "Omega Project," pp. 223-26. Also see chapter five in this book.

4Ring, *Omega Project*.

5Ibid., chaps. 5-6.

6Ibid., pp. 168-72.

7Bruce Greyson, "Can Science Explain the Dear-Death Experience?" *Journal of Near-Death Studies* 8 (Winter 1989): 87.

8Stanislav Grof and Christina Grof, eds., *Spiritual Emergency* (Los Angeles: Jeremy P. Tarcher, 1989), pp. 2-26.

9Jacques Vallee, *Dimensions* (Chicago: Contemporary Books, 1988), pp. 278-81.

10See articles by Brooks Alexander, John Ankerberg and John Weldon, William Alnor, and Tal Brooke in *Journal of the Spiritual Counterfeits Project* 17 (1992) for an excellent overview of this topic from a Christian perspective.

11In this survey people were "committed" if they met a minimum standard as defined by their own religious tradition. For Protestants the criteria for commitment were church attendance, membership in a denomination, frequency of personal prayer, belief in life after death and the rated importance of religion in the person's life. Respondents were classified as "committed" if they registered some activity in all five categories.

[12]Reported in Kenneth Woodward, "The Rites of Americans," *Newsweek*, November 29, 1993, p. 81.

[13]William Alnor, "The Alien Obsession," *Journal of the Spiritual Counterfeits Project* 17 (1992): 28-37.

[14]Kenneth L. Woodward, "Angels," *Newsweek*, December 27, 1993, pp. 52-57.

[15]See J. I. Packer, *Knowing God* (Downers Grove, Ill.: InterVarsity Press, 1973), pp. 31-42.